Local Habitations

Local Habitations

Regionalism in the Early Novels of George Eliot

Henry Auster

Harvard University Press
Cambridge, Massachusetts | 1970

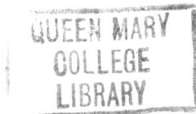

15748

Distributed in Great Britain by Oxford University Press, London
Publication of this book has been aided by a grant from
the Hyder Edward Rollins Fund
Library of Congress Catalog Card Number 74-116734
SBN 674-53676-2
Printed in the United States of America

To My Father and the Memory of My Mother

A human life, I think, should be well
rooted in some spot of a native land.
— Daniel Deronda

Preface

Since George Eliot has not suffered in recent years from critical neglect, a few words of explanation to introduce a new study of her work may not be inappropriate. The present book is a much diminished realization of a project that originally was intended to deal with the regional elements in the novels of George Eliot, Thomas Hardy, and D. H. Lawrence. In tracing the responses of the three writers to the dissolution of the stable, organic, predominantly rural society that persisted well into the nineteenth century, I was going to draw on and satisfy longstanding personal interests in the condition of uprootedness, the provincial basis of much of English fiction, the relation between the novelist and his society, and the effects of social change on narrative form.

My interest in these questions has remained constant, but I have had to limit drastically the scope of the discussion. Soon after beginning to look seriously through scholarly and critical material on regionalism, I became convinced that my initial scheme was not practicable. On the one hand, the regional novel in England appeared still to be a relatively obscure and neglected topic. It would be necessary, therefore, before launching into an examination of particular works, to descrbe regionalism at some length, placing it in its proper context in literary history, outlining the issues related to it, and applying it in a general way to the discussion of the novels themselves. On the other hand, however, regionalism in English fiction, while generally scorned as a matter for serious study, had certainly not gone unnoticed: comments, opinions, definitions, even one or two brief discussions were sprinkled in various places and needed only to be brought together and compared for a pattern (assuming that there was one) to emerge.

Thus, since I was not really interested in undertaking an exhaustive study of regionalism, I could to a large extent rely in the preliminary part of my task on secondary sources; but even so, the kind of survey and arrangement of materials that I had in mind would demand, it soon became clear, a good deal of space. It would be desirable, also, to have a point of view, a specific focus that would give direction to such a broad introduction. The consideration of the work of the three novelists with which I had started was put out of the question then and there, especially since the novels themselves, the very reason for the study, demanded, as I discovered with time, to be treated with great detail. The most sensible course, then, appeared to be to confine my attention primarily to the work of George Eliot alone and, as I became convinced, to her early work at that. My interest in regionalism and the perspective afforded by the introduction suggested an interpretation of her achievement that I hoped would be fresh, interesting, and substantial enough to stand by itself.

Part One of this study, therefore, is an attempt to define the subject and to suggest the direction and emphases to be followed. In the three short initial chapters, I argue the validity of regarding George Eliot as a regional novelist. While many critics have alluded to her characteristic regionalism, none has deliberately explored this aspect of her work, perhaps because regionalism is generally defined too narrowly and confused with restricted provincialism. But as the few thoughtful discussions of the subject show, local attachments do not have to make a novelist's work parochial; on the contrary, they can, when exploited by a powerful, genuinely creative intelligence, direct it, nourish it, and enrich it.

Regionalism, then, flexibly understood, carries over as the unifying concern into Part Two. In considering George Eliot's early novels, I do not pursue systematically every issue raised in Part One, but try instead to respond as fully as I can to the distinctive character of each book. Because my basic interest remains the same throughout and reflects the underlying similarity of theme, setting, and social perspective in all four books, the unity of concern from chapter to chapter should not be greatly obscured. Regardless of the initial approach, the analysis of each novel dwells on the author's view of provincial existence, her presentation of physical environment and communal activity, and the significance of the natural and social contexts in the moral and psychological life of the individual.

In singling out a particular aspect of a writer's achievements, one risks, by the process of abstraction and concentrated study, attributing to that one aspect undue prominence. While I believe that regionalism in fiction has been unjustly scorned and George Eliot's regionalism has been neglected, I offer this discussion not as an attempt to override earlier commentaries on her novels but as a complementary effort to fill a gap of considerable importance that they have left behind. It is impossible nowadays to write responsibly about authors of George Eliot's stature without becoming heavily indebted to the work of other critics: the extent and nature of my obligation to them will presently become apparent. Through agreement and disagreement with other views, my own perceptions were sharpened, and I have been able to define my judgments with greater precision than I could have done otherwise. I hope that what is original in my contribution repays to some extent the debt I have incurred.

But in the writing of this book, I have also incurred debts that can be specified easily and that it is pleasant to acknowledge here. I thank first Professor Jerome Hamilton Buckley, who read the original manuscript, for his valuable criticism and advice and his invaluable encouragement and friendship. His example as a gentleman, teacher, and scholar I shall always cherish. I am most grateful to Dr. Monroe Engel, who also read the original version of the book and offered not only helpful suggestions for its improvement but moral support and a standard of analytical and stylistic excellence and rigor which I feel I have satisfied with only imperfect success. I am indebted as well to my friend Frank Bidart: early in the process he painstakingly scrutinized the manuscript, chapter by chapter, with a keen eye for faults of expression and exposition, but also with an infectious and nourishing enthusiasm for the work as a whole. Finally, conscious of the inadequacy of a mere statement of gratitude, I thank my wife, whose criticism, patience, and encouragement have sustained me in every stage of my studies.

A slightly different version of this study was presented in May 1966 as a doctoral dissertation to the Department of English of Harvard University, and was awarded the Howard Mumford Jones Prize. The preparation of the book was made easier by a grant from the Canaday Humanities Fund in the summer of 1968, the help of which I gratefully acknowledge.

H. A.

Leverett House
Cambridge, Massachusetts
June 1969

Contents

Part One

The Background

---

1   The Critics Surveyed:

Responses to George Eliot's Regionalism

Some books are to be tasted, others to be swallowed,
and some few to be chewed and digested.
           — Sir Francis Bacon

i

The full-length studies of George Eliot that have appeared since 1959 testify to the variety of approaches to which her work lends itself. There is, for example, Reva Stump's detailed dissection of the imagery in three of the novels,[1] Jerome Thale's rather more flexible and inclusive essays on all the major books,[2] the challenging, subtle, and impressive analyses of her distinctive narrative form and technique by Barbara Hardy and by W. J. Harvey,[3] and the lucid and informed considerations by Bernard J. Paris and by U. C. Knoepflmacher of the fiction against the background of ideas and concerns which influenced her most and which she espoused and elaborated.[4] An even greater range of treatment, varying considerably in value, is evident in the ever-increasing number of essays devoted to her works in scholarly and critical journals. The greatness of George Eliot's achievement is today, once again, taken for granted, and her admirers no longer find it necessary to preface their remarks with the apologetic or assertive pleas on her behalf that were apparently so necessary not too long ago.[5]

Although of recent date in this century, George Eliot's emergence as a novelist of the first rank, a writer to be read with the utmost seriousness, parallels the high esteem that she enjoyed during much of her career. Up to the publication of *Daniel Deronda*, the reviewers of her work and commentators on it met each new novel of

[1] Reva Stump, *Movement and Vision in George Eliot's Novels* (Seattle, 1959).

[2] Jerome Thale, *The Novels of George Eliot* (New York, 1959).

[3] Barbara Hardy, *The Novels of George Eliot* (London, 1959); W. J. Harvey, *The Art of George Eliot* (London, 1961).

[4] Bernard J. Paris, *Experiments in Life: George Eliot's Quest for Values* (Detroit, 1965); U. C. Knoepflmacher, *Religious Humanism and the Victorian Novel: George Eliot, Walter Pater, and Samuel Butler* (Princeton, 1965). Knoepflmacher's fine book, *George Eliot's Early Novels: The Limits of Realism* (Berkeley and Los Angeles, 1968), which discusses the same body of work and touches on many of the same points (though from a different perspective) as I do, came out too late for me to use in this study. Laurence Lerner's *The Truthtellers: Jane Austen, George Eliot, D. H. Lawrence* (London, 1967) was also published too recently for my use here.

[5] See, for example, Lord David Cecil, *Early Victorian Novelists* (New York, 1935) and F. R. Leavis, *The Great Tradition* (London, 1948). The security of George Eliot's status as a major, classic English novelist owes much to the scholarship of Gordon S. Haight. His edition of her letters as well as the definitive *George Eliot: A Biography* (New York and Oxford, 1968) — which came out too late for me to use it in this study — are the outstanding achievements of the work of many years. All present and future students of George Eliot must feel grateful to him.

hers, with the possible exception of *Romola*,[6] with higher praise than the last, and firmly claimed for her a place with the great figures of English fiction: Jane Austen, Scott, Dickens, and Thackeray. Her contemporaries were impressed by the philosophical range and texture of her work and its moral dedication; they admired her powers of characterization and ability to portray English society with complexity and insight; and, just as she and George Henry Lewes expected, they enjoyed her humor and pathos.[7] While most readers agreed that the plots of her novels were static and awkwardly contrived, they had no doubt that her characteristic strengths more than made up for this weakness.

One of the critics who complained about George Eliot's artificial plots and weak endings was Henry James,[8] who also wondered at her lack of devotion to "the game of art." The novel, he wrote in 1885, was for her "not primarily a picture of life, capable of deriving a high value from its form, but a moralized fable, the last word of a philosophy endeavoring to teach by example."[9] James must have had in mind her familiar habit, especially in the early novels, of halting the narrative in order to chat with the reader, explain the situation, and

[6] *The Athenaeum* (11 July 1863), in finding *Romola* "impressive but laboured" (p. 46), voiced the ambivalent feelings George Eliot's contemporaries had about the book. *The Westminster Review*, XXIV n.s. (1863), called it "its author's greatest work" (p. 344) but regretted "that *Romola* is an Italian story, and a story of the fifteenth century" (p. 351). Henry James, who thought that it was "on the whole the finest thing she wrote," believed nevertheless that it was seriously flawed by pedantry: "It is overladen with learning, it smells of the lamp," he wrote in *The Atlantic Monthly*, LV (1885), 675.

[7] "Humor and pathos" were required by Victorian critics as standard novelistic accomplishments. As George Eliot tells it, G. H. Lewes used to encourage her at the very outset of her career by telling her: " 'You have wit, description, and philosophy — those go a good way towards the production of a novel. It is worthwhile for you to try the experiment' . . . when I read to him the first part of 'Amos,' he had no longer any doubt about my ability to carry out the plan. The scene at Cross Farm, he said, satisfied him that I had the very element he had been doubtful about — it was clear I could write good dialogue. There still remained the question whether I could command any pathos; and that was to be decided by the mode in which I treated Milly's death . . . I read it to G. when he came home. We both cried over it, and then he came up to me and kissed me, saying, 'I think your pathos is better than your fun.' " J. W. Cross, *George Eliot's Life as Related in Her Letters and Journals* (Edinburgh and London, 1885), I, 416–417 — hereafter referred to as *Life*.

[8] Specifically in *Adam Bede* and *Felix Holt* — see Henry James, "The Novels of George Eliot," *Atlantic Monthly*, XVIII (1866), 479–492, reprinted in *Views and Reviews* (Boston, 1902); and "Felix Holt, the Radical," *The Nation*, III (1866), 127–128, reprinted in *Notes and Reviews* (Cambridge, Mass., 1921).

[9] Henry James, "George Eliot's Life," *Atlantic Monthly*, LV (1885), 673, reprinted in *Partial Portraits* (1888).

point the moral, as well as the poetic justice that rules her fictional world. But though a moral and often a moralistic writer, George Eliot took particular pride in her psychological realism and repeatedly expressed an aversion for overt didacticism in art. In view, therefore, of her professions and even, as most critics have come to recognize, her practice, the opinion that James expresses is not completely fair or accurate.[10] It did, however, set the note for the deflation to which her literary reputation was subjected during the next fifty years.

But while he described her shortcomings as an artist, James also dwelt on the distinctive virtues of George Eliot's novels. In an early essay he noted with some reserve that her sympathies were with "the common people": "She is as unmistakably a painter of *bourgeois* life as Thackeray was a painter of the life of drawing-rooms." [11] Although he commended the authenticity and intimate ease with which she handles her material, he found that in "Janet's Repentance," the third of the *Scenes of Clerical Life*, those excellent qualities tend to impair the structure of the story:

> ... the stern and tragical character of the subject has been en-feeblcd by the over-diffuseness of the narrative and the excess of local touches. The abundance of the author's recollections and observations of village life clogs the dramatic movement, over which she has as yet a comparatively slight control. In her subsequent works the stouter fabric of the story is better able to support this heavy drapery of humor and digression.[12]

Not long before this essay, James reviewed *Felix Holt* in *The Nation*, and here he reserved his highest praise for the local touches and personal recollections that fill the book's first chapter. Paying tribute to George Eliot's "humanity," which "colors all her other gifts — her humor, her morality and her exquisite rhetoric," he wrote,

[10] She did not undertake to write a Positivist novel because, as she explained to Frederic Harrison, "I think aesthetic teaching is the highest of all teaching because it deals with life in its highest complexity. But if it ceases to be purely aesthetic — if it lapses anywhere from the picture to the diagram — it becomes the most offensive of all teaching." *The George Eliot Letters*, ed. Gordon S. Haight (New Haven and London: Yale University Press, 1955), IV, 300 — hereafter referred to in the text as *Letters*. See also her "Notes on Form in Art," in *The Essays of George Eliot*, ed. Thomas Pinney (London: Routledge and Kegan Paul, 1963), pp. 431–436 — hereafter referred to in the text as *Essays*. Leavis, Barbara Hardy, and Harvey all examine James's strictures and find them mistaken or irrelevant.
[11] *Atlantic Monthly*, XVIII, 480.
[12] *Ibid.*, 482.

It is as a broad picture of midland country life in England, thirty years ago, that "Felix Holt" is, to our taste, most interesting. On this subject the author writes from a full mind, with a wealth of fancy, of suggestion, of illustration, at the command of no other English writer, bearing you along on the broad and placid rises of her speech, with a kind of retarding persuasiveness which allows her conjured images to sink slowly into your very brain . . . Against the solid and deep-colored background offered by this chapter, in connection with a hundred other passages and touches, she has placed a vast number of rustic figures. We have no space to discriminate them; we can only say that in their aggregate they leave a vivid sense of that multiplicity of eccentricities, and humors, and quaintnesses, and simple *bizarreries*, which appears to belong of right to old English villages.[13]

In thus seizing on the regional and provincial element in George Eliot's fiction, Henry James defined one of the most powerful attractions which her writing held for the Victorian reader. It was the detailed, authentic, and sympathetic depiction of rural life and society in her first four books that won her popularity as an author and came to be recognized as her distinctive quality. *Middlemarch*, her greatest triumph, was the culmination of a series of "studies of provincial life."

Although the regional quality of her work never quite lost its hold on the interest and affection of George Eliot's readers and their nostalgic weakness for rustic charm, it was at least in part responsible for the decline of her literary reputation between the 1890s and the 1940s. The critical cliché about her accomplishment that was widely accepted during that time posited a sharp cleavage between her early novels (*Scenes of Clerical Life* to *Silas Marner*) and the later ones (*Romola* to *Daniel Deronda*).[14] Frederic Harrison's enthusiasm for

[13] *The Nation*, III, 128.
[14] See, for example, Mathilde Parlett, who writes in "The Influence of Contemporary Criticism on George Eliot," *Studies in Philology*, XXX (1933), 103: "The critics of George Eliot are substantially agreed in (1) the division of her works into two groups — her early realistic fiction and the later philosophical novels; (2) their recognition of the differentiae that characterize each group; and (3) their analyses of the causes that produced the change. Having agreed thus far, the critics have then divided into two schools — those who insist upon the superior merits of the early novels and those who claim preëminence for the later works. Of recent years the ranks of the second school have thinned rapidly, and it would seem to be only a question of time before there shall be unanimity of opinion on this point also." Miss Parlett, who has proved a false prophet on the last point, believes that George Eliot changed her manner in response to the moralistic quibbles of reviewers of her early works and their misunderstanding, resulting from her reticence and use of implication, of her philosophy. But

Adam Bede, for example, is representative of the stand taken by the older critics, although most of them would probably insist that the spontaneity and observation that he admires there are present also in *The Mill on the Floss*, *Silas Marner*, and even the apprentice work, *Scenes of Clerical Life*. For Harrison, however, who prized George Eliot's resources as "an eye-witness," *Adam Bede* was "the only one of her works . . . which we feel to be inevitable, spontaneous, written out of the abundance of enjoyment and experience. It is of all her books the heartiest, the wittiest, the most cheerful, or rather the least desponding." [15]

The reviewer of Cross's *Life* in *The Edinburgh Review* put the highest value on *The Mill on the Floss*, but his account is based on the same assumptions about the nature of George Eliot's work and development as Harrison's. With rhetorical flourish and considerable detail, he describes her first period of authorship, which ended with *Silas Marner*: "She had now come to an end of that reservoir of first impressions and original conceptions which had been accumulating in the long slow years of her imaginative and ambitious youth. From henceforward the strain is changed. A different region of life and different developments attract her." He seems to regret that her stock of reminiscences of provincial life should have been so quickly exhausted, and that she was forced to turn from the sympathetic depiction of humble life to "the problems of a more advanced civilisation" and the analysis of the educated and sophisticated classes:

> It is difficult to express how great the difference is when, instead of being seen from among the farmyard ricks, the landscape is looked at across the velvet glades of a park. The very perspective alters the sense of differing magnitudes. The peasant class, with all its natural preoccupations, the respectable farmers, the rural artisans, limited by the country doctor and clergyman, the highest eminences known, were all familiar to her mind as "household words," and drawn with the utmost force of an art which was nature . . . But the time for that limitation was over, and, herself living in a different world, she began to feel it expedient to follow the necessities and more intricate problems of a different sphere.[16]

since the early novels show a much greater freedom in the use of explicit commentary and authorial intrusion, this seems to me a very dubious view.

[15] Frederic Harrison, "George Eliot's Place in Literature," *The Forum*, XX (1895), 71.

[16] "The Life and Letters of George Eliot," CLXI (1885), 546–547.

Essentially as simplified and extravagant as Harrison's opinion, this wordy judgment is typical of the way in which the late nineteenth and early twentieth century thought of George Eliot's career: it consisted of two phases, of which the second was by far the less successful and made her entire achievement seem somewhat disappointing. Cross was commended for his devotion, but criticized because in his anxiety to prove the novelist's superiority, he awoke instead in the public "a general sense of the inadequate, of promises unfulfilled and expectations deceived." [17]

It is still common in our own time to divide George Eliot's work into two groups: the fresh, reminiscential, and comic "romances" of her "youth" and the massive, analytical, and profound novels of her "maturity." Modern critics seem occasionally even to be echoing the terms of the Victorian discussion; the comparative evaluation of the two stages of her career, however, has been gradually reversed. Virginia Woolf, for example, writing in the 1920s, practically echoes the feelings of the "Scotch Reviewer" just quoted in her enthusiasm for George Eliot's early works, but her estimate of *Middlemarch* is much higher than that expressed by eminent Victorians like her father.[18] She speaks of the "beauty of those first books" and the convincing fulness with which the characters and their surroundings are depicted: "we move among them, now bored, now sympathetic, but always with that unquestioning acceptance of all they say and do, which we accord to the great originals only." Pointing to the "flood of memory and humour" through which George Eliot recreates "the whole fabric of ancient rural England," she praises the sense of naturalness and spontaneity that characterizes the early work and "leaves us with little consciousness that there is anything to criticise." But though her way of accounting for the change in the novelist's manner still resembles the nineteenth-century view, she shows a new respect for the productions of her maturity. Far from having diminished, George Eliot's power is at its highest in *Middlemarch*, "the magnificent book which with all its imperfections is one of the few English novels written for grown-up people. But the world of fields

[17] *Ibid.*, 516.
[18] Leslie Stephen thought that "the immediate success of *Middlemarch* may have been proportioned rather to the author's reputation than to its intrinsic merits. It certainly lacks the peculiar charm of the early work..." *George Eliot* (New York and London, 1902), p. 173.

and farms no longer contents her. In real life she had sought her fortunes elsewhere." And, as Virginia Woolf goes on to observe, "when the first flush of creative energy was exhausted and self-confidence had come to her, she wrote more and more from the personal standpoint, but she did so without the unhesitating abandonment of the young." [19]

Since Virginia Woolf's essay, critics have asserted with increasing decisiveness the preeminence of the later books,[20] and today the status of *Middlemarch* as her most successful novel, perhaps even the greatest achievement in English fiction, is firmly established. From whatever direction writers may approach her work, they tend to regard the analysis of *Middlemarch* as the climax of their efforts. If they see fit to refer at all in one way or another to the regional spirit inherent in her books, they generally take the view that in that novel she finally outgrew it and came to concentrate singlemindedly on more profound and universal issues than in *Scenes of Clerical Life* or *Silas Marner*.

F. R. Leavis, in calling for a revaluation of "the great tradition" of the English novel, mocks the taste of the older admirers of George Eliot: "At the risk of appearing priggish one may suggest that there is a tendency to overrate charm. Certainly charm is overrated when it is preferred to maturity." [21] Energetically he proceeds on that basis to put her first books in what he regards as a proper perspective. As he makes a vigorous effort to rescue *The Mill on the Floss* from its traditional place among the early novels, he finds the writing in *Scenes of Clerical Life* promising and intelligent but artistically clumsy, describes *Adam Bede* with some condescension as "unmistakably qualified to be a popular classic," possessing attractions that "are as plain as they are genuine" and familiar,[22] and dismisses *Silas*

[19] "George Eliot," *The Common Reader* [*First Series*] (London, 1925), pp. 211, 213, 214.
[20] The similar shift in critical attitudes toward Dickens's novels — the modern enthusiasm for his later, "darker" work — is well known. The parallel has been noticed also by Allan P. Casson in "The Early Novels of George Eliot" (unpublished Ph.D. dissertation, Harvard University, 1960), pp. 25–26.
[21] *The Great Tradition*, p. 35.
[22] *Ibid.*, p. 36. In the foreword to the Signet Classics edition (1961) of *Adam Bede*, Leavis discusses the novel and its representation of rural society with a measure of respect and seriousness that indicates an abandonment of his early condescension. The essay is reprinted in *Anna Karenina and Other Essays* (London, 1967).

Marner as "a charming minor masterpiece." [23] Leavis's judgment is penetrating and largely just, but he falls into simplification and exaggeration; Barbara Hardy and W. J. Harvey, who are greatly indebted to his pioneering essay, offer in their books many fine discriminations refining his critical gusto.

ii

The latest considerations of George Eliot's work, including the studies by Mrs. Hardy and Mr. Harvey, evince very little interest in her regionalism, but they do recognize and discuss related questions: her concern with social change and relationships, the importance of the community and secondary background characters in her novels, and the nature of her "unheroic" realism.[24] Earlier criticism, which is on the whole much more general than the specialized approaches of recent years, has also perceived and examined such issues. Joan Bennett's study, for example, is largely concerned with the pattern that she sees as central in every novel of George Eliot's: the unfolding of an individual drama within a copiously rendered social medium. Drawing on this insight, Mrs. Bennett is able to make more precise, comprehensive, and enlightening evaluations of the separate works than many more ingenious critics. She finds that George Eliot's best books derive their strength from "the degree of success with which she gives life to the social world surrounding her central characters." [25] Her early work, which ends, according to general agreement, with *Silas Marner*, is distinguished by the remarkable assurance with which "she plants those characters in the environ-

---

[23] *Ibid.*, p. 46.

[24] See, for example, Reva Stump, pp. 68–74; Thale, pp. 36–48, 91–98, 115–120, 142–147; Barbara Hardy, pp. 15–31; Harvey, pp. 148–161 — an effective rebuttal to Leavis's early, disparaging views of *Adam Bede*; and Paris, pp. 45–49, 193–222.

[25] *George Eliot: Her Mind and Art* (Cambridge: Cambridge University Press, 1948), p. 82. Mrs. Bennett's incisive definition of this pattern has been developed in several recent essays concerned with the detailed study of the narrative organization in George Eliot's novels. See, for example, David R. Carroll, "Unity Through Analogy: An Interpretation of *Middlemarch*," *Victorian Studies*, II (1958–59), 305–316; "The Unity of *Daniel Deronda*," *Essays in Criticism*, IX (1959), 369–380; and *"Felix Holt*: Society as Protagonist," *Nineteenth-Century Fiction*, XVII (1962–63), 237–252 . See also Fred C. Thomson, "The Theme of Alienation in *Silas Marner*," *Nineteenth-Century Fiction*, XX (June 1965), 69–84 and Quentin Anderson, "George Eliot in *Middlemarch*," *From Dickens to Hardy*, ed. Boris Ford (Penguin Books, 1958), pp. 274–283. See also Thomas Pinney's article "The Authority of the Past in the Novels of George Eliot," *Nineteenth-Century Fiction*, XXI (1966), especially pp. 135–140.

ment with which she had been familiar since her childhood." It is *Middlemarch*, however, that is her masterpiece: "though certain excellencies must be sought elsewhere, *Middlemarch* is her widest and deepest study of the interpenetration between the life of a community and the individual lives that compose it." As Mrs. Bennett notes, in writing her greatest novel, George Eliot did not suppress or reject her local attachments and knowledge but continued to rely on them. Having gained "a more assured command of her art," she returned "to the environment she most fully understood" and exploited it as effectively, if not as buoyantly, as in her first efforts.[26]

Joan Bennett's recognition of the persistent influence which her native region exercised over George Eliot's writing is quite traditional. From the outset, her readers knew that she depended on Warwickshire as the setting for her stories and drew on her memories of events, impressions, and characters of her formative provincial years, even on the gossip gleaned in childhood, for the rough material of plots and atmosphere. The inhabitants of Nuneaton were quick to claim *Scenes of Clerical Life* as a portrait of their community, and readers familiar with Staffordshire and Derbyshire soon recognized the scene of *Adam Bede* and identified Hayslope as the village of Ellastone in North Staffordshire. The concrete, precise, and affectionate details of the characterizations and setting indicated that the author was actually acquainted with the people and places in the stories; indeed George Eliot was several times moved to insist that she was writing fiction, not biography or history. "Mr. Tryan is not a portrait of any clergyman living or dead," she wrote to her publisher, John Blackwood, who had received a protest from a Rev. W. P. Jones against the depiction of his brother as the hero of "Janet's Repentance." "He is an ideal character, but I hope probable enough to resemble more than one evangelical clergyman of his day ... As to the rest of my story, so far as its elements were suggested by real persons, those persons have been, to use good Mr. Jones's phrase, 'long in eternity'" (*Letters*, II, 375-376). Later, while relating the "History of 'Adam Bede'" in her Journal, she distinguishes in the same way her fiction from the facts that inspired it:

> The germ of "Adam Bede" was an anecdote told me by my Methodist Aunt Samuel ... an anecdote from her own experience ...
> The character of Adam, and one or two incidents connected with

[26] Joan Bennett, pp. 82–83.

him were suggested by my Father's early life; but Adam is not my father any more than Dinah is my aunt. Indeed, there is not a single *portrait* in "Adam Bede"; only the suggestions of experience wrought up into new combinations. (*Letters*, II, 502–503)

But though she denied that she was simply transcribing from memory, George Eliot freely acknowledged her reliance on the experiences and observations of her past. In 1859, as she was in the middle of writing *The Mill on the Floss*, she wrote to her friend, Barbara Bodichon:

> ... at present my mind works with the most freedom and the keenest sense of poetry in my remotest past, and there are many strata to be worked through before I can begin to use *artistically* any material I may gather in the present. Curiously enough, à propos of your remark about "Adam Bede" there is much less "out of my own life" in that book — i.e. the materials are much more a combination from imperfectly known and widely sundered elements than the "Clerical Scenes." (*Letters*, III, 128–129)

Although the poetry of the past of which she speaks suffuses *The Mill on the Floss* more conspicuously than her other novels, George Eliot did not exhaust the rich stores of her memory until the very end of her career, when she set *Daniel Deronda* in the 1860s. As the title of one of her last essays indicates, she is constantly "Looking Backward," whether it is to society's past or her own. All her novels, with the exception of *Romola* and *Daniel Deronda*, are the products of her working through the strata of her first thirty years in the Midlands. *The Mill on the Floss* is easily recognized as the most personal, searching, and intimately biographical of her books, but *Silas Marner* and *Felix Holt* were also conceived and designed around scenes, incidents, and figures culled from the past (*Letters*, III, 382; *Life*, I, 25, 27; II, 291). As Mrs. Bennett suggests, *Middlemarch* marks yet another return to her provincial youth, although here the transmutation of personal experience is subtler and more complicated than in the earlier books.[27] It seems mistaken, therefore, at least from the point of view of content, to insist, in the manner of the Victorian readers of George Eliot and some modern critics, on a sudden and

[27] See especially Gordon S. Haight, "George Eliot's Originals," *From Jane Austen to Joseph Conrad*, ed. Robert C. Rathburn and Martin Steinmann (Minneapolis, 1958), 177–193, for inclusive treatment of the actual persons who are thought to have suggested George Eliot's characterizations. The same information can also be collected from the biographical and "topographical" works cited in note 30.

drastic transformation in interest and approach between *Silas Marner* and *Felix Holt*. To be sure, there are real and important changes that can be discovered in her work, but they are part of a gradual and continuous development rather than the result of an abrupt shift in direction.

Only in her "Renaissance" novel and her "modern" novel does she fail to use the provincial setting that gives a sense of continuity and progression to her other major fiction. And the two exceptions actually support the pattern and prove the rule, for it was while working on *Romola* that George Eliot said:

> It is the habit of my imagination to strive after as full a vision of the medium in which a character moves as of the character itself. The psychological causes which prompted me to give such details of Florentine life and history as I have given, are precisely the same as those which determined me in giving the details of English village life in "Silas Marner," or the "Dodson" life, out of which were developed the destinies of poor Tom and Maggie. (*Letters*, IV, 97)

But laborious research in the archives of Florence could never altogether supply the vital breath that inspires the regional books, and in the same letter George Eliot admitted her "tendency to excess" in the effort to build up a full vision of the background in *Romola*. As for *Daniel Deronda*, the sophisticated, cosmopolitan, rootless world in which the story is set is an important element in her deliberate exploration of the aimlessness and incoherence of modern life.

> In this book the absence of an enveloping society for either Gwendolen or Daniel is a part of the author's central conception. Both characters are incomplete because they have been deprived of such a soil in which to grow. Gwendolen's selfishness and narrowness of vision and Daniel's quest for some communal tie to direct his altruistic aspirations are the outcome of a lack, in the early life of each, of just such a background as Hayslope provided for the characters in *Adam Bede*, the Dodson-Tulliver world for Maggie, or Middlemarch for Dorothea.[28]

The importance of George Eliot's attachment to the Midlands can thus be verified by the variety of ways in which it finds expres-

[28] Joan Bennett, p. 83. For complementary discussions of the conflict between individuals and their communities, see Reva Stump, pp. 68–109, and George J. Worth, "The Intruder Motif in George Eliot's Fiction," *Six Studies in Nineteenth-Century English Literature and Thought*, ed. Harold J. Orel and George J. Worth (Lawrence, Kansas, 1962), pp. 55–68.

sion in her books. In the now formidable number of studies devoted to her life and work, a full, detailed, and balanced attempt at such verification is lacking. We have instead many biographical tributes to her enduring regionalism,[29] the rather more detailed historical, biographical, and topographical studies dedicated to the exact identification of every person, place, and event in her fiction,[30] and a number of essays dealing in part or in their entirety with her realism in presenting rural society, class structure, and political changes, and her historical perspective and accuracy.[31] With the aid of these, with some attention to the question of regionalism in general, and particularly through a close study of the early novels, I wish in the succeeding pages to attempt an elucidation of the nature, function, and evolution of George Eliot's regionalism.

Regionalism in English fiction, as distinct from American, when regarded at all, is normally regarded as something of a curiosity, and a curiosity of no significance. Enduring literature, it is said, is universal: only second-rate writers are regional. I understand this

[29] For example, Mathilde Blind, *George Eliot* (Boston, 1904), pp. xiii–xviii, 18, 84–85; George Willis Cooke, *George Eliot* (Boston and New York, 1883), pp. 216–220; Mary H. Deakin, *The Early Life of George Eliot* (Manchester, 1913), pp. 113–134, 139–149. (This book is still a most useful biographical and critical account of George Eliot's early life and contains surprisingly "modern" estimates of the works.) Anne Fremantle, *George Eliot* (London, 1933), pp. 18–19, 77, 87, 93, 126–127; Blanche Colton Williams, *George Eliot* (New York, 1936), pp. 14–26, 129–141, 147–157, 265–270; Lawrence and Elisabeth Hanson, *Marian Evans and George Eliot* (London, 1952), pp. 9, 202, 205–206.

[30] For example, Rose G. Kingsley, "George Eliot's Country," *Century Magazine*, XXX (1885), 339–352; S. Parkinson, *Scenes from the George Eliot Country* (Leeds, 1888); Lady Newdigate-Newdegate, *The Cheverels of Cheverel Manor* (London, 1898); James T. Foard, "Features of Fact and Fancy in the Works of George Eliot," *Manchester Quarterly*, IX (1890), 28–54; Charles S. Olcott, *George Eliot: Scenes and People in Her Novels* (New York, 1910); Charles G. Harper, "The George Eliot Country," *The Living Age*, CCCIII (1919), 416–419; Dorothy Dodds, *The George Eliot Country*, ed. F. J. Cross (Nuneaton: The George Eliot Fellowship, 1952). See also a letter from Bert G. Hornback in *TLS* (21 December 1967), p. 1239.

[31] The best of these, by far, is Claude T. Bissell, "Social Analysis in the Novels of George Eliot," *ELH*, XVIII (1951), 221–239. See also T. E. Kebbel, "Village Life According to George Eliot," *Fraser's Magazine*, XXIII n.s. (1881), 263–276; C. Kegan Paul, "The Rustic of George Eliot and Thomas Hardy," *Merry England*, I (1883), 40–51; Walter Francis Wright, "George Eliot as Industrial Reformer," *PMLA*, LVI (1941), 1107–15; Asa Briggs, "*Middlemarch* and the Doctors," *Cambridge Journal* (1947–48), 749–762; Jerome Beaty, "History by Indirection: The Era of Reform in *Middlemarch*," *Victorian Studies*, I (1957–58), 173–179; William J. Hyde, "George Eliot and the Climate of Realism," *PMLA*, LXXII (1957), 147–164; John M. Prest, *The Industrial Revolution in Coventry* (London, 1960); A. J. Sambrook, "The Natural Historian of Our Social Classes," *English*, XIV (1962–63), 130–134.

14

attitude and even agree with it in part; where I demur is at the implication that first-rate writers, who are universal in their concerns, can never be regional. It is inaccurate to confuse regional with parochial literature, for successful regional works, as Claude Simpson puts it, "transcend mere localism in their theme, though clearly gaining strength from the immediacy and flavor of local detail." [32]

If distinguished novelists can be regional and at the same time retain a general appeal, their regionalism becomes a matter of literary interest. An examination of regional elements in a work of fiction often reveals a good deal not only about the author's concerns but about his technique, his way of investing the particular, precisely observed locale and its traditions, customs, and personalities with implications of far-reaching significance. Such an examination can also relate with some precision a writer's ideas and metaphysical preoccupations, his view of life, to actual conditions and experiences of a local origin. Faulkner lends himself easily to an approach of this kind, and so does Hardy — indeed Douglas Brown's fine monograph discussing Hardy largely in terms of his response to the plight of the agricultural laborer is a good example of the direction such inquiries can follow.[33] Where appropriate, attention to regional elements can thus cast valuable light on a novelist's social attitudes and his awareness of sweeping changes.

As we have seen, George Eliot's regional ties have been widely noticed, but they have not excited much sustained or deliberate interest. Loved by the general reader of the nineteenth century and the stalwart sentimentalists of the twentieth, her regionalism has been disregarded by most of the eminent students of her work. They have devoted themselves instead, properly enough and — many of them — profitably as well, to exploring her imagery, narrative form, ethics, religion, and ideology. For my part, I hope in what follows to supplement the tried techniques that have been applied to her novels, to show how essential their regional spirit is, to suggest that regionalism is not the insignificant, purely local mannerism it has generally been considered, and to justify my own nostalgia for the "charm," cosiness, and satisfying vision of social coherence that mark her early books.

[32] *The Local Colorists: American Short Stories, 1857–1900* (New York, 1960), p. 12.
[33] *Thomas Hardy* (London, 1954).

2 Country Matters: Regionalism, Realism, and George Eliot's Fiction

It was a happy opening of a rich and unworked mine when Miss Edgeworth gave her humourously descriptive tales of Irish life to the world — most happy if, as Sir Walter Scott declares, they had the merit of first suggesting to him the idea of a series of stories illustrative of the character and manners of his own country.
— The Westminster Review (1853)

i

Only rarely have modern critics of any stature concerned themselves, even briefly, with the subject of regionalism; when they have
done so their attitude has generally been one of condescension, if not
outright scorn. We have seen, for example, how firmly F. R. Leavis
deprecates the "charm" associated with regional fiction; his wife
expresses her disdain for the genre with still greater decisiveness and
acerbity. Refusing "to consider that subject as more serious than a
future academic classification," Q. D. Leavis describes the regional
novel as "some commonplace work of fiction made interesting to the
Boots Library public by a painstaking application of rural local colour
(the popular reputation of so poor a novel as *Under the Greenwood
Tree* is perhaps explicable thus)." She does admit the possibility that
"a novel noticeably grounded in the regional" can achieve "artistic
distinction," but asks whether the success of such a work does not
depend more on its general literary excellencies than its regional
basis. "It would hardly occur to most people," she adds, "to think of
Wuthering Heights, for instance, as a regional novel, or even *The
Mill on the Floss*." [1]

Now at the risk of appearing eccentric, I confess that I do think
of *Wuthering Heights* as, among other things, a regional novel; this
is also how I regard *The Mill on the Floss*, and with greater assurance
about the importance of its regionalism. As her "even" indicates,
Mrs. Leavis too believes that *The Mill on the Floss* is more distinctly
regional than *Wuthering Heights*; significantly, she does not mention
Adam Bede, in which the regional spirit is unmistakably dominant.
She asserts her low estimate of *Under the Greenwood Tree* with the
casualness of a long-standing aversion to Hardy, and emphasizes in
her description of the regional novel the mediocrity of much of the
kind. Any literary form, of course, can be reduced in definition by
such a stress, but I cannot really take issue with Mrs. Leavis since
I agree with her main point: if a regional novel is to win distinction,
it must succeed as "a work of art like any other great novel." Few
would question this argument, but it does not demolish regionalism
as a subject for responsible literary consideration. Because of the
way the imagination of certain writers functions, the regional element
is more than "merely a factor contributing incidentally to [the]

[1] "Regional Novels," *Scrutiny*, IV (1935–36), 440.

greatness"[2] of their work. Regionalism then becomes a more interesting problem than Mrs. Leavis supposes.

Critics who defend regional fiction against the charges of narrowness and triviality that are frequently leveled against it normally begin by differentiating it from local color writing, which strives for nothing more interesting or revealing than anecdotal or antiquarian quaintness. Regionalism, on the other hand, as F. W. Morgan, a sociologist, has observed, is distinguished by "absorption in a particular locality; absorption and not merely interest."[3] It is, according to Thomas J. Hardy, "the work of writers who realize that man is the product of the soil, and that the characters of the story and the environment are essential to one another."[4] Phyllis Bentley, herself a noted regional author, remarks that a "writer of genius . . . can see human destiny through his chosen region" despite the tendency of the regional form to encourage "prosaic pedestrianism" and to survey "Yorkshire rather than human destiny."[5] Thus, while the borderline between regional and local color literature is not easily defined or maintained, it is recognizable, particularly on the basis of artistic merit — the magnitude of a work's aim and the quality of its success. Harry Bernard, a Canadian critic, remarks on the ease with which regionalism is confused with the literature of terror, folklore, localism, and provincialism,[6] but he argues nevertheless that there is no necessary contradiction between regionalism and universality in literature:

> . . . le régionalisme vrai assure leur vigeur à maints chefs-d'oeuvres classiques. Roman de l'avarice, l'*Eugénie Grandet* de Balzac se trouve aussi un roman de la province française, et plus particulièrement de l'Anjou . . . Le raisonnement ne s'applique qu'à la France. Quoi de plus régional, et de plus national à la fois, que les romans de Charlotte et d'Emily Brontë, de George Eliot, de Thomas Hardy, d'Arnold Bennett?[7]

[2] *Ibid.*
[3] F. W. Morgan, "Three Aspects of Regional Consciousness," *The Sociological Review*, XXI (1939), 84.
[4] Thomas J. Hardy, "Regional Romance," *Books on the Shelf* (London, 1934), p. 204.
[5] Phyllis Bentley, *The English Regional Novel* (London: George Allen and Unwin, 1941), pp. 44-45.
[6] Harry Bernard, *Le Roman régionaliste aux États-Unis, 1913–1940* (Montréal, 1949), p. 30.
[7] *Ibid.*, p. 31.

Phyllis Bentley has also noticed the link between regionalism and national awareness to which Bernard refers. In her pamphlet, *The English Regional Novel* (which, brief and modest as it is, appears to be the fullest consideration in English of the subject), she defines the regional novel as "the national novel carried to one degree further of subdivision; it is a novel which, concentrating on a particular part, a particular region of a nation, depicts the life of that region in such a way that the reader is conscious of the characteristics which are unique to that region and differentiate it from others in the common motherland." [8] Bernard clearly depends on this statement for his own definition of regionalism, but he strives for slightly greater precision than Miss Bentley:

> Comme l'indique le terme, il s'interesse à la région, celle-ci plus ou moins étendue, plus ou moins détérminée et qui concourt avec d'autres régions, à former l'ensemble du territoire d'un pays. Il en fixe les traits physiques et surtout l'atmosphère, exploite sa légende et son passé, montre ses habitants, insiste sur les particularismes de leur langage, leur culture, de leur habitudes de vie.[9]

It is on the basis of deduction from novels like George Eliot's that theories of regionalism are formulated. Her work, and especially her early work, meets fully and exactly the requirements most consistently laid down in the definitions of regional fiction. If she was not actually, as Thomas J. Hardy believes, the first novelist who "discovered an English region as something in itself considerable, fascinating," [10] she remains the first distinctly major author to exploit the discovery. For Phyllis Bentley she is one of the four great writers (the others are Charlotte Brontë, Trollope, and Hardy) "who created, developed, and possibly perfected the English regional novel." [11] Other students of regionalism rank her at least as high.

ii

As the definitions of Miss Bentley and Harry Bernard imply, regional fiction grows out of not merely regional consciousness but

[8] P. 7.
[9] *Le Roman régionaliste aux États-Unis*, p. 31.
[10] *Books on the Shelf*, p. 208.
[11] *The English Regional Novel*, p. 13.

a sense of national unity underlying the local diversity. Neither critic, however, makes much of the larger dimension or considers in any detail the possible influence of Sir Walter Scott on the growth of English regionalism. Miss Bentley explains the appearance of the regional novel in an acute but uncomplicated fashion:

> The reason why regional fiction flowered in this period [the nineteenth and twentieth centuries] is, I think, precisely that improvement in communications which during the same period is tending to render the regions themselves less regional. Yorkshire did not know it was Yorkshire, nor Somerset Somerset, until the frequent travel made possible by improved communications showed Yorkshiremen and Somersetmen other counties, so that they realized how different was their own.[12]

A much fuller account, both speculative and historical, of the evolution of regionalism in England can be found in Lucien Leclaire's *Le Roman régionaliste dans les Îles Britanniques, 1800–1950*, which is probably the most exhaustive treatment of the subject.[13] Leclaire divides the development of the regional novel into three periods: (1) 1800–1830, when there appeared under the influence of Maria Edgeworth and Sir Walter Scott the "national" novel of Ireland and Scotland; (2) 1830–1870, the years of the unintentional, unself-conscious regional novel ("Le roman régionaliste 'par surcroît' "); and (3) 1870–1950, during which time the form matured and increased in number and variety.[14]

The roots of regionalism he finds in the romantic movement, particularly in the influence of Rousseau and the work of Wordsworth and Crabbe. (Cowper, whom Leclaire does not mention, also must have contributed to the new interest in provincial life and locality.) The enthusiasm for nature, with its fondness for the picturesque and pastoral as well as its eye for observed facts, the democratic impulse of individualism and respect for the common man and humble exis-

---

[12] *Ibid.*, p. 12.
[13] Paris, 1954.
[14] Leclaire distinguishes four principal but overlapping forms and stages in this final phase: (1) picturesque regionalism (1870–1895), e.g., Thomas Hardy, Richard Jefferies, R. L. Stevenson; (2) sentimental regionalism (1890–1914), e.g., J. M. Barrie, Arthur Quiller-Couch, Katherine Tynan; (3) realistic and naturalistic regionalism (1900–1925), e.g., George Douglas, Arnold Bennett, Hugh Walpole; and (4) interpretive (critical, purposeful) regionalism (1920–1939), e.g., D. H. Lawrence, Francis Brett-Young, J. C. Powys. Post-war regionalism he treats as a fifth phase.

tence, and the precedent set by the eighteenth-century novel's depiction of country life, all encouraged novelists in the early years of the nineteenth century to turn their attention to the environment with which they were most familiar. Of the pioneer efforts in the direction of regionalism only the novels of John Galt were authentically regional, localized in a particular, precisely observed, homely setting, and concerned with the faithful depiction of everyday activity.[15] But the crucial impulse, as Leclaire at times recognizes, seems to have come from the works of Scott, which were not really regional in scope or interest but were immensely popular and influential.

That Scott gave a great impetus to the English novel in the direction of romantic adventure and historical reconstruction is a commonplace of literary history; less familiar is his part in creating a taste for more mundane and local narratives. Victorian critics, however, were well aware of the dual nature of his influence. David Masson, for example, believed that had Scott "betaken himself to prose fiction at first, instead of deferring his exercises in it to a mature age . . . he would have taken rank both among the romance-writers of the Gothic picturesque and among the painters of contemporary life and manners . . ."[16] Scott may be "the father of the Modern Historical Novel,"[17] but Masson speaks with special emphasis of his "passion for the real in History . . . and his Scotticism,"[18] and admires his ability to "blend the interest of romantic adventure with that of homely and humorous representation of manners."[19] Scott had acknowledged, as Masson notes, his indebtedness to Maria Edgeworth's Irish stories for the decisive inspiration behind *Waverley*,[20] and it is as a nationalist writer that he excels: "Scott is greatest in his Scotticism."[21] His love of natural scenery and the past, essentially limited "to a particular region geographically and a particular era chronologically,"[22] derives from his love of his country.

Although a trace of chauvinism may be detected in Masson's

[15] Leclaire, pp. 30–33, 41–42.
[16] David Masson, *British Novelists and Their Styles* (Cambridge, 1859), pp. 189–190.
[17] *Ibid.*, p. 197.
[18] *Ibid.*, p. 190.
[19] *Ibid.*, p. 192.
[20] *Ibid.*, p. 190.
[21] *Ibid.*, p. 204.
[22] *Ibid.*, p. 167.

repeated assertions of his countryman's nationalistic feelings, his estimate of Scott's effect on the novel in England is sound enough. Modern writers on regional fiction have confirmed the link, which he seems almost to take for granted, between Scott's "Scotticism" and English regionalism. Leclaire regards Scott as a seminal figure in the development of the regional novel, though not himself a regionalist; and F. W. Morgan, noting that in the nineteenth century Scott's "interest in locality in the past became an interest in locality in the present," defines the nature of his influence with considerable literary acumen. He writes that in the Waverley novels "local colour in time led to local colour in place. They were full of a feeling for landscape and local humours, which stamped them as original and outstanding. Scott, in fact, established the topographical novel by giving the background of neighbourhood an absorbing interest and importance." [23]

In a recent general discussion of Scott, John Henry Raleigh indirectly corroborates the findings of the critics who have a special interest in regionalism. He shows that Scott remained popular in the nineteenth century because he anticipated in his novels many of the aims and concerns which Victorian readers came to expect in fiction. His object was "to describe men rather than manners, to show possessions common to men in all stages of society," [24] to set his heroes and events firmly in a historical context, and to extend the social range of the novel so that it included not simply the traditional middle-class characters but figures of the nobility and peasantry as well. [25] These were also George Eliot's aims, and when the connection is made, it becomes clear why she should have cherished Scott all her life.

She shared with him, first of all, a social vision that stemmed from a life of relative mobility and openness. Masson, in describing Scott's familiarity not only with the scenery and history of his country but also with its people, cites the author's own comments: " 'having had from his infancy,' as he says, 'free and unrestrained communication with all ranks of his countrymen, from the Scottish peer to the Scottish ploughman,' he knew their ways, their dialect, their modes

[23] *The Sociological Review*, XXI, 83.
[24] John Henry Raleigh, "What Scott Meant to the Victorians," *Victorian Studies*, VII (1963–64), 12.
[25] *Ibid.*, 13–14. See also Kathleen Tillotson, *Novels of the Eighteen-Forties* (Oxford, 1954), p. 142, on Scott's influence in making low characters and regional settings acceptable in fiction, and pp. 86–91, on the extension in this period of the social and geographic range of the novel.

of thought, their humours, as intimately as any Scotchman breathing." [26] Similar knowledge is apparent in George Eliot's fiction, and
she demurely boasts of it in "Looking Backward," an obliquely autobiographical essay in her last publication, *Impressions of Theophrastus Such*:

> . . . I am rather fond of the mental furniture I got by having a
> father who was well acquainted with all ranks of his neighbours
> . . . A chief misfortune of high birth is that it usually shuts a
> man out from the large sympathetic knowledge of human experi-
> ence which comes from contact with various classes on their
> own level, and in my father's time that entail of social ignorance
> had not been disturbed as we see it now . . . Hence I have always
> thought that the most fortunate Britons are those whose experi-
> ence has given them a practical share in many aspects of the
> national lot, who have lived long among the mixed commonalty,
> roughing it with them under difficulties, knowing how their food
> tastes to them, and getting acquainted with their notions and
> motives not by inference from traditional types in literature or
> from philosophical theories, but from daily fellowship and ob-
> servation.

As her father's constant companion for several years, George
Eliot, as she says, "profited by his popularity" and acquired some of
his social experience and knowledge. Later in this discussion, especially in Chapter 3, I will have occasion to comment more fully on
the sociological interest in her work, and particularly the sense of
change, evident even in "Looking Backward," that permeates the
novels. At this point, however, it seems best to proceed with the
examination of the influences that could have shaped her novelistic
interests and techniques. Raleigh offers an illuminating hint on the
nature of these influences when he compares Scott to Wordsworth
and tries to account for their popularity in the nineteenth century.
They were, as George Eliot's biographers tell us, her favorite authors,
but according to Raleigh they were also, if not the favorite authors
of the Victorians, at least "the two single most important influences"
on them.[27] Although he does not connect Scott and Wordsworth with
George Eliot, his description of what her contemporaries admired in
their work makes clear at least her affinity with them. He speaks of

[26] *British Novelists*, p. 173.
[27] *Victorian Studies*, VII, 18.

the three major ways in which the two romantics "overlapped and reinforced one another":

> First, and most obvious, is the turn from city to country for background ... The second way is Scott and Wordsworth's ability to describe landscape so effectively that they add a new dimension, in the imagination of the observer, to the landscape itself ... A third way in which [they] coincided was in their pictures of common life. Scott himself said repeatedly that he agreed with the Preface to the *Lyrical Ballads*, especially with its notion that, among the lowly, human passion received more strong and direct expression.[28]

The other qualities of Scott which Raleigh believes attracted Victorian readers are not related to the idea of regionalism, but they should at least be mentioned, if only to underline the closeness between his literary concerns and George Eliot's. For she resembles and probably exceeds him in his effort to achieve moral seriousness and truthfulness, his affectionate regard for the past, his secular and conservative view of history as process and development, and his sense of the losses inherent in progress as well as of the inevitability of change. Raleigh also finds in Scott's novels "the faint stirrings of feminism": "Negatively, in his conventional heroines like Rose of *Waverley* he showed how frivolous, passionless and uninteresting are unemancipated women. Positively, in Flora MacIvor, Di Vernon, and Jeanie Deans, he showed what a woman could be, if free, or partially free."[29] The comment brings to mind George Eliot's heroines and the feminine contrasts that recur in her novels: Hetty and Dinah, Lucy and Maggie, Tessa and Romola, Mrs. Transome and Esther, Rosamond (or Celia) and Dorothea, Gwendolen and Mirah — in each case the model of conventional, merely ornamental womanhood is unfavorably compared with the exceptional, individualistic, and idealistically enterprising woman.[30]

iii

Although Leclaire fails to give full weight to Scott's role in the development of English regional fiction, his survey of the cultural

[28] *Ibid.*
[29] *Ibid.*, 19.
[30] See also Lloyd Fernando, "George Eliot, Feminism, and Dorothea Brooke," *Review of English Literature*, IV (1963), 76–90.

background against which that development occurred is competent and concise. Writing of the years 1830-1870, he comments on the influence of political reform, social change, wider education, and better transportation on the growth of the regional novel and finds that in its initial state regionalism was on the whole not deliberate or self-conscious. Novelists were encouraged by the examples of Maria Edgeworth and of Scott to write about the places they knew personally; in handling intimately familiar settings they naturally came to employ a concrete and precise style, buttressed by authentic detail, by facts observed at first hand and fondly remembered. (Hence derives the accurate location, temporal as well as spatial, of many novels in this period.)[31] For in reaction to social and industrial developments, writers and their audience recalled with mingled nostalgia and concern the rural order of another day. At first the interest in country life remained apart from the fictional treatment of current problems, but after Charlotte Brontë's *Shirley* (1849) and Mrs. Gaskell's *North and South* (1855) they came to be frequently combined.[32]

In the forties and fifties, however, the purely rural novel, with its vein of pastoral sentiment, still continued to flourish. George Eliot's first books, from *Scenes of Clerical Life* (1858) to *Silas Marner* (1861), seem to me to fall, at least superficially, into this category, for in them a wistful regard for a lost way of life tends to prevail (at least until parts of *The Mill on the Floss* and *Silas Marner*) over her historical perspective and sensitivity to contemporary issues. But in spite of their concern with the rustic past — or rather because of it — these novels, together with their more ephemeral counterparts, met a genuine need of the time. As Gillian Beer writes of early rural fiction:

> The industrial encroachments on the landscape, instead of undermining the literary image of the countryside as the source of beauty and the home of morality, gave to it rather the added

[31] Leclaire, pp. 84–90. See also Kathleen Tillotson, pp. 91–115, on the emergence in the 1840s of the "genius of place" in the English novel and the frequent temporal shift of the action to a "period twenty to sixty years earlier" than the writing; and Harvey, pp. 115–117, and John Holloway, *The Victorian Sage* (London, 1953), pp. 116–121, on the "temporal scale" of George Eliot's novels.

[32] Phyllis Bentley calls *Shirley* "the first great English regional novel" (p. 14); she notes also that the working class characters and dialect in *Mary Barton* and *North and South* constituted important innovations in the development of the regional novel (p. 17).

27

intensity of a vanishing world. It is as if the integral image of the countryside was an emotional and literary necessity to the reading public of the earlier nineteenth century, feeling itself perhaps newly divorced from an agrarian past.[33]

The power of pastoral literature to attract Victorian readers requires very little authentication. It may be enough to point again to the popularity of Scott and, especially, of Wordsworth. Indeed, David Masson's tone in justifying the novel of country life recalls "the love of rural objects and natural scenery" that first drew John Stuart Mill to Wordsworth's poems [34] or "the extraordinary power with which Wordsworth feels the joy offered to us in nature" that Arnold admired.[35] Masson is worried that "so many of us, cooped up in cities and chained to this part or that of the crowded machinery of complex civilization, have all but lost our acquaintance with our ancient mother earth." He sees in the rural novel a chance of escape, of maintaining a healing contact with nature:

> . . . is it not well, is it not medicinal that . . . in the pages of our novelists, as in those of our narrative poets, we should be taken away in the imagination from our common social haunts, and placed in situations where Nature still exerts upon Humanity the unbroken magnetism of her inanimate bulk, soothing into peace in the quiet meadows, whispering of the unearthly in the depths of a forest, telling tales of the past in some solitary crumbling ruin, moaning her sorrow in the gusts of a moor at midnight, or dashing the eternal monotone of her many voices against a cliff-embattled shore? [36]

It is only fair to mention that this effusion, with its somewhat Gothic delight in entrancement and its fashionable literary allusion to Tennyson's "Ulysses," was first delivered in a lecture room. But despite its rhetorical inflation and circumlocution, the passage is obviously sincere, reflecting in its dislike of the city a tradition of thought which reaches at least from Wordsworth to our own day. It may be ironic (suggestively, perhaps) that so sentimental an appeal should have

---

[33] Gillian Beer, "Charles Kingsley and the Literary Image of the Countryside," *Victorian Studies*, VIII (March 1965), 244.

[34] *Autobiography of John Stuart Mill* (New York: Columbia University Press, 1924), pp. 103–104.

[35] "Wordsworth," *Essays in Criticism, Second Series* (London and New York, 1888), p. 153.

[36] *British Novelists*, p. 28.

been published in the same year as *The Origin of Species*, with its rather more disturbing view of the natural world, yet it is to just this kind of longing for communion with nature that the first novelists of rural life catered.

George Eliot, although she has her moments of nostalgia and even occasionally of melodrama, deliberately rejects in all her work the sentimental, idealized treatment of the country and the essentially condescending attitude to the passing rural order that many of the early writers, especially in the 1820s and 1830s, favored. She neglected, however, as they did, to leave "some record of the worsening conditions of the peasant and small farmer and of the drift to the towns which Cobbett records in the 1820's." [37] But it is not through ignorance or indifference that she fails to portray the squalor, misery, and injustice of the countryside. When she began her career as a novelist in the late 1850s, the fictional expositions of the "Condition-of-England Question" by Disraeli, Mrs. Gaskell, Dickens, and Charles Kingsley were already well known. George Eliot's aims were different: she was intent not on drawing attention to the suffering of the poor but on expressing her view of life. She was a genuinely intellectual person with a conservative bent of mind, and the problems that she thought important, the problems to which she constantly returned, were ethical and psychological — internal, permanent, and ultimate rather than external, circumstantial, and immediate. She was stirred most strongly by moral and emotional themes transcending in relevance the limits of the provincial environment in which she first perceived them; at the same time, her penetrating vision and intelligence imbued the setting in which she located her human dramas with far-reaching significance. To the extent that her imagination was directed by what she knew best and cherished most, the condition of the poor, as a general social issue, could be included in her

[37] Gillian Beer, 244. On the absence of poverty in the fiction of the time, see Kebbel, *Fraser's Magazine*, XXIII, 275, where by a curious twist of logic he concludes that since George Eliot presented rural life as generally comfortable, "the hardships of the village poor were to some extent exaggerated" by such writers as Cobbett and Crabbe. But see also Wright, *PMLA*, LVI, 1108: "We find nowhere in her works any description of the home conditions of the very poor and only one incident revealing violence — the latter mainly free from sentiment ... But what George Eliot omitted of historical detail she compensated for by approaching social questions with a vast philosophical background that gave her a perspective superior to that of her novel-writing predecessors and contemporaries."

29

pictures of regional life only incidentally and with questionable success, as in the depiction of the careworn miners in *Felix Holt*.[38] V. S. Pritchett has described well the direction of her literary interests, at least in her early novels: "In the mid-Victorian England of the railway and the drift to the towns, George Eliot was harking back to the last of the yeomen, among whom she was born and who brought out the warmth, the humour, the strength of her nature." [39]

As a regionalist, then, George Eliot is neither pastoral and romantic nor self-consciously topical. Her novels are prompted by personal interests and affections, by her aesthetic instincts and intimate knowledge of her material. In helping her to achieve an art of lasting value, such motives also strengthen her regionalism and give it a quality of philosophical resonance; they represent the "pure" elements without which novels cannot be interesting in themselves as well as for their local color. Lucien Leclaire, who discusses this problem in a synoptic "Essai de définition" at the end of his study, speaks of the deadening effect of regional fiction in which some element, whether picturesque, topographical, or documentary, is to be found in excess. Similarly, he says, a lack of perspective in viewing a region — inordinately local enthusiasms and prejudices, for example — can bring about a fatal imbalance in a novel and limit its interest.[40] George Eliot's works are singularly free from such flaws: although their locale is recognizably that of the Midlands, there is nothing insistent or inevitable about the identification, as there is, say, with Hardy's Wessex. Phyllis Bentley, in defining George Eliot's regionalism, finds that her "fictitious topography is extensive and corresponds fairly closely to reality, but it does not draw the reader's attention as does that of Trollope." Conceding that her plots and themes are not strictly regional, Miss Bentley insists on the regionalism of "a great many of the episodes, the incidents, of her stories," and "many of her main, important characters." Regional characters, she explains, "are those who wrest a living directly from the soil," and she points to the Poysers and the Tullivers, to Silas Marner and Caleb Garth. Finally,

[38] With characteristic caution she declared in a letter: "But though I saw a great deal of the Poor in my early youth, I have been for so many years aloof from all practical experience in relation to them, that I am conscious of my incompetence to judge how far it would be wise to use existing arrangements rather than to try and supersede them" (*Letters*, VI, 46–47).
[39] *The Living Novel* (London: Chatto and Windus, 1946), p. 85.
[40] *Le Roman régionaliste dans les îles Britanniques*, pp. 260–262.

she comments on George Eliot's moderation in the use of dialect
(according to Leclaire, the most telling "local color" element in any
regional work):

> She handles [dialect] very effectively, with far fewer apostrophes
> and phonetic spellings than Charlotte Brontë or Mrs. Gaskell.
> This she did deliberately, following a theory of her own. In a
> letter to the philologist Skeat she explained this theory, telling
> him that her inclination to be as close as she could in her render-
> ing of dialect, both in words and spelling, "was constantly
> checked by the artistic duty of being generally intelligible . . ." [41]

In her employment of other obviously regional features, George
Eliot is guided by the same thoughtful restraint that marks her use
of dialect. Never permitting the strictly local characters of the environment to dominate her, she succeeds nevertheless in giving us
the authentic spirit of the place. What we recall about "the George
Eliot country" is not its correspondence to the Midland shires but
rather the rural, deeply provincial quality of its life.[42] In her work
we find embodied the sympathy that Leclaire considers to be the
only constant and quintessential elements of regionalism: "les rap-
ports entre l'auteur et son milieu, d'un part, et le sujet de son oeuvre
d'autre part." [43] George Eliot can be judged, particularly by the terms
of Leclaire's definition and summation, a regional novelist of the most
genuine and valuable kind:

> . . . lorsqu'à la présentation régionale se joint aussi *la nécessité
> régionale du thème*, c'est à dire, en somme, lorsque, par une
> véritable synthèse organique le milieu naturel intervient dans la
> destinée des personnages, de sorte que le cadre et les hommes
> sont intimement solidaires, alors l'on obtient un roman régional-
> iste au sens le plus complet du terme, dont la valeur intrinsèque
> ne depend plus que du talent de son auteur.[44]

[41] See also William Edward A. Axon, "George Eliot's Use of Dialect," *Stray
Chapters in Literature, Folklore, and Archeology* (Manchester, 1888), p. 163:
"With the reticence of genius, George Eliot obtains her effects with the slightest
possible expenditure of material. She contrives to give the impression of provincial speech without importing any great number of unfamiliar words into the
text."
[42] As Lord David Cecil says of *Middlemarch*: "She did not have a vision of
Barchester or Cranford and then invent situations on which to hang her pictures
of this vision; she had a vision of society and the impression of certain principles,
and then embodied it in a picture of a specific place" (*Early Victorian Novelists*,
p. 264).
[43] *Le Roman régionaliste dans les îles Britanniques*, p. 257.
[44] *Ibid.*, p. 260.

iv

The distinctive features of regional fiction — the copious use and detailed depiction of a well-known setting, characters who belong to the working and middle classes, an atmosphere of everyday activity, dialogue in common, often colorfully indigenous language — all encourage a realistic manner. As Leclaire abundantly demonstrates, realism, which is almost an organic property of the traditional novel in general,[45] is practically inevitable in regional narratives. For George Eliot, the realistic (by which she meant truthful) presentation of life was the most essential quality in art. She developed her aesthetic theory, in which realism served as an indispensable means to "the extension of our sympathies," long before she began to write fiction. In her critical essays for *The Westminster Review*, it was realism that she took as her principal criterion in evaluating the works she was discussing; and it was realism — moral, psychological, social, and topographical — that she espoused as the chief merit in fiction. In reviewing *Modern Painters* she was particularly delighted to find that Ruskin shared her belief:

> The truth of infinite value that he teaches is realism — the doctrine that all truth and beauty are to be attained by a humble and faithful study of nature, and not by substituting vague forms, bred by imagination on the mists of feeling, in place of definite, substantial reality. The thorough acceptance of this doctrine would remould our life; and he who teaches its application to any one department of human activity with such power as Mr. Ruskin's, is a prophet for his generation.[46]

[45] For discussions of realism and the novel, see especially Northrop Frye, *Anatomy of Criticism* (Princeton, 1957) pp. 303–314 (first published as "The Four Forms of Fiction," *Hudson Review*, II [1950], 582–595); the symposium on realism in *Comparative Literature*, III (1951), especially the essays by Robert Gorham Davis, Henry Hatfield, and Harry Levin; Ian Watt, *The Rise of the Novel* (London, 1957), pp. 9–34.

[46] *Westminster Review*, LXV (1856), 343–344. In an article on "George Eliot's Novels," *The Quarterly Review*, CVIII (1860), 469–499, finding her altogether too realistic for its taste, accused her of following "that very dangerous model, Mr. Ruskin." But Ruskin himself would have rejected her as a disciple: he disliked her interest in commonplace facts and objected particularly to *The Mill on the Floss* (in *Fiction, Fair and Foul*, I and V), whose characters he considered "the sweepings out of a Pentonville omnibus." It was out of "personal regard for her," that he abstained from criticizing George Eliot when she was alive [see *The Works of John Ruskin*, ed. E. T. Cook and Alexander Wedderburn (London, 1907) XXVII, 377]. On the relation between George Eliot and Ruskin, see also Darrel Mansell, Jr., "Ruskin and George Eliot's Realism," *Criticism* (Summer 1965), pp. 203–216.

32

She opposed falsification and sentimentalization in art, literature, and theology; the sarcastic attacks on Edward Young's poetry
and on John Cumming, and the equally scathing treatment of pastoral
idylls in painting and fiction [47] exemplify the fervor of her opposition.
Her critical perspective was characteristically far-sighted, comprehensive, fully thought out, and morally directed.

> Art is the nearest thing to life; it is a mode of amplifying ex-
> perience and extending our contact with our fellow-men beyond
> the bounds of our personal lot. All the more sacred is the task
> of the artist when he undertakes to paint the life of the People.
> Falsification here is far more pernicious than in the more artifi-
> cial aspects of life. It is not so very serious that we should have
> false ideas about evanescent fashions — about the manners and
> conversations of beaux and duchesses; but it *is* serious that our
> sympathy with the perennial joys and struggles, the toil, the
> tragedy, and the humour in the life of our more heavily-laden
> fellow-men, should be perverted, and turned towards a false
> object instead of the true one ... We want to be taught to feel,
> not for the heroic artisan or the sentimental peasant, but for the
> peasant in all his coarse apathy, and the artisan in all his sus-
> picious selfishness. (*Essays*, p. 271)

The passage comes from "The Natural History of German Life," an
extended review of Wilhelm Heinrich von Riehl's *Die bürgerliche
Gesellschaft* (1851) and *Land und Leute* (1853). Written in July
1856, the essay anticipates in its main principles the familiar and
only partly humorous apologies for Amos Barton in *Scenes of Clerical
Life* and for "the Reverend Adolphus Irwine" in *Adam Bede*. Although
she subtly refined these principles in her later work, George Eliot
always remained faithful to their spirit.

Her realism, however, is not the realism of Zola or even Flau-
bert. It is not based on a massive, detailed, quasi-photographic transcription of physical reality. She is ruled in her work by certain
feelings and ideas about the nature of man, society, and the moral
order, and her selection of the facts of existence, while firmly based
on objective observation, is guided by her attitudes and colored by her
comprehensive affection.[48] Although she was from the beginning of

---

[47] "Evangelical Teaching: Dr. Cumming," "Worldliness and Other-Worldli-
ness: The Poet Young," and "Silly Novels by Lady Novelists"; all three are reprinted in *Essays*.
[48] Knoepflmacher, *Religious Humanism*, pp. 60–61, 118–122, writes about

her career complimented by most critics for the verisimilitude with which she portrayed humble life, there were soon readers, alerted perhaps by the didactic authorial intrusions in the early novels and the increasingly explicit embodiment of "the doctrine of consequences" in the late ones, who questioned the authenticity of her version of reality. "George Eliot," wrote one such caviler, "has frequently been praised for her realism . . . If by 'realism' is meant the exact reproduction of the facts of life, George Eliot is not a realist. She is too fond of inculcating ethical doctrines to descend to a minute study of the actual." [49]

Such skepticism about the extent and genuineness of her realism has been most often focused on the moral determinism (akin at times to Carlyle's "Natural Supernaturalism") that governs the world of her fiction and on the implausibility of certain of her characters. But more relevant to my present concern is what some critics regard as her failure to depict the very lowest segment of the rural population, the laborers and peasants as distinct from the craftsmen and tenant farmers. Walter J. Hyde, who notes this omission, comments that she did not actually ignore humble types but dealt with them only to the extent that her sense of decorum and narrative necessity dictated.

> For George Eliot there would be no falsehood, yet no obscenity . . . The *real* peasant . . . whenever glimpses of him are unfolded, appears with underdeveloped suggestions of a naturalistic treatment. He is, like the laborers who attack the railway surveyors in *Middlemarch*, ignorant as well as surly and suspicious. He is usually slow and clumsy of speech, for his head is vacant of thought . . . An animal's existence is the peasant's lot. [50]

She was thus not entirely inconsistent with her declared approval of the frank presentation of the coarseness of lower-class characters. But in the review of Riehl, where she made the declaration, she called for sympathy as well as truthfulness in depicting laborers and peasants, and the gentle condescension and amiable humor with which

George Eliot's "idealistic realism" from a similar perspective. See also the discussions of her literary theory cited in note 52.

[49] D. F. Hannigan, "Prospective Transformation of the Novel," *Westminster Review*, CXL (1893), 257.

[50] Hyde, *PMLA*, LXXII, 154–157. See also Paul, *Merry England*, I; H. C. Minchin, "George Eliot: Some Observations," *Fortnightly Review*, CXII (1919), 896–903; and C. W. Meadowcroft, Jr., *The Place of Eden Phillpotts in English Peasant Drama* (Philadelphia, 1924), pp. 10–14.

she describes such figures in *Adam Bede* or *Silas Marner* accord well with her critical pronouncements. To imply that she regards the peasant as simply brutish is to ignore the compassion which Ferdinand Brunetière defined as the distinctive and transcendent quality of George Eliot's realism. Adopting her terms, he contrasted the warm concern and tenderness for humble characters evident in her novels and those of other English realists with the detachment and even hostility of the French naturalists: "Une sympathie profonde pour ces 'monotones existences,' et pour ces 'vulgaires laboureurs' qu'il aime à mettre en scène est l'âme même du naturalisme anglais. Le naturalisme français, au contraire . . . ne respire que dédain et mépris pour ses Bouvard et ses Pécuchet." [51]

George Eliot's realism, besides being warmed by her humanity, was also controlled by her philosophy. Her novels rest on a substantially worked out and critically tested set of principles, of which the most important and characteristic are fidelity to experience and at the same time imaginative and edifying transmutation of experience. Students of her theory of fiction have associated such transmutation with the increased intellectuality of her late works. "The greatest change in her creed as a novelist," writes Richard Stang, "was in the importance of the place of ideas in the design of the novel . . . in her periodical reviews, her emphasis was on the novel as a picture of real life. She came more and more, however, to believe that the only true line of development for the English novel must lie in what Arnold called 'the application of ideas to life.' " [52] Reflecting this change is her abandonment of the inarticulate characters, humble forms of existence, and predominantly rural settings of the early novels for the depiction of "ordinary causes" acting on individuals with exceptionally large views of life, intense aspirations, and a capacity for moral growth and self-knowledge. [53]

[51] Ferdinand Brunetière, *Le Roman naturaliste* (Paris, 7th ed., 1896), p. 213.
[52] Richard Stang, "The Literary Criticism of George Eliot," *PMLA*, LXXII (1957), 961; cf. Alice R. Kaminsky, "George Eliot, George Henry Lewes, and the Novel," *PMLA*, LXX (1955), 997–1013. Mrs. Kaminsky, relying on P. Bourl'honne, *George Eliot: Éssai de biographie intellectuelle et morale, 1819–1854* (Paris, 1933), suggests that it was Lewes who showed George Eliot a way of going beyond the factual realism she had subscribed to in her early work. Gordon S. Haight, however, is skeptical of the extent of influence she attributes to Lewes; see "George Eliot's Theory of Fiction," *Victorian Newsletter*, no. 10 (Fall 1956), pp. 1–2.
[53] See also Barbara Hardy, p. 14, where she makes the same point and uses

While such development does not in itself constitute a departure from strict realism, the growing conspicuousness of the moral vision, with its painstaking linking of cause and effect, does occasionally in the late novels strain the limits of ordinary credulity. Her vision rests on a questionable belief in the inevitable rebounding of past deeds upon the doer and the operation of a moral law in an apparently secular universe. But when this vision is convincingly fleshed out, when it is fully and carefully realized, the reader is not provoked to argue with it. In *Middlemarch*, for example, one simply does not sense any dogmatic arbitrariness in the way the novel's various entanglements are resolved. The underlying ethical design is so perfectly dramatized, made concrete and particular, that the narrative, far from being stultified, gains coherence as well as depth from the moral vision. The events and relationships seem to unfold with all the naturalness, substantiality, and necessity of real life.[54] As W. J. Harvey, in discussing the problem of George Eliot's determinism, very aptly observes:

> ... the impression we derive from the novels is not that of a malignant Fate or of an impersonal historical force; it is rather a full portrayal of the "necessary combinations through which life is manifested" ... we must remember always to distinguish between her philosophy and the successful effect of her creative powers ... between the kind of inevitability which derives from the philosophy and the impression of inevitability which is the effect of a successful aesthetic whole.[55]

v

George Eliot would probably not have conceded that her mature manner, philosophical and at times even visionary though it was,

---

it to modify the simplifications of Mario Praz, *The Hero in Eclipse in Victorian Fiction*, trans. Angus Davidson (London, 1956), pp. 319–382. It is on this development of her work that Thomas Seccombe in his article on George Eliot in the eleventh edition of the *Encyclopaedia Britannica* must have based his contrast between Jane Austen, who "dealt with familiar domestic types," and George Eliot, who "excelled in the presentation of extraordinary souls."

[54] For the resolution of this seeming paradox see Paris, especially pp. 242–250, "The Reconciliation of Realism and Moralism," and George Levine, "Determinism and Responsibility in the Works of George Eliot," *PMLA*, LXXVII (1962), 268–279.

[55] *The Art of George Eliot* (London: Chatto and Windus, 1961), p. 50. I am grateful to Mrs. W. J. Harvey for allowing me to quote here and subsequently from her late husband's book.

violated her realistic credo. "There has been no change in the point of view from which I regard our life since I wrote my first fiction," she said in 1876. "The principles which are at the root of my effort to paint Dinah Morris are equally at the root of my effort to paint Mordecai" (*Letters*, VI, 318). The enlarged scope and ambition from *Romola* on, the pronounced intellectuality and symbolic texture of *Romola* and *Daniel Deronda*, can thus be seen as extending rather than betraying her notion of realism. Sharing the view of George Henry Lewes that the antithesis of "Realism . . . is not Idealism, but Falsism," [56] that realism is the accurate but significant (and therefore selective) imitation of life, she fused into a coherent personal vision the facts culled from experience and observation. Her description of the creative process, written in 1879, is directed against the photographic transcription of appearances and upholds the validity of the mind's distilling action:

> . . . powerful imagination is not false outward vision, but intense inward representation, and a creative energy constantly fed by susceptibility to the veriest minutiae of experience, which it reproduces and constructs in fresh and fresh wholes . . . a breadth of ideal association which informs every material object, every incidental fact with far-reaching memories and stored residues of passion . . .[57]

Coleridgean as her affirmation of the truth of imaginative transmutation is,[58] it is not far removed from modern and flexible conceptions of realism. In spite of the ethical vision that controls her writing, her aims and technique generally meet the stipulations laid down by theorists of realism: verisimilitude, representativeness, and objec-

[56] "Realism in Art: Recent German Fiction," *Westminster Review*, LXX (1858), 492. By "Falsism" Lewes means any distorted rendering of experience in the interest of romance and sentimentality. Since his elaboration of the Idealism-Falsism opposition curiously recalls George Eliot's own strictures in "The Natural History of German Life" (1856) against the idyllic misrepresentation of rural life, he would seem to be following up her suggestion. John Blackwood records that she said to him (in 1861): "Any real observation of life and character must be limited, and the imagination must fill in and give life to the picture" (*Letters*, III, 427).

[57] "How We Come to Give Ourselves False Testimonials, and Believe in Them," *Impressions of Theophrastus Such*.

[58] Coleridge, in the *Biographia Literaria*, Chapter XIII, defines the secondary imagination as an echo of the primary, an "agent of all human perception": "It dissolves, diffuses, dissipates, in order to recreate . . . to idealize and to unify."

tivity.[59] Although in the second part of this study I discuss in some detail George Eliot's reliance on realistic techniques and her departures from them, it is not my ambition here to attempt a full-blown definition of realism. But I would like at least to indicate how she fulfills the basic imperatives of the mode.

In all her writings, including the correspondence, we find numerous expressions of her devotion to the principle of verisimilitude. Always determined to achieve "as full a vision of the medium in which a character moves as of the character itself," she sought to breathe into her novels a sense of "real life," to conjure up an environment which would seem palpable and authentic and characters who would be credible and compelling. She therefore avoided scrupulously any melodramatic simplification in sketching the motives and behavior of her people, and disapproved of such contrivance in the work of others. As early as February 1853 she writes in a letter: " 'Ruth,' with all its merits, will not be an enduring classical fiction — will it? Mrs. Gaskell seems to me to be constantly misled by a love of sharp contrasts — of 'dramatic' effects. She is not contented with the subdued colouring — the half tints of real life" (*Letters*, II, 86). Truth to life was her constant criterion, but it was her own sense of what was true, of course, that guided her. Writing in 1857 to John Blackwood, she defined the tenets that ruled her in delineating character and defended the credibility of her figures: "My artistic bent is directed not at all to the presentation of eminently irreproachable characters, but to the presentation of mixed human beings in such a way as to call forth tolerant judgment, pity, and sympathy. And I cannot stir a step from what I *feel* to be *true* in character" (*Letters*, II, 299).

It is through her interest in "mixed human beings" that she imbues her work with a sense of representativeness. In her earliest novels she repeatedly declares her concern with the normal, the common, and even the commonplace; as she justifies that concern, she manages to ennoble it. The ethically directed, almost evangelical and humanitarian quality of her realism is made quite plain in such declarations. In a famous passage in *Adam Bede*, for example, she says:

[59] See George J. Becker, "Realism: An Essay in Definition," *Modern Language Quarterly*, X (1949), 184–197; also the symposium on realism in *Comparative Literature*, III (1951).

These fellow-mortals, every one, must be accepted as they are: you can neither straighten their noses, nor brighten their wit, nor rectify their dispositions; and it is these people — amongst whom your life is passed — that it is needful you should tolerate, pity, and love: it is these more or less ugly, stupid, inconsistent people, whose movements of goodness you should be able to admire — for whom you should cherish all possible hopes, all possible patience. And I would not, even if I had the choice, be the clever novelist who could create a world so much better than this, in which we get up in the morning to do our daily work, that you would be likely to turn a harder, colder eye on the dusty streets and the common green fields — on the real breathing men and women, who can be chilled by your indifference or injured by your prejudice; who can be cheered and helped onward by your fellow-feeling, your forbearance, your outspoken, brave justice.[60]

Even when, as many critics have noted,[61] she extended her range and concentrated on depicting characters of exceptional vitality and intelligence, she retained her interest in the mundane. But in her late novels ordinary people are seen as part of the background against which the extraordinary individuals move. Too much can be made, however, of the contrast between the two phases of her career: the difference is one of emphasis, not subject matter. From the beginning she treats the commonplace as the context in which the outstanding person has to function, with which he or she has to come to terms, accepting its limitations and recognizing its capacity for love, beauty, goodness, and strength. Thus, although Amos Barton gives his name to George Eliot's first story, it is his wife Milly, "a large, fair, gentle Madonna" with "a sublime capacity for loving," who is presented with

[60] Chapter XVII. Subsequent references to George Eliot's novels will be included in the text; the Standard Edition (Edinburgh and London: William Blackwood and Sons [1897]) is used throughout.

[61] For example, Alice Kaminsky writes of George Eliot's ambition to describe "deeper truths ... higher mental life" and "human behavior in relation to a more complex environment" than in *Adam Bede*, *The Mill on the Floss*, and *Silas Marner* (*PMLA*, LXX, 1009). Robert M. O'Clair notes in Chapter 2 of his unpublished Ph.D. dissertation, "A Critical Study of George Eliot's *Middlemarch*" (Harvard University, 1956) that *Felix Holt* marks the end of George Eliot's interest in simple rural characters — she now focuses on businessmen, professional men, and the aristocracy — but *Romola*, which preceded *Felix Holt*, signifies the change still more dramatically. Barbara Hardy defines the change in terms of the intelligence and articulateness of the protagonists and insists on its gradualism, for only Amos Barton and Silas Marner "may be called entirely unheroic" (p. 14). And even Silas, as I suggest in Chapter VII, has a heroic quality, especially in contrast with his environment.

the greatest intensity and admiration. Mr. Gilfil, the protagonist of the second story, appears drab, but the narrative, in disclosing the circumstances that have left his life without a source of inspiration, restores to him some of the impressiveness he had in his youth. And in the third story of the *Scenes of Clerical Life*, the two central figures, Janet Dempster and Mr. Tryan, are clearly imposing in stature. Similarly, though each of the chief characters in *Adam Bede* is marked by some human imperfection, none is really commonplace, certainly not Adam himself.[62] ("I will not pretend that his was an ordinary character among workmen," says the author of him in Chapter XIX; "He was not an average man.") Arguing from the obverse point of view about the later books, it is manifest that in *Middlemarch*, for example, the protagonists are at least as exposed to the working of "ordinary causes" as their average fellow creatures; moreover, in contending against the abrasive entanglements and frustrations of ordinary experience, they prove to be rather less exceptional than they at first appeared, either to themselves or the reader. Indeed, a correct estimate of themselves and their position in the world is the chastening lesson that most of her characters have to learn: in one form or another Lydgate's "spots of commonness" mark everyone and are therefore representative of general human limitations.

Objectivity is already implicit in George Eliot's quest for verisimilitude and representativeness, but it appears also in the characteristic fairness and compassion with which she treats almost all her fictional personages. Mr. Dempster in "Janet's Repentance," Dunstan Cass in *Silas Marner*, Raffles in *Middlemarch* are among the very few of her villains who appear as simply villainous; even the most criminal figure in her novels, Tito Melema in *Romola*, is seen from the inside, and his defects and rationalizations are analyzed with understanding. Her portraits of Casaubon and Bulstrode are better known and much more striking examples than Tito of the forbearance, the fully rounded objectivity with which she regards her characters.

[62] Adam and Dinah have traditionally been considered failures in characterization because of what was thought their faultlessness. Modern critics, however, have shown that neither is really *perfectly* good or is intended by the author to seem so. See, for example, the contrast between Gerald Bullett's view of Adam in *George Eliot: Her Life and Books* (New Haven, 1948), pp. 182–185 and Joan Bennett's (pp. 109–110). See also George R. Creeger, "An Interpretation of *Adam Bede*," *ELH*, XXIII (1956), 218–236; Reva Stump, pp. 37–51; Barbara Hardy, pp. 32–46; Harvey, pp. 179–184; and Paris, pp. 149–156.

Her comprehensive vision and ability to render convincingly a variety of points of view are essentially a form of "negative capability." Supported by her social experience and insight as well as her aesthetic intelligence, she depicts successfully not only different individuals but different classes, and includes in her presentation much of the social spectrum of her time. V. S. Pritchett writes that in *Adam Bede* she "knows the country hierarchy and how a squire is this kind of man, a yeoman another, a teacher, a publican, a doctor, a clergyman another. They are more than themselves; they are their group as well. In this they recall the characters of Balzac." [63] But as she shows in *Middlemarch* and especially in *Daniel Deronda*, she can move with great facility from the country kitchen to the elegant drawing room. She prided herself on the breadth of her social knowledge, and the critics, who have come to admire the way she employs that knowledge in her novels, have justified her pride.[64]

[63] *The Living Novel*, p. 87.

[64] Remarking on the objectivity of the account of St. Ogg's in *The Mill on the Floss*, Claude Bissell says: "George Eliot, by the strength of her personality and the happy alliance of circumstances, was never closely identified for any length of time with any one social group or any one class. She is, as it were, removed from the world of petty aspirations and petty conflicts that dog the author whose social status is a cause for personal concern ... No other Victorian novelist moves more firmly and confidently through almost the entire range of nineteenth-century society. There are gaps, of course, but the total picture is a tribute to her catholicity of vision. Her success with rural types and with the world of middle-class commercialism is well known. Not so well known, perhaps, is her success with a more sophisticated and aristocratic society, the kind of society that Dickens entered at his peril" (*ELH*, XVIII, 226–227).

3   Toward Social History: Continuity and Development
in George Eliot's Fiction

*Local character, habits, institutions, modes of
thought and observation, are all the result of
a long process, different in different parts of
England. They are only to be seen and understood by a sympathetic searcher and observer who
looks upon each part of England in the light of
its past, who sees that past not only in ancient
buildings here and there, but on the whole face
of the land, and in the hearts and lives of its
inhabitants.*
— Mandell Creighton

i

Although in her late novels George Eliot captures the life of the upper classes with skill and felicity, her special strength, as has been widely recognized, resides in the depiction of what Wordsworth called "humble and rustic life." Wordsworth's influence on her is generally assumed to have been profound, but few critics have tried to define in any detail its exact nature.[1] Her affinity with the poet extends beyond their common interest in the countryside. They shared also, as has been pointed out, the same conception of literature, the notion that it should be true to life but edifying: "He believed poetry should be impregnated with moral ideas; she believed the same of the novel. He was the advocate of a realism which led the mind and spirit through external reality to the true, transcendental reality, and (though using a different terminology) so was she."[2] As that external reality, both chose to deal with rural life and, focusing on its generalizing possibilities, invested it with a representative significance. In the Preface to the *Lyrical Ballads*, in which we find one of the earliest and most trenchant accounts of the cultural effects of growing industrialization and urbanization in England, Wordsworth justifies his use of country life as material for poetry in terms that could apply also to George Eliot's practice as a novelist:

> Humble and rustic life was generally chosen, because in that condition the essential passions of the heart find a better soil in which they can attain their maturity, are less under restraint, and speak a plainer and more emphatic language; because in that condition of life our elementary feelings co-exist in a state of greater simplicity, and, consequently, may be more accurately contemplated and more forcibly communicated; because the manners of rural life germinate from those elementary feelings, and, from the necessary character of rural occupations, are more easily comprehended, and are more durable; and, lastly, because in that condition the passions of men are incorporated with the beautiful and permanent forms of nature.

[1] As Thomas Pinney notes, no full analysis of Wordsworth's influence on George Eliot exists, although all critics and biographers take note of it. See Pinney, "George Eliot's Reading of Wordsworth: The Record," *Victorian Newsletter*, no. 24 (Fall 1963), pp. 20–22, where, among other items, he lists the mottoes for novels, chapter epigraphs, and quotations from Wordsworth and allusions to him in the fiction, essays, and letters.
[2] James D. Rust, "The Art of Fiction in George Eliot's Reviews," *Review of English Studies*, VII n.s. (1956), 172.

45

George Eliot chose in her early novels to write about ordinary provincial experience because she was intimately acquainted with it and because she wanted, as is clear in her review of Riehl and her pleas in *Scenes of Clerical Life*, *Adam Bede*, and *The Mill on the Floss*, to make the life of the rural working classes known to her largely bourgeois audience, to make it appear interesting and sympathetic. But also, in her constant reading of Wordsworth, she must have been impressed by his description and exploitation of the literary values of rural circumstances. In discussing the novels themselves, I hope to show how her own writing relies on those values, how she repeatedly contrasts the atmosphere of her stories with the life of her urban, intellectual readers only to call attention to the essential uniformity of human nature and the continuity between the simple past and the increasingly complex present. Here, as part of the critical background for that discussion, I wish simply to suggest in a general way the nature of her affinity with Wordsworth.

R. H. Hutton, one of the ablest of George Eliot's first critics, in discussing her early work focuses on her depiction of "manners of the simplest and most genuine kind — of the rural farmers and labourers — of the half-educated portion of the country middle-class, who have learnt no educated reticence." [3] Although he does not mention Wordsworth, his central notion is one of the most important principles in the 1800 Preface — by 1860, the date of Hutton's essay, the radical ideas of Wordsworth's manifesto had apparently become diffused into fairly natural critical attitudes, if not yet commonplaces. Thus what Hutton seizes on as basic in George Eliot is also central to what she has in common with Wordsworth. Arguing that cultivated society tends to suppress the "deeper instincts and emotions in which all men share more or less deeply; which are in the strictest sense personal, and yet in the strictest sense universal," Hutton suggests that George Eliot obtains her peculiar strength from dealing with such instincts and emotions in their relatively pristine state. By way of contrast he adds that "the means of studying these broader aspects of human life are much fewer in the educated society which Miss Austen and Mr. Thackeray draw, than in the country towns, mills,

[3] R. H. Hutton, "The Novels of George Eliot," *National Review*, XI (1860), 194; enlarged and reprinted as "George Eliot as Author" in *Essays on Some of the Modern Guides of English Thought* (London, 1887), pp. 151–268.

and farmhouses which are dotted about George Eliot's *Scenes from*
[*sic*] *Clerical Life* and her more elaborate tales." [4]

The contrast that Hutton draws between the literary opportunities offered by "rural" and "polite" societies is of course somewhat
exaggerated. Henry James, who might well have conceded that the
treatment in novels of cultivated people was subject to some restrictions, would undoubtedly have asserted that such restrictions constituted a valuable challenge, not an obstacle, for the writer intent on
exploring profound, universal human issues. George Eliot seems to
have been prompted by some such belief, as well as by a desire to
confront directly the spirit of her age, when she extended the scope
of her work and, moving beyond the rather limited social dimensions
of her early novels, took as her principal subject in *Romola, Felix
Holt, Middlemarch,* and *Daniel Deronda* the life of refined and complex society and the problems of articulate and sophisticated individuals. In her review of Riehl she had invited some "man of sufficient
moral and intellectual breadth" to

> ... devote himself to studying the natural history of our social
> classes, especially of the small shopkeepers, artisans, and peas-
> antry, — the degree in which they are influenced by local condi-
> tions, their maxims and habits, the points of view from which
> they regard their religious teachers, and the degree to which they
> are influenced by religious doctrines, the interactions of the
> various classes on each other, and what are the tendencies in
> their position towards disintegration or towards development.
> (*Essays,* pp. 272–273)

She herself did not undertake the task of the sociologist, but she
does give us in her novels the fruits of her own observation. The
issues she defined in "The Natural History of German Life" — the
influences of environment on society, the characteristic principles
and models of behavior evolved by each social group, the relevance of
religion to everyday life, the responsiveness of the social structure to
historical change — are all dealt with, indirectly rather than directly,
in the narratives. Her novels, it has been suggested, can thus be seen
"in one aspect as the work of a natural historian of social classes, as
exercises in human ecology — observing and relating the creature
to its surroundings." [5] Such a definition helps to fix for us an element

[4] *Ibid.,* p. 196.
[5] A. J. Sambrook, *English,* XIV, 131.

in George Eliot's writing that is as prominent in the early novels as in the late, but that in the former is vividly embodied through her distinctly regional views and associations, through local memories and attachments.

ii

The authenticity, if not the range, of George Eliot's depiction of society impressed her earliest critics, some of whom trusted it so far that they based historical generalizations on it. Modern students of her work have been more circumspect, but they too find her writings historically useful and revealing, if only in confirming findings obtained through more orthodox and authoritative means than fiction. Asa Briggs and John Prest thus employ *Middlemarch* as a valuable aid in their studies in English history — Briggs in investigating medical training and reform in the nineteenth century,[6] and Prest in describing the industrial revolution in Coventry.[7] Jerome Beaty, a literary scholar, finds in the same novel greater historical relevance than the two historians, but he stresses that the historical material is always used "dramatically, within the story, as part of the lives of the characters." [8] It is "the subtlety and indirectness" with which George Eliot uses history, he suggests, "which largely accounts for the average reader's impression that there are only a few minor references to political history in *Middlemarch* and his feeling that this is not in any sense a 'historical novel.' " [9]

Another critic, Graham Hough, who values George Eliot's sense

[6] *Cambridge Journal*, I, 749–762.

[7] In *The Industrial Revolution in Coventry*, p. 145, Prest says about *Middlemarch*: "This great novel is valuable as a picture of society, and of the relations of classes, of the spread of scandal, and of fashion. It does not matter whether one can identify in Mr. Vincy an actual ribbon-manufacturer, provided that Mr. Vincy himself is not an improbable one. Nor does it matter whether Mr. Bulstrode is an actual banker, Mr. Brooke and Sir John Chettam actual landlords, or Lydgate an actual doctor. Each of them stands for a class, and it is the way they talk about and behave to each other that matters to the historian. If one agrees that George Eliot had the skill and opportunity to portray this kind of historical fact, then one may safely infer that in *Middlemarch* George Eliot has laid a large part of Coventry society bare to the roots."

[8] *Victorian Studies*, I, 175.

[9] *Ibid.*, 177. Carroll, in *Victorian Studies*, II, 305–316, uses Beaty's findings to show George Eliot's technique of correspondence, parallelism, and reinforcement between private and public affairs. On the unobtrusive, functional use of political issues in *Middlemarch*, see also Bissell, *ELH*, XVIII, 238.

of history very highly indeed, believes that "if we really want to know what it felt like to live in pre-Reform Bill England, we will not find out from *Emma* or *Pickwick*; we have to go to *Felix Holt* or *Middlemarch*, duller books but much more like the real thing." [10] The qualification seems old-fashioned today and a little timid, particularly in the light of his praise of George Eliot's "massive handling of the everyday stuff of life." She treats history without the resonance, as Beaty puts it, of "momentous occasion," for she sees it as belonging to the daily existence of her characters. The historical dimension in her novels thus really constitutes an integral part of the "massive realism" that Hough admires. And she gains much of this effect because of her concern with the working life of men and women, which she renders vividly through a considered attention to technical and practical details and a keen power of observation and significant selection. Sensitive to the many connections between psychological, moral, and social spheres, she is particularly successful in suggesting the interpenetration of public and private lives. She presents with unexcelled insight and concreteness the effects on each other of a man's work and his character, and sees, as few novelists before or after have seen, the "separate" segments of normal existence as forming a whole. All her heroic characters — men like Adam Bede, Felix Holt, Caleb Garth, Daniel Deronda; women like Dinah Morris, Maggie Tulliver, Romola, Dorothea Brooke — have to strive to discover vocations in which they can most fully express themselves. Lydgate in *Middlemarch* has found his calling, but he is frustrated by personal limitations, the "spots of commonness" that divide his life into two parts: the strictly professional one, to which he applies all his zeal and impressive intelligence, and the personal one, which he regards as almost incidental and which ruins him because he fails to take it seriously in time. In presenting his medical interests and ambitions, the author is just as detailed, perceptive, and informed as she is in presenting the illusions of his domestic and social life.

The specificity with which she presents Lydgate's situation and others like it is one of her greatest and most distinctive virtues as a novelist. It springs not simply from aesthetic control or strong empathy, but from responsiveness to social conditions and a deep, in-

[10] Graham Hough, "Novelist-Philosopher: George Eliot," *Horizon*, XVII (1948), 51.

stinctive knowledge of provincial existence. She knew, as David Daiches says,

> ... what a doctor's life and studies were really like; she understood the problems of the banker and the landlord; she was aware of the difficulties of the scholar who wanted to make a name for himself by originality as well as she knew the daily routine of the farmer and the auctioneer. And she brought all this knowledge into her best novels with a deep sense of what a society at work was really like . . .[11]

The same detailed authenticity we feel in *Middlemarch* can be found also in her other works, as she presents Adam Bede's carpentry and Mrs. Poyser's housekeeping, the business dealings, general economy, and law suits of St. Ogg's, the obscure agricultural world of *Silas Marner*, and the political and legal chicanery in *Felix Holt*.

She achieves her "massive realism," the sense of particularity and intimacy, not through a simple massing of facts but through the expression, at once objective and sympathetic, of her regional feelings. Authentic and concrete as she is in depicting the life of the provinces, she manages "to avoid the quality of documentary in most of her novels" because "her material is bound to her by actual experience or by personal association and is transformed by memory and reflection. She is giving her version of a way of life that, although it is rooted in the past, continues to exist powerfully in her imagination." [12] Late in life, in the rather sentimental mood of "Looking Backward," she wrote of the pull of local attachments formed in youth:

> I cherish my childish loves — the memory of that warm little nest where my affections were fledged. Since then I have learned to care for foreign countries, for literatures foreign and ancient, for the life of Continental towns dozing around old cathedrals, for the life of London, half sleepless with eager thought and strife . . . I belong to the "Nation of London." Why? There have been many voluntary exiles in the world, and probably in the very first exodus of the patriarchal Aryans . . . some of those who sallied forth went for the sake of a loved companionship, when they would willingly have kept sight of the familiar plains, and of the hills to which they had first lifted up their eyes.

[11] David Daiches, "The Return of George Eliot," *The Nation*, CXCIV (1962), 518.
[12] Bissell, *ELH*, XVIII, 224.

Toward Social History:
Continuity and Development
in George Eliot's Fiction

William Hale White, who knew her when both were boarding at John Chapman's curious establishment, was impressed by the tenacity of her regional ties and particularly by the way she embodied them in her work.[13] Recalling perhaps her own words in the passage just cited, he wrote that her

> . . . youthful impressions were cherished with affection and were the root of a sweet and healthy conservatism. In later life she did not cast herself loose, but applied herself with all her natural strength and with all her stores of the newest thought to display and interpret the Warwickshire of her childhood, its fields, its villages, their inhabitants and their beliefs . . . She owed to them the foundation of what she was, but they, through her, became vocal.[14]

It is fashionable today to disparage the strain of reminiscence in George Eliot's first stories and with it the early critics, like White, who found in that strain her greatest merit as a writer. But in asserting its importance we need not deplore, as many of them did, its diminished influence in the late novels; on the other hand, when we affirm the superiority of the later novels we can do so without scoffing at the "charm" of the early ones. For if we consider her regionalism as merely charming, we may miss not only the moral overtones of the spirit of place in her work or the dependence of her imagination on her provincial past, but also the way in which the meaning of even the "mature" novels is related to her regional consciousness. It may be going too far to say that we "cannot separate the literary works of George Eliot from the geographical surroundings of her youth," [15] but it is true that in making the separation we neglect an element of basic importance to a full understanding of her work. The presentation of social and physical background in her novels is full and wholly convincing; it would be difficult to deny

[13] See Wilfred H. Stone, "Hale White and George Eliot," *University of Toronto Quarterly*, XXV (1955–56), 437–451. Stephen Merton, in "George Eliot and William Hale White," *Victorian Newsletter*, no. 25 (Spring 1964), pp. 13–15, covers some of the same material but makes no mention of Stone's essay. Both writers point to the similarities between White's admiration for George Eliot and Mark Rutherford's attachment to Teresa in *The Autobiography of Mark Rutherford*.
[14] William Hale White, *Last Pages from a Journal* (London, 1915), pp. 136–137.
[15] Edward A. Parry, "The Humour of George Eliot," *Fortnightly Review*, CXII (1919), 881.

that its success depends in large part on the working of her memory, on her affectionate involvement with her past. As one Victorian reviewer observed: "Only an intense love for the country — for the work-a-day people, and for the leisurely life that was going on about her — could have printed the pictures of it so deeply in her imagination." [16]

iii

The question of background in fiction, of the quality and detail with which setting should be presented, has long been the center of critical controversy, especially since Virginia Woolf's essay "Mr. Bennett and Mrs. Brown." In the essay, she objects to Arnold Bennett's minute description of physical surroundings and appearances because it fails to yield a true picture of reality. Robert Liddell, who believes that the novel aims primarily at "the delineation of character in action," seems to support her position: for him "the landscape is merely incidental" and the function of background is simply "limitative, to keep the characters still, and to allow us to concentrate upon them and upon the happenings." [17]

Liddell's definition of fiction, however, seems to be too narrow and inappropriately cast in Aristotelian terms better suited to the drama. To see the novel as the representation of characters in action is to ignore its special capacity for comprehensiveness, social perspective, and concrete depiction. Such theoretical pronouncements should be contrasted with the practice of great novelists like Dickens, Tolstoy, Hardy, or Faulkner, who rely in their work on a closely rendered setting which they invest with symbolic suggestiveness and use as an integral part of the narrative design. "Novelists who make much of scene painting," writes Lord David Cecil, "do so because the setting of their tale is an essential part of their theme. Either the action is connected with the setting or the setting is symbolic of the human drama." [18] John Wain, who in his own novels draws on the realistic tradition as well as sometimes on the regional, sees the question of "how much background ought to be brought in" as calling

[16] "George Eliot," *Blackwood's Edinburgh Magazine*, CXXIX (1881), 255.
[17] Robert Liddell, *A Treatise on the Novel* (London, 1947), pp. 111–112.
[18] Lord David Cecil, "A Note on Jane Austen's Scenery," *The Fine Art of Reading and Other Literary Studies* (Indianapolis, 1957), p. 163.

for "one of the major decisions that faces a writer of fiction." It is, he says, part of "the old problem of Art and Information, or the Imagination and Facts," and its solution depends on a novelist's conception of his task and, ultimately, of life:

> Take any human being — a cabinet minister, a crossing-sweeper, a burglar or a bishop — and try to explain what makes him live his life in that way and on those assumptions. Immediately you have to widen your scope and explain how he was formed by his environment, and continues to be held in a certain shape, induced to look in certain directions, and think in certain patterns, by that environment. Which is itself controlled and created by — what? [19]

The questions Wain raises were obviously the same questions that interested George Eliot; in answering them she was guided by her social experience and insight and her feelings for her native region. Her background and temperament thus equipped her exceptionally well to construct in her novels the comprehensive and substantial settings dictated by her philosophical, social, and aesthetic views. The locale of her novels has been justly admired for being concrete and exact. "She never leaves her stories in the skies, as it were, but gives them a local habitation in time and space," [20] ran a typical Victorian comment; and an early French admirer praised her writing, with some extravagance, for the "exactitude *topographique* irréprochable qui marque les plans du paysage . . . avec une rigueur toute géométrique." [21] Modern critics, who respect functionality in art, have emphasized also the thematic resonance of her descriptions and pointed out that in her work, as a Belgian writer, Irène Simon, says, "Le milieu, l'atmosphère sociale, le climat de l'époque, jouent . . . un rôle essentiel; ils expliquent ou confirment certaines attitudes ou tendances. Ce ne sont pas des simples cadres qui limitent le tableau, mais des thèmes de base où les melodies individuelles prennent naissance." [22]

As the comment implies, George Eliot's use of natural descrip-

---

[19] John Wain, "Oysters and a Novelist's Art," *New Republic*, CLI (1964), 24.

[20] "George Eliot as a Novelist," *Westminster Review*, LIV n.s. (1878), 116.

[21] Émile Montégut, "George Eliot: Les oeuvres et la doctrine morale," *Revue des deux mondes*, LVI (1883), 309; reprinted in *Écrivains modernes de l'Angleterre* (Paris, 1885).

[22] Irène Simon, *Formes du roman anglais de Dickens à Joyce* (Liège, 1949), p. 132.

tion is essentially of the same order as her social analysis and depiction of working life. It shows, like other aspects of her achievement, a development that can be traced from the early novels to the late. Beginning in *Scenes of Clerical Life* with scrupulously accurate representations of actual places recalled from her youth, she moved to an imaginative and emblematic use of physical environment in *Adam Bede* and *Silas Marner*. In these novels the descriptions, while concrete and realistic, are imbued with symbolic significance and play a part in the moral and narrative structure; we need only recall here the carpenter shop, the Rectory, and Mrs. Poyser's kitchen, or Squire Cass's Red House, the parlor of the Rainbow, and Silas Marner's cottage.[23] In *The Mill on the Floss*, the elements involved are somewhat different, for here the author constructs the setting from recollections of her childhood home at Griff in Warwickshire and from the deliberate observation of the town of Gainsborough in Lincolnshire, which serves as St. Ogg's. Impressionism, realism, and symbolism merge and overlap in the fond, frankly nostalgic picture of Dorlcote Mill, the ironic account of the town, and the portentous and, I think, overdone use of the river with its associated imagery.

In *Romola*, she tries as usual to present "as full a vision of the medium" as of the characters, and the result, though labored and artificial, is certainly nothing if not full. Though the book is not the resounding fiasco which it is generally assumed to be, its use of setting differs from the English novels in both aim and effect. The important events in *Romola*, as is most often the case in George Eliot, are intellectual and moral; but whereas in the regional novels these events are almost invariably connected with the environment,

---

[23] Creeger, in *ELH*, XXIII, discusses at length the most prominent example of the symbolic use of landscape in *Adam Bede*, the contrast between Loamshire and Stonyshire; some of his exaggerations are effectively modified by R. A. Foakes, "*Adam Bede* Reconsidered," *English*, XII (1958–59), 173–176, who stresses the idealizing element of pastoral romance in the novel. Casson in the dissertation already cited, and F. W. Willey, in "George Eliot and the Conventions of the Novel" (unpublished Ph.D. dissertation, Harvard University, 1962), rely on Frye's definition of the forms of prose fiction and find in *Adam Bede* a synthesis of realism and idealization, i.e., of the novel and the romance. In his discussions of *Adam Bede*, Willey makes some acute observations on the symbolic significance of landscape and the characters' responses to it. O'Clair finds a similar technique employed in *Middlemarch*. In *Nineteenth-Century Fiction*, XX, Thomson ably discusses the symbolic use of setting in *Silas Marner* and finds, like Foakes, Casson, and F. W. Willey on *Adam Bede*, that the novel evinces "a neat balance of realism and quasi-supernaturalism" (p. 72).

here they remain apart from it. The English Midlands of the nineteenth century she knows feelingly; her knowledge of fifteenth-century Florence is bookish and a little ostentatious. Handling the setting more as a *tour de force* than an organic part of the design, piling up detail for its own sake, for its picturesque effect, she fails to bring the locale to life. "After this [the writing of *Romola*]," Oscar Browning says, "George Eliot paused. She apparently recognized that her real strength lay in the English novel." [24] And Leslie Stephen, commenting on the change from *Romola* to *Felix Holt*, observes wryly: "We have got back from Florence of the Renaissance to the English midlands during the Reform Bill agitation, and for that we may be thankful." [25]

The reliance on landscape and interiors for emphasis and meaning is noticeably diminished in *Felix Holt*. Apart from the introductory chapter, which is largely discursive and analytical, there is little natural description here, and the spirit of locality, though strong and recognizable, lacks the particularity and warmth of the early books. Interaction between individual and community is dramatized in terms of plot and the political and economic activity in the background; place has only a small part in this dramatization.[26]

In *Middlemarch*, too, there is a comparative absence of physical description, but it is compensated for by the depth and inclusiveness of the author's vision and her heightened intellectual and aesthetic assurance. She handles with much greater variety and vividness than in *Felix Holt* the nonphysical elements determining the lives of the characters and the atmosphere of the community. Private ambition, moral promptings, emotional and intellectual drives are displayed with a wholly convincing sense of their intricacy and interconnectedness; and the social pressures which limit and direct individual action — the economic, political, cultural undercurrents of everyday life — are shown in all their relentlessness and challenge. The environment itself, complex and relatively extensive as it is, is always a felt presence, intensely and palpably *there* in spite of a lack of emphasis on material surroundings. We do not really know what the town of

[24] Oscar Browning, *Life of George Eliot* (London, 1890), p. 94.
[25] *George Eliot*, pp. 150–151.
[26] Carroll, in *Nineteenth-Century Fiction*, XVII, 240, sees in the novel a sustained parallelism between the development of the private narrative, the social, economic, and political events in Treby Magna, and the scattered allusions to the state of England.

Middlemarch looks like but, knowing its people — all of them, as it may at times seem — knowing their occupations and desires, their thoughts and their talk, we do know what it *is* like. As Quentin Anderson has pointed out, in *Middlemarch* George Eliot surveys not a natural landscape but "what may be called a landscape of opinion." He characterizes "the book's use of the physical world by referring to George Eliot's own sense of Warwickshire as a physical locale which has been wholly humanized." Drawing a contrast with "the affectionate sense of nature . . . which suffuses *Adam Bede*," he writes,

> Nothing comparable to the description of Hetty Sorrel in Mrs. Poyser's dairy can enter into *Middlemarch*, not because it is a more "intellectual" book, but because its immediacies are not things seen but things felt and believed. . . . we know almost nothing of the appearance of Middlemarch itself, although our sense of the life of the town as a community is very full indeed, ranging as it does from a pot-house to the Green Dragon, the town's best inn, from horse-dealers, auctioneers, the grocers to the lawyers, physicians, merchants, clergymen, and landowners who stand at the head of the scale.[27]

Daniel Deronda, which is not concerned with the variety and fullness of provincial life, has a richness of its own and exceeds, at least in ambition, the scope of *Middlemarch*. If physical background plays here a smaller part than in *Romola* — George Eliot's other non-regional novel — it is used with far greater effectiveness. For when in *Daniel Deronda* a scene is singled out for particular description, it is designed to contribute to the overall meaning of the book: the responses of the characters to the choir of the old abbey church that Grandcourt has had converted into stables are as significant as, say, Dorothea Brooke's reactions in *Middlemarch* to Lowick or to Rome. But the setting, though it very clearly supports the theme and story, is quite without the instinctive sense of place with which George Eliot depicted the town of Middlemarch. The lack is hardly inappropriate: the action of the novel is fairly wide-ranging, the atmosphere worldly and sophisticated — there is really no effective central setting — and the theme is essentially that of rootlessness.

Indeed *Daniel Deronda* seems to derive, in spite of its cosmo-

[27] From *Dickens to Hardy*, p. 280. S. L. Bethell, in "The Novels of George Eliot," *Criterion*, XVIII (1938–39), 47, and O'Clair, in Chapter 2 of his thesis, have also remarked on the comparative absence of natural description in *Middlemarch*.

politanism, from George Eliot's lifelong effort to commemorate, resolve, and make intelligible her mixed feelings about the provincial society in which she has grown up: it is an implicit demonstration — a negative one, as it were — of the need for the stability and continuity offered by that society. *Middlemarch*, on the other hand, is a much more direct expression of her attachment to the life of the Midlands and her continued contemplation of it. Although its "immediacies are not things seen but things felt and believed," the background is all-important — it is part of the novel's point, its *raison d'être*. Perhaps more than ever in her work "the question arises," as Arnold Kettle remarks, "as to whether background is the right word to use." [28]

iv

Most critics who have called attention to George Eliot's regionalism have stressed that her roots are not simply in her native provinces but in the early nineteenth century. All but one of her English novels are set in that period, the period of her youth and, as in *Adam Bede* and *Silas Marner*, of her father's youth as well; they show a condition of life that was already becoming a thing of memory when she began to write. She herself was clearly conscious not only of the changes in English life taking place during her time, but also of the possible effect of fiction which, like her own, represented a closely knit world rapidly passing out of existence. Provincial in its limitations and compensations, this world was accumulating in its gathering obsolescence a great store of nostalgic power and ready contrasts with the present. She frequently draws on that store and, interrupting her narratives to address the reader, chides him for the ignorance about the past and casual contempt for it that she has attributed to him. By means of ironic and sometimes ponderously humorous expostulations, she attempts to persuade her contemporaries that the agrarian order forming the background of her stories is full of human interest and worthwhile activity, and that the obscure lives she describes have at least a potential for love and exaltation, for warmth, dignity, and tragedy.

Standing alone and pressing forward a simple lesson, such

[28] Arnold Kettle, *An Introduction to the English Novel* (London, 1951), I, 177.

passages might be ineffective, but in George Eliot they gain power from their close relation to the narrative, to the characters, settings, and events on which they comment and which they themselves serve to reinforce. She brings the past to life through immersion in her material: the informed sympathy with which she regards the milieu of her novels, the warmth, detail, and solidity of her vision, help to give her provincial pictures a compelling strength. The dramatization and explicit commentary bring out the coherence as well as the narrowness of the organic community and convey a sense of the changes gradually loosening the network of relations of the preceding epoch. Recognizing the necessity of technical and intellectual advancement, she is also aware of the cost that progress exacts from moral and cultural traditions. In a premonitory and generally implicit way, she expresses in her work the modern longing for harmony and cohesiveness. Later novelists, responding with increasing urgency, explicitness, and precision to "the sick hurry and divided aims" of modern life, have again and again taken as their subject the many-faceted dislocation apparent in society. George Eliot, however, modern in education and consciousness but "born early enough in the last century to see an England which has almost completely passed away," [29] was able to anticipate their concern without losing sight of the rural past. Her enduring regional attachments provided her with a source of personal and aesthetic direction: looking backward, she drew on the experiences and observations of her youth not only for narrative material but also for moral and social standards which might still apply to the world of her maturity.

Like many other Victorians who criticized their society and brooded about the "Signs of the Times," George Eliot was responding not so much to the growth of industry and cities as to the accompanying breakup of established patterns of behavior and relationships. The problem is, of course, still with us and in a more aggravated form than she knew it. "Instead of the community, urban or rural, we have, almost universally, suburbanism. We dwell where we find it convenient or where we can, pay our rates and taxes if we have to, and live in agglomerations united only by contiguity, the system of transport and the supply of gas, water and electricity." [30] George

[29] White, *Last Pages*, p. 136.
[30] F. R. Leavis and Denys Thompson, *Culture and Environment* (London, 1933), p. 2.

Eliot certainly did not live under these conditions, although she was made uneasy by their prefiguration and discussed in *Daniel Deronda* the symptoms of social fragmentations. She did not look out, as Robert Liddell says Jane Austen or Hardy did, "at country villages inhabited by labourers and landowners, by clergyman and doctors and their female dependents, by people who belonged there, and were functionally connected with the place." [31] But it was to such an organic community, whose death has been long deplored, that she was in many ways attracted, even as she perceived its limitations and took note in her novels of its erosion.

John McCormick, in discussing the antecedents of the modern novel in English, deals briefly but acutely with the way she anticipates in her novels the theme of social disintegration preoccupying modern authors. Comparing the shifts in writers' attitudes to their society and relating these shifts to social changes, he divides the history of the English novel from the nineteenth century on into three phases. In the first phase the novelist is essentially committed to overt social goals and values, sees society as a coherent and an intelligible organization, and works at transcribing its operation. The second phase is one of social questioning, of interest moving from society to the individual, and the point of view from the comic to the tragic. The third and modern phase, ushered in by the "catastrophe" of the Great War, is marked by "the loss of old certainties," and the isolation "of man from man and group from group." [32] Now George Eliot's work belongs chronologically in McCormick's first phase, but he rightly perceives that there are elements in it which indicate her consciousness of the advancing dissolution of the traditional order: "In the wide cast of her intellectual net, George Eliot apprehended the breaking up of Victorian society — we think of the countrymen near Middlemarch meeting the surveyors for the railroad with pitchforks — thus anticipating the novelists of the second phase." [33]

George Eliot's early novels depict provincial England before the modern fragmentation became evident or, as in *The Mill on the Floss*, in the initial stages of the process. The community of Warwickshire in the late eighteenth- and early nineteenth-century setting of *Adam Bede* and *Silas Marner* is presented in such a way as to em-

[31] Robert Liddell, *Some Principles of Fiction* (London, 1953), p. 23.
[32] John McCormick, *Catastrophe and Imagination* (London, 1957), p. 41.
[33] *Ibid.*, pp. 27–28.

phasize the changes that have occurred by the 1860s, but also so as
to bring the two periods closer together by highlighting the continuity
that underlies the changes. Thus the Victorian reader, his interests
aroused by the picturesque concreteness and regional sentiment, is
made aware of the values embodied in the vanishing rural order and
of the losses he has incurred in his pursuit of progress. But *The Mill
on the Floss* also has links with *Felix Holt* and *Middlemarch*, in which
the provincial community is studied more closely and objectively
than in the earlier books; the social changes, which previously had
been only implied in the narrator's perspective and digressions, are
now made part of the story. The three novels are set in roughly the
same period, between 1829 and 1832, and are with some subtlety
made more immediately relevant to the Victorian present than the
"rustic" works. Claude Bissell, for example, remarks on the suggestion of social mobility in *The Mill on the Floss* and links it with the
pronounced sense of flux in the society of *Middlemarch*, "where ideas,
no less than economic stakes, can divide or unite." In *Middlemarch*,
too, he notes another aspect of the development in the author's social
vision: "The number of malcontents, of those who try to burst out
of their social mould, has, in this novel, greatly increased. St. Oggs
could throw up only a Maggie and a Philip, but most of the leading
characters in *Middlemarch* are jarred into dissatisfaction and sometimes even into active rebellion." [34]

Aliens as well as malcontents actually appear in all of George
Eliot's fiction, early as well as late. But even remembering the un-
happy ending of *The Mill on the Floss* or the somberness and bleakness that color much of *Silas Marner*, it is clear that in *Felix Holt* and
Middlemarch her treatment of provincial life has taken on a new and
darker hue, a more complex expression, responsive to the stresses of
the time. She is still dealing with communal existence, of course, and
with the relationship between the individual and society; *Middlemarch* is, among other things, an unexcelled portrait of a closely knit
community. But the tensions threatening to crack the solidity of the
structure, the book's subversive elements, should not be ignored. Raymond Williams, when he discusses the nature and requirements of
the modern realistic novel, uses *Middlemarch* as a model of the genre,
but a model that cannot be emulated any more because the genuine

[34] *ELH*, XVIII, 238.

community on which it depends, "a community of persons linked not merely by one kind of relationship — work or friendship or family — but many interlocking kinds," is no longer available. The argument is a just one, but he simplifies the nature of *Middlemarch* in order to illustrate his point.

As Williams describes the dilemma of the contemporary novelist, who has no stable society to write about, it is not difficult to see that George Eliot was at least on the threshold of that dilemma:

> . . . the links between persons in most contemporary novels are relatively single, temporary, discontinuous. And this was a change in society . . . before it was a change in literary form. Again, related to this . . . the characteristic experience of our century is that of asserting and preserving an individuality . . . as compared with the characteristic nineteenth-century experience of finding a place and making a settlement. The ordinary Victorian novel ends, as every parodist knows, with a series of settlements, of new engagements and formal relationships, whereas the ordinary twentieth-century novel ends with a man going away on his own, having extricated himself from a dominating situation, and found himself in so doing. Again, this actually happened, before it became a common literary pattern.[35]

Now it should be clear from the ending of *The Mill on the Floss*, the theme of alienation and precarious settlement in *Silas Marner*, the muted resolution of *Middlemarch*, the nearly tragic close of the "good half" of *Daniel Deronda*, and the essentially austere spirit of all of George Eliot's work that she is not, in Williams's own terms, a typical Victorian novelist.[36] She stands really between two worlds: one is the stable, coherent society of the Midlands, which she remembers from her youth and to which she is powerfully drawn, even as she rejects its parochialism, and the other is the more or less modern world of the second half of the nineteenth century, to which she is committed by her intellectual interests, by almost her whole personality, in fact, but a world whose rootlessness and restlessness, superficiality and discontinuity, make her gravely anxious.

[35] Raymond Williams, *The Long Revolution* (London, 1961), p. 286.

[36] In "Thomas Hardy," *Critical Quarterly*, VI (1964), 351, Williams himself has acknowledged this, for he sees a special tradition of social criticism in the novel connecting George Eliot, Hardy, and D. H. Lawrence. Each of the three, because of background and aesthetic practice, was "separate from the dominant social and literary culture." There is a danger, however, in putting too much stress on the eccentricity of George Eliot's intellectual position: as has been frequently noted, she was in many ways a representative Victorian figure.

v

When, in 1954, George Dangerfield, reviewing the first three volumes of *The George Eliot Letters*, somewhat grudgingly prepared to "admit her once again to the company of the great English novelists," he cited as a strong reason "her deep provincialism." The remarkable body of work that has in the interval been devoted to George Eliot has made it certain that more sophisticated and readily impressive merits will be named in acclaiming her greatness. But I hope that the preceding discussion has suggested some of the directions in which a study of her provincialism — what I prefer to call her regionalism — may lead. Mr. Dangerfield's remarks provide a useful résumé and confirmation of my extended attempt to justify this subject. He writes that George Eliot's

> ... most persistent theme — "the stealthy convergence of human lots . . . a slow pressure of effects from one life upon another" — rose from her remembered experience of the complex relations between municipal town and country parish, between Church and Chapel, squirearchy and yeomanry, artisan and laborer. And the tragic element in "The Mill on the Floss" and in "Middlemarch" is partly the result of a clash between the rural-provincial world, where everybody knew his place, and the emerging urban-genteel world, where nobody had really any place to know. In "The Mill on the Floss," Maggie Tulliver — an idealization of George Eliot in her youth — is a displaced person.[37]

There is, however, much more to be said, and Part Two of this book, which offers a detailed examination of the regional elements in George Eliot's first four works of fiction, will carry on the argument. Regionalism is there seen as one possible, but very natural, approach, *a* key rather than *the* key, to her novels. I do regard regionalism as the foundation of her work, but it is a foundation from which she built upward and away, expanding her scope, moving beyond the particularity of personal connections to place and community toward a consideration of issues which have an obviously universal relevance.

Like Hardy and Lawrence after her, George Eliot began her career as an author with an interest in precise locality, an attachment to the life and region which she recalled from her youth. Place has

[37] George Dangerfield, "A Great Victorian Intelligence," *The Nation*, CLXXIX (1954), 334.

a powerful pull on her imagination in the early novels, and she represents it with massive, wide-ranging detail, conjuring up a vivid sense of an actual, concretely felt neighborhood. The compactness of the setting and the almost organic orderliness of existence help her to unravel at leisure the relationships and conflicts that provide the matter for intrigue. Life in such circumstances can be seen clearly, steadily, and whole: the relative simplicity of the provincial situation gives her the opportunity to generalize and to create without much trouble an impression of moral definiteness and social comprehensiveness. As Hardy wrote of his regional setting in the first chapter of *The Woodlanders*: "from time to time, dramas of a grandeur and unity truly Sophoclean are enacted in the real, by virtue of the concentrated passions and closely-knit interdependence of the lives therein."

In her late books, she came to master settings and situations that were complex, sophisticated, and "modern." Through her work, as much as through the work of Hardy and Lawrence, can be traced an increasing responsiveness to the cluster of great and startling changes — economic, social, political, intellectual, spiritual, and psychological — that were disturbing the nineteenth century and shaping the twentieth. In the work of all three, the growing sense of the difficulty of life, the concern with cultural change and modern dilemmas, goes hand in hand with a nostalgic view of a simpler, greener past and a resolute, or stoical, or gloomy and prophetic glance at the future. The regional setting offered itself first to George Eliot as a convenient paradigm for comprehending fate, society, the individual, and the relations between them, for sifting the accidental, superficial, and fleeting in the human situation from the universal, essential, and permanent. But the problems which confronted her gradually proved too sweeping and pressing to be contained comfortably within the bounds of pure regionalism; again like Hardy and Lawrence later, she found it necessary to extend the scope of her work, modify her technique, and adjust her ideas. She strove in this effort not only to define and dramatize the modern situation, to suggest possible ways of coping with it, but also to preserve and transplant the enduring values she had embodied in her regional novels, the values of "her deep provincialism."

Part Two
The Fiction

4 Pillars of Community:
Scenes of Clerical Life

For clergy are men as well as other folks.
— Henry Fielding

i

David Masson's lectures on *British Novelists and Their Styles*, one of the earliest serious works on the subject, came out in 1859, about a year after the publication of *Scenes of Clerical Life*. In the course of tracing the development of fiction in English and attempting to project some future directions for the novel, Masson classifies roughly according to content and primary concern what has recently been done. One of his categories is "the novel of English life and manners," which, unlike its Irish and Scottish counterparts, has not had an "express nationality of character." He attributes this lack largely to the regional distinctness of English life. Only recently, he writes, have English novelists turned to examine with any closeness the life and manners of their society. Locating their stories in their native counties, many have presented the national culture through a provincial perspective:

> Miss Brontë made a refreshing innovation in English novel-writing when she drew her characters and scenes and even portions of her dialect from her native Yorkshire; Mrs. Gaskell has followed with her pictures of artisan life, and her specimens of provincial dialect in Lancashire; and Mr. Kingsley has broken ground as an artist, in Devonshire and other counties. There are rich fields of yet unbooked English life both in northern and in southern England; and the literary centralization of English life in London has been owing, perhaps, to the centralization of the literary craft itself there.[1]

In keeping with his schematic approach to the criticism of fiction, Masson seems here to be almost calling for a burst of novels of local color, depicting England, county by county, for the relish of natives and the admiration of tourists. But in mentioning Charlotte Brontë and Mrs. Gaskell, what he is in fact referring to is the better sort of regional novel. He associates this kind of novel with a realistic treatment of material and therefore with the Pre-Raphaelites. Acknowledging "the persevering and painstaking accuracy" of the novelists of the eighteenth century, Masson nonetheless insists on the originality of the "more general and conscious" realism of his contemporaries. He calls attention particularly to their "more resolute and careful" treatment of matters that are familiar and their "greater

---

[1] *British Novelists and Their Styles*, p. 220.

indifference to traditional ideas of beauty," as a result of which they freely depict "facts and objects accounted common, disagreeable, or even painful." [2]

The latest work cited in *British Novelists* is *Adam Bede*, which must have appeared just in time for Masson to bring his remarks up to date by alluding to it near the end of his book. Quite rightly, he sees George Eliot's first novel as belonging in the regional and realistic tradition established by recent writers like "Miss Brontë, Mrs. Gaskell, Miss Mulock and others," whose work he has been describing. Surprisingly, though, he seems not to have read *Scenes of Clerical Life* [3] ("The Sad Fortunes of the Reverend Amos Barton," the first story, was published in *Blackwood's Magazine* in January 1857), for he writes of *Adam Bede* as if it were a first work: "at this moment readers are hailing the advent of a new artist of the Real school, in the author of *Adam Bede*." [4] The neglect in such a context of George Eliot's first work of fiction is puzzling: at the very least it has cost Masson's discussion the added force and vividness that an apt and topical illustration could have provided. For *Scenes of Clerical Life*, in its use of regional setting and dialect, its fidelity to actual, recollected experiences, characters, and locale, its morally directed insistence on the importance of the commonplace, exemplifies the extension of the novel's scope with which Masson credited the "new" English realists.

[2] *Ibid.*, pp. 258–259.
[3] It is surprising for a man of his position and interests. David Masson arrived in London from Aberdeen and Edinburgh University in 1847, and quickly established himself as a literary scholar, critic, and reviewer. In 1852 he was appointed professor of English Literature at University College, London. In May of that year he wrote an article in *The Leader* which George Eliot knew to be his (*Letters*, II, 48); she writes of meeting him in February 1853 (*Letters*, II, 89). There are in the *Letters* scattered references to Masson and his works, and there is a note from him thanking George Eliot for admiring his monumental biography of Milton (1859–1880). In view, then, of such contacts and the general closeness of literary life in London, it is odd that Masson seems not to have read George Eliot's first book. He must surely have read some of her essays in *The Westminster Review*, and it may be that in one of these ("The Natural History of German Life") he found a suggestion for his comment in *British Novelists* (p. 259): "It is as if, proceeding on the theory that the British novel in its totality, should be a Natural History of British Life, individual novelists were acting farther on the principle of subdivision of labour, and working out separately the natural histories of separate counties and parishes."
[4] *British Novelists and Their Styles*, p. 260. For Masson, the complementary "school" to the "Real" is the "Ideal or Romantic," of which Dickens is the leading exponent (p. 248).

As a kind of triptych of "English life and manners," George Eliot's first depiction of provincial society is characteristically retrospective. In their tone of wry, oddly unsentimental, and persuasively sensible nostalgia for bygone simplicities of social structure and behavior, the three stories anticipate much of George Eliot's later writing. The tone and point of view have, of course, strong autobiographical roots and are directed at the natural weakness for nostalgia which the Victorian reader was expected to harbor, but they also perform a valid and important function in the narratives. Thus, in "The Sad Fortunes of the Reverend Amos Barton," what might otherwise have been a drab story is given an emotional interest and infused with a certain softness through the personal and affectionate, half-reminiscing and half-dramatic mode of narration.

The little drama, pathetic yet ludicrous, is also set in a full and vivid context: the Shepperton Church, which is being reconstructed while the story proceeds, the theme of doctrinal strains and changes, and the communal life captured in warm detail, all help to create an impression of breadth and substance in the background. The tale of Amos Barton, the "superlatively middling" curate, well-intentioned but awkward and insensitive in executing his duties, and of his incongruously happy marriage, his innocuous but offensive involvement with a worldly *coquette*, his unpopularity among the shocked parishioners, and his sad recovery of their sympathy and esteem is little more than a touching anecdote. But around this anecdote George Eliot has created a village community whose activity, interconnections, and leading principles overshadow the private tragicomedy of the Bartons.[5]

[5] In "Amos Barton," writes Barbara Hardy, quoting George Eliot, "the subject and the theme is [the] voice of ordinary tones" (*The Novels of George Eliot*, p. 18); she is referring to the unheroic Amos, a portrait of human inadequacy. But Mrs. Hardy underestimates the amount of space and quality of attention devoted to depicting the nature of the Shepperton community and its reactions to the situation of the Bartons. The people of Shepperton are also unheroic and, in their way, inadequate, but the friendship and help which at the end they extend to Amos despite their earlier disapproval of him is a kind of response to the author's address to the reader: "I wish to stir your sympathy with commonplace troubles — to win your tears for real sorrow: sorrow such as may live next door to you..." ("The Sad Fortunes of the Rev. Amos Barton," Ch. VII). Mrs. Hardy writes very well about the choric, causal, ironic role of the community in "Amos Barton," but in viewing the story as a personal tragedy she places the emphasis where it does not clearly belong. Thomas A. Noble, who has made a full-length study of *Scenes of Clerical Life*, seems in this respect to be in a stronger position, for he discusses the stories as dramatizations of the

The mere plot — if it can be called that — exists to bring into play the collective character and representative but individualized personalities of the community. The moral delusions, the complacency, narrowness, and materialistic, self-centered practicality of "bucolic society five-and-twenty years ago" are brought to life with an assured indirectness of manner. Against these — and suggested with the same dramatic understatement — are placed the special qualities for which George Eliot cherished provincial nature: the underlying good sense, the instinctive, if not informed, moral rightness rooted in long established attitudes and values, and the warmth and sympathy that can be called forth by need. These complementary states of the rural soul are expressed through dialogue, narration, and commentary and are subtly linked with the underlying interest, present in all of George Eliot's fiction, in social history, in the counterpoint of continuity and change, the satisfactions of stability, and the challenges and expenses of progress.

From the beginning, then, George Eliot is concerned with individual fate in a social context, but in her first story, perhaps because of the colorlessness of the nominal hero, the emphasis seems to be on the context rather than the individual.[6] That the background — the structure of rural society, the quality of its daily life, the intimacy and interdependence of its relationships — is unusually important in "Amos Barton" is suggested in the tone and perspective of the opening, the weight given to the "choric" scenes, their location and the special function they perform, and in the structure of the narrative. At the very outset, the personal affection for the village life of twenty-five years before and the wryly ironic regret with which its disappearance is viewed set the tone for this story and the two that follow: "Shepperton Church was a very different-looking building five-and-twenty years ago. To be sure, its substantial stone tower looks at you through its intelligent eye, the clock, with the friendly expression of former days; but in everything else what changes!" With fond detail and reflective commentary extending the signifi-

eighteenth-century doctrine of sympathy (*George Eliot's "Scenes of Clerical Life"* [New Haven, 1965]).

[6] Thus the equilibrium between public and private lives which Mrs. Bennett has found to be quintessential in the structure of "the typical George Eliot novel" is lacking here. The absence of equilibrium is more striking in George Eliot's last novel, *Daniel Deronda*, in which, as Mrs. Bennett has noted, the lack of satisfactory communal ties is a crucial part of the theme.

cance of the description from the particular, personal, and concrete to the general, social, and historical, the church is described as it once was and now is. The architectural alterations (initiated by Amos Barton) are linked with the material and technical innovations of the nineteenth century and with reform in general:

> Immense improvement! says the well-regulated mind which un-intermittingly rejoices in the New Police, the Tithe Commuta-tion Act, the penny-post, and all guarantees of human advance-ment, and has no moments when conservative-reforming intel-lect takes a nap, while imagination does a little Toryism by the sly, revelling in regret that dear, old, brown, crumbling, pictur-esque inefficiency is everywhere giving place to spick-and-span new-painted, new-varnished efficiency, which will yield endless diagrams, plans, elevations, and sections, but alas! no picture. (Chapter I)

The attitude itself may appear sentimental, but it is justified and made resilient by the self-aware, self-mocking humor of the narrator and the controlled strength of his attachment to the locale and the past.

From physical changes, the recollections pass to the doctrinal developments, which were also beginning to be felt distinctly at the time of the story. Here the perspective is extended still further into the past, both through the narrator's childhood reminiscences and the mention of Mr. Gilfil's curacy, which preceded Mr. Barton's. Thus, the time span, reaching out to the remote past and at the same time to the present (that is, 1856, the time of the writing), establishes a thread of continuity that intertwines with the discussion of the changes.[7] Similarly, the personal references of the narrator, the ac-count of the church choir and the village's taste in religious music, and the teasing, familiar allusion to Mr. Gilfil, all create a convincing sense of environment, felt firmly by the author and therefore also by the reader. The recollection of religious tensions, with its allusion to the Catholic Emancipation Bill and the rise of Dissent in the com-munity, stems from this environment, and the narrative smoothly passes to Amos Barton who, as the curate of Shepperton, is a crucial figure in the atmosphere of innovation and reform.[8]

[7] See Daniel P. Deneau, "A Note on George Eliot's 'Amos Barton' — Reticence and Chronology," *Notes and Queries*, n.s. VI (1959), 450–451.
[8] Appropriate to my emphasis on the significance of community life in "Amos

Of course, as we are made to sense at once and are soon explicitly told, Amos Barton is not up to the job.[9] But more important than his failures is his standing in the community. The "landscape of opinion," which Quentin Anderson defines as the dominant subject in *Middlemarch*, is even more conspicuous in "Amos Barton," and its prominence accounts for the gradual, indirect way in which the protagonist himself is introduced into the story. For after the narrative point of view has been established, the social atmosphere suggested, and the vehicle of the plot — the poverty of the Bartons — indicated, it is the community's opinion of the curate, not the curate himself, that is brought to the forefront: "What was thought of this problem, and of the man who had to work it out, by some of the well-to-do inhabitants of Shepperton, two years or more after Mr. Barton's arrival among them, you shall hear if you will accompany me to Cross Farm."

Since the opinions of Mrs. Patten's visitors are not expressed with the stilted directness and artificial display of information which the narrator's promise may suggest but rather arise naturally out of a completely credible conversation between distinctly realized persons, we learn a great deal directly and indirectly about the people themselves and their social lives as well as about Amos. Although their discussion is cast in a nostalgic perspective by the narrator's delight over such remembered delights as "real farmhouse cream," there is nothing misty eyed about the characterization of these natives

---

Barton" and the two other stories, but particularly apt at this point, is William A. Sibbald's comment: "Regarded collectively, the 'Scenes' had an interest beyond that inspired by their respective themes. They gave in vivid detail a picture of life in rural and provincial England as it existed seventy to a hundred years ago, a picture which no formal history could or can supply. The past was re-created, bygone phases of life and thought were re-captured, the social and religious forces leavening society re-vitalised and brought into action. The French Revolution, the rise and fall of Napoleon; and, at home, the social ferment that ended in the transfer of political power from an aristocratic oligarchy to the middle-class; the religious upheaval that had for its main issue the Tractarian movement of 1833 — all happened within the period covered by the 'Scenes' ... Life in the 'Scenes,' therefore, was of the old leisurely type that vanished on the advent of industrialism; frankly insular, provincial, even parochial, with one connecting link to relate it to the larger national issues that made for history — the Church." "George Eliot's Place in Literature," *Westminster Review*, CLXIII (1905), 336–337.

[9] In Chapter II, George Eliot observes: "Alas for the worthy man who, like that candle, gets himself into the wrong place! It is only the very largest souls who will be able to appreciate and pity him — who will discern and love the sincerity of purpose amid all the bungling feebleness of achievement."

of "the George Eliot country." They are seen clearly, objectively, humorously and, in spite of their moral and intellectual deficiencies, with respect and sympathy. The humor here is not, as it is in some instances in *Scenes of Clerical Life*, heavy-handed: the tone of the disquisition on "real farmhouse cream" and the jocular contempt for the "miserable town-bred reader" support the mood of the initial description of the church. By these means, the personal feeling for the environment and its spirit is made clear and functional. The cozy setting and the brief, knowing introductions of Mr. Pilgrim, Mrs. Patten, and Mrs. Hackit yield the same effects. By conveying a sense of the narrator's personality and his intimacy with the place and characters, they evoke a temptingly congenial atmosphere and elicit our interest and trust — in fact, they charm us.

The effectiveness of this scene can be attributed to many elements but especially to the characterization, the dramatic sense of relationship between characters, and the fully suggested social atmosphere in which the discussion takes place. The characterization is marked by an economical but sustained unraveling of the sharply observed individualities of the spokesmen of the small community. Mrs. Hackit's aggressive prudence and shrewd, satiric quickness are suggested at once in her supposition that "sixpences grew on the bents of Cross Farm." As she is more fully introduced to the reader, the quiet wit, specific comments, and implied suggestions of the description substantiate and vivify that first impression:

> Mrs. Hackit declines cream; she has so long abstained from it with an eye to the weekly butter-money, that abstinence, wedded to habit, has begotten aversion. She is a thin woman with a chronic liver-complaint, which would have secured her Mr. Pilgrim's entire regard and unreserved good word, even if he had not been in awe of her tongue, which was as sharp as his own lancet. She has brought her knitting — no frivolous fancy knitting, but a substantial woollen stocking; the click-click of her knitting-needles is the running accompaniment to all her conversation, and in her utmost enjoyment of spoiling a friend's self-satisfaction, she was never known to spoil a stocking. (Chapter I)

The tone of this sketch is carefully modulated: Mrs. Hackit is observed accurately but with an affection and intimacy that temper the satire applied to her. Her hard qualities, the social manner that expresses these, and the respect with which, because of them, she is treated are suggested, but softly, so that she is felt to be, at worst, somewhat crusty and not unkind. The contrasting portrait of Mrs. Patten that immediately follows the paragraph just quoted indirectly confirms the favorable impression of Mrs. Hackit. Here the humor and disclosure work against the character rather than for her: "Mrs. Patten does not admire this excessive click-clicking activity. Quiescence in an easy chair, under the sense of compound interest perpetually accumulating, has long seemed an ample function to her, and she does her malevolence gently." The last detail is quickly supported: Mrs. Patten, described, unlike Mrs. Hackit, in terms that reduce her moral stature ("a pretty little old woman of eighty," and so on), intends to leave her money "to a distant relation of her husband's," not to her devoted niece, Janet. Janet's devotion, however, though selfless, is selfless in a distastefully sycophantic way: "Janet seemed always to identify herself with her aunt's personality, holding her own under protest." Thus, in the characterization of the demure and complacent Mrs. Patten ("Now, Mr. Hackit, I've never been a sinner . . . If I'm not to be saved, I know as many as are in a bad way"), her petty spitefulness and hypocrisy are strongly implied; whereas in the picture of Mrs. Hackit it is her latent kindness and human responsibility that are held in reserve and gradually revealed. Not only does she defend Amos Barton while the others malign him, but she (unlike Mr. Pilgrim, for example) has thought seriously about his activities, especially his attempt (smacking of Evangelicalism) to reach the poor by preaching to them in their own neighborhood:

> "Well, I don't know about that," said Mrs. Hackit, who had always the courage of her opinion, "but I know, some of our labourers and stockingers as used never to come to church, come to the cottage, and that's better than never hearing anything good from week's end to week's end. And there's that Track Society as Mr. Barton has begun — I've seen more o' the poor people with going tracking, than all the time I've lived in the parish before. (Chapter I)

Mrs. Hackit's statements in the first chapter and later are given a quality of weight and authority that the other characters (with the slight exception, in Chapter VI, of the kind, practical, intelligent Mr. Cleves, the first of George Eliot's ideal clergymen) do not possess.

Related to the perception and finely controlled rendering in depth of individual characters is George Eliot's ability to suggest with a minimum of effort the connections between people, whether multiple interactions of neighbors or family relationships. She does this through dialogue as well as commentary, through the implied juxtaposition of contrasting personalities (as in the case of Mrs. Hackit and Mrs. Patten), through highlighting the views that people have of one another (Mr. Pilgrim's opinion of Mrs. Hackit, Mrs. Patten's of Mr. Hackit, Mrs. Hackit's — the entire community's, for that matter — of Amos and Milly Barton, and so on), but especially through the recurrent use of such group and conversation scenes as those at Cross Farm and Milby Vicarage. In these scenes, by showing her characters communicating with each other on the basis of their distinctive qualities and opinions as well as their common social roots, George Eliot dramatizes not only the nature of their interrelationships, but also the structure of their society and their place in it. And because the characters and their relations are so effectively suggested, the larger social vision can be embodied with economy and impact. Since in "Amos Barton," as in her other fiction, this extension of view is always arranged around the plot itself, the group scenes serve as vivid illustrations, from the point of view of society, of the intertwining of public and private lives. George Eliot's regional consciousness is so instinctive, so natural to her, and she controls it so intelligently that though the extensive connections between the individual and community may not form her principal theme, they do in all of her work consistently provide a rich accompaniment to it. Mrs. Hardy has put this point well:

> Apart from its role as background and its equally prominent role as agent — from *Amos Barton* to *Middlemarch* the collective personality of the community acts as a causal agent, making and breaking relations — the chorus has also a formal function. Like the narrator's voice it interrupts the track of the protagonist and is the chief source of that narrative irony which is important in making George Eliot's tragic statement . . . One man's tragedy is everyone else's comedy . . . There is usually also the moment when one man's tragedy becomes everyone's tragedy.[10]

Much of this choric work can be done, as it is in *Middlemarch*, through commentary and exposition. In "Amos Barton," in spite of the omniscient narrative voice, George Eliot does not greatly rely on

[10] *The Novels of George Eliot* (London: The Athlone Press, 1959), p. 21.

general or straightforward depiction of the social or physical background. When she does on occasion resort to it, she does so unobtrusively but authoritatively, with a relevance and precision of detail that stem from intimately known and remembered experience. The opening passage describing Shepperton Church reveals these qualities very clearly and most fully. In the middle of Chapter II, a rather different scene, complementary to the first, is described as a setting for "the workhouse, euphuistically called the 'College'."

> The College was a huge square stone building, standing on the best apology for an elevation of ground that could be seen for about ten miles round Shepperton. A flat ugly district this; depressing enough to look at even on the brightest days. The roads are black with coal-dust, the brick houses dingy with smoke; and at that time — the time of handloom weavers — every other cottage had a loom at its window, where you might see a pale, sickly-looking man or woman pressing a narrow chest against a board, and doing a sort of tread-mill work with legs and arms.

Coming right after the harassed but warm atmosphere of the Bartons' home (an atmosphere infused with the loving and capable influence of Milly Barton), the bleakness of this passage startles the reader and enforces the already strong suggestion of the precariousness of the Bartons' happiness. It both broadens and deepens our sense of the environment, and serves as an appropriate transition to the College and its inhabitants, the difficulty of Mr. Barton's duties, and his pathetic but understandable inadequacy in fulfilling them. As in the Cross Farm conversation, the brief, wryly factual introductory remarks about the people in the workhouse are directly descriptive and sometimes analytical. Also descriptive and analytical is the story in Chapter II of the Countess' real background and the suspicious fantasies that public opinion in Milby has woven about it. Similarly, in the account of the Clerical Meeting at Milby Vicarage, each of the attending clergymen is briefly characterized and implicitly judged.

In the course of such summary sketches, some specific information about the social context is often casually given, but most often strategic disclosures of this sort are made allusively, during conversations or arguments. These revealing comments are used to inform the reader both about the nature of the social situation in its various aspects — for example, religious habits, moral values, economic concerns, class structure, political issues of various scope, local activity — and the immediately relevant facts of the plot, which, of course, is hardly separable from the social situation. The gossip of Mrs. Patten's visitors and the incidental commentary are full of informative details that give the background its broad concreteness and vitality. The ambiguous social position of Mr. Pilgrim, for example, is suggested briefly with almost self-evident illustration:

> ... the doctor from the nearest market-town [Milby], who, though occasionally affecting aristocratic airs, and giving late dinners with enigmatic side-dishes and poisonous port, is never so comfortable as when he is relaxing his professional legs in one of those excellent farmhouses where the mice are sleek and the mistress sickly. (Chapter I)

Apart from the information about Mr. Pilgrim himself and the broad hint of a heart anxious for status as well as profit, this aside is a clue to the element of social mobility in the community and the position of physicians. At the same time, it also contributes to creating the atmosphere of warm coziness in which the conversation takes place. When we are told that Mr. Pilgrim "hated the Rev. Amos for two reasons — because he had called in a new doctor, recently settled in Shepperton; and because, being himself a dabbler in drugs, he had the credit of having cured a patient of Mr. Pilgrim's," the effect of social suggestiveness is the same. In a similar vein are the comments about Mrs. Patten's background ("a lady's-maid, and married for her beauty"), her money, and her respect for Mr. Hackit, "a shrewd substantial man, whose advice about crops is always worth listening to, and who is too well off to want to borrow money." Such apparently casual observations are crucial in building up a general sense of the morals and manners of provincial life.

In the words of the characters themselves more precise information is disclosed: it concerns principally Amos Barton, his standing in the community, and the community's reaction to his clerical innovations. But in the process of learning about Amos and piecing together the facts most pertinent to the plot itself, the reader is helped to set this particular fiction in the context of history and the movement of religious opinion in provincial England. The contextual location is present in the description of the Church and in Mrs. Hackit's stout defense of Mr. Barton; it appears even in Mr. Pilgrim's reference to Mr. Barton as "a confounded Methodistical, meddlesome chap, who must be putting his finger in every pie"; in Mr. Hackit's relation of the argument about hymn singing; in the misapprehending rumors that link Mr. Barton with Dissent ("They say his father was a Dissenting shoemaker," says Mr. Pilgrim); and in the various remarks made by the narrator as well as the characters themselves about preaching, ritual decorum, and the Evangelical and Tractarian Movements.[11]

Such religious and historical allusions recur consistently in all of George Eliot's novels, and reflect the central importance of religious movements not only in her own youth as a provincial bluestocking but in the general life of the region and the time of which she is writing. The importance of the Church and its clergymen was moral, secular, and institutional at least as much as it was doctrinal or spiritual. We see this, of course, in George Eliot's characterizations of the clerics she admires, men such as Mr. Gilfil, Mr. Irwine, or Mr. Farebrother,[12] and also in the prominently social nature and reverberations of Amos Barton's "sad fortunes." As the "landscape of opinion" is gradually displayed, it is seen that Barton is disliked by most of his parishioners and "clerical brethren" because of his unprepossessing demeanor, his lack of tact, charm, and intelligence. Mr. Pilgrim's grudge against him is private, as is Mrs. Patten's — but both have in a way been called forth by his professional and personal insensitivity. "When Mr. Barton comes to see me, he talks about nothing but my sins and my need o' marcy," complains Mrs. Patten; and the same lack of feeling is evident in his ineffectual ministrations to the inmates of the workhouse. "So your snuff is all gone, eh?" he asks Mrs. Brick, and deflates her "visionary hope" of a handout with "Ah, well! You'll soon be going where there is no more snuff. You'll be in need of mercy then. You must remember that you may have to seek for mercy and not find it, just as you're seeking for snuff" (Chapter II).

---

[11] See especially the end of Chapter II.
[12] The secular ties of clerical existence are also illustrated obliquely in Dr. Kenn's dilemma — superficially similar to Amos Barton's since both clergymen antagonize their parishioners by sheltering "disreputable" young women — in *The Mill on the Floss*. In spite of his high-minded faith, Dr. Kenn has to submit to social pressures and narrow scrupulousness. Though St. Ogg's is of all George Eliot's communities the least touched by religious feelings, the novel itself, through the prevailing perspective and Maggie's temperament and aspirations, may be the most essentially religious of all her fiction.

Mrs. Hackit, who speaks up for Amos, does so largely out of admiration and sympathy for his wife: *"I* like Mr. Barton. I think he's a good sort o' man, for all he's not overburthen'd i' th' upper storey; and his wife's as nice a lady-like woman as I'd wish to see. How nice she keeps her children! and little enough money to do't with . . ." (Chapter I). Poverty, gnawing though genteel, is the Bartons' most plaguing trouble, as Mrs. Hackit sensibly perceives, and the saddest of Amos's fortunes is his wife's death; both are worldly and temporal in nature rather than religious and have social connections and consequences. Tied to the Bartons' indigence is the "subplot" of the story and its only intrigue: Caroline Czerlaski's prolonged and inconsiderate sojourn in their home and the added strains, both domestic and communal, which it creates. Every action in such a small, tightly knit society has wide repercussions. Amos Barton's unpopularity is the result of many apparently inconsequential acts and oversights, and his innocent but misunderstood friendship with the still less popular, practically ostracized Countess makes his position in the village almost impossible. What saves him and unites him again to the community is the general outflow of sympathy at the death of his wife and the respect for his deep grief.

The story is constructed in such a way as to give emphasis to the broad perspective and extensive reverberations. Chapter I sketches in the social background and introduces Barton through the views of him as a clergyman and individual held by several members of his congregation. In the second chapter, after a vignette of the Bartons' domestic happiness under difficulties and a brief mention of the Countess, we are given another picture of the community, not so much through Barton's eyes but as seen from his interests and standpoint. In the third chapter the Countess is introduced and judged, but the nature of the plot and her involvement in it begin to be made clear only through the conversation of Mr. Ely and Mr. Farquhar — socially the most distinguished persons in the story — as they exchange opinions about her and Mr. Barton. Because of Mr. Ely's supercilious reserve the exchange is largely one-sided. The popular view of the Countess and her actual background (much duller and more commonplace than the sensational fantasies concocted by "the good people of Milby") are given in Chapter IV, and the note of realistic deflation is continued in Chapter V, where the narrator appeals for the reader's interest in the average virtues of the hero and demands sympathy for his failings and troubles. Mr. Barton's troubles are then recalled, the community's concern, especially about his wife, is displayed, and his official activity and his interest in the Countess, with the further displeasure this causes the town, are described.

At this point, near the end of the fifth chapter and roughly at the middle of the story, the preparatory portion of the narrative is complete. We now have a good sense both of the environment and the nature of the protagonist and his problems, and we already suspect the way in which these are going to be related and developed. With the appearance of Caroline at Milly Barton's door, the "push from a malignant destiny" begins to be felt. Chapter VI, the opening, as it were, of the second half of the story, begins symmetrically at Cross Farm, with another discussion of Mr. Barton by the already familiar cast; this discussion is continued at a more refined level but also in a more spiteful tone by Mr. Barton's fellow clergy at Milby Vicarage. Chapters VII and VIII are more consistently concerned with the Bartons' private life and tragedy than any other section of the story, but even here references to the extra-domestic life can be found: Milly Barton's death, for example, is observed largely through the grieved eyes of Mrs. Hackit, who has by this time come almost to embody the essential character of the community.

In Chapter IX, the sympathetic response of the parish is described in some detail. Mr. Barton is taken back into the fold and, as if to stress his new connection with the small society, the altered and reconstructed church — a result, if we recall the several earlier references to this, of his initiative and effort, material proof of his mark on the people of Shepperton — is reopened. The time is May, which combines with the occasion and the sense of social harmony to suggest a note of mellow triumph that qualifies the pathos of Mrs. Barton's death. The triumph is in turn qualified by Mr. Barton's removal, but it is far from quenched: the emphasis in the end is put, as it has been throughout, on Mr. Barton's standing in the community. He is now firmly accepted by it (when the story opens he is still a newcomer, having lived in Shepperton a mere two years), and has in turn developed roots that attach him to the town:

> . . . Shepperton had become the place where he most wished to
> stay — where he had friends who knew his sorrows — where he

lived close to Milly's grave. To part from that grave seemed like parting with Milly a second time; for Amos was one who clung to all the material links between his mind and the past.

The short tenth and final chapter (preceding the still shorter conclusion) dwells on representative reactions in the town to Mr. Barton's departure and illustrates further the theme of social integration. It mingles moods of affirmation and sadness that derive from Amos Barton's achievement and his loss of genuine local ties: "Amos failed to touch the spring of goodness by his sermons, but he touched it effectually by his sorrows; and there was now a real bond between him and his flock." It is the genuineness of this bond that makes the departure so painful; what frightens and depresses him is "the separation from the loved and familiar, and the chilling entrance on the new and strange."

ii

"Amos Barton" is probably the most successful story in *Scenes of Clerical Life*. Its realism, in governing conception, characterization, suggestion of environment, and narrative development, is consistent and genuine. The realism is characteristically qualified and enriched by George Eliot's wish to show the fortitude and suffering, the tragedy and triumph, to which even the most drab and limited character can rise and which make his circumstances both interesting and sympathetic.[13] It is also, from my point of view, the most interesting of the three and, for this reason, has had to be treated with some fulness. In neither of the other stories does George Eliot coordinate as successfully as in "Amos Barton" private with public narrative interest or relate as fully the leading characters to their background. Neither in "Mr. Gilfil's Love-Story" nor even in "Janet's Repentance" does she exploit as effectively the diverse aspects of her

[13] Noble, in *George Eliot's "Scenes of Clerical Life,"* also thinks of it as the best of the stories "because it is truest to life, full of homely realistic detail and free alike from startling incident and strong passion" (p. 15). Henry James liked "Amos Barton" best ("The Novels of George Eliot," p. 481), but Leslie Stephen preferred "Mr. Gilfil's Love-Story," which he called "almost faultless" (*George Eliot*, p. 58). In an article on "George Eliot's Anti-Romantic Romance: 'Mr. Gilfil's Love-Story' " (*Victorian Newsletter*, no. 31 [Spring 1967], pp. 15–19), in language more fervent than Stephen's, U. C. Knoepflmacher voices the same preference for the middle story largely on the basis of its "skillful interpenetration of two separate orders of reality" — the romantic and the ordinary.

regional interest. In the last two stories, the regionalism is largely anecdotal and topographic. The elements that interest me in this study, George Eliot's easy sense of environment and character, her inclusive interest in social structure, in the manners and morals of the provincial community — these are present, to be sure, in "Mr. Gilfil's Love-Story" and in "Janet's Repentance." But in the second story, they do not form a central object of interest and in the third, though much space is devoted to a fairly direct analysis of the people of Milby and their shifting opinions of the main figures, these things remain separate — or at least more so than in "Amos Barton" — from the main narrative.

In "Janet's Repentance," the relatively poor connection between plot and social background is disturbing because the story of the Dempsters and Mr. Tryan quite clearly *belongs* in the locale — it is not merely a local legend. But though Mr. Gilfil himself belongs in Shepperton, his love story is a local legend and (apart from being the great personal tragedy of his life) nothing more — it simply happened to take place in the region. We can see this clearly in the absence, after the first chapter, of the convivial gatherings in which the private events of the plot are discussed and judged by the minor characters representing the community. Mrs. Hardy implies that the difference between this story and the two others is one of structure. Commenting on the shifting point of view in *Scenes of Clerical Life* "from misunderstood man to misunderstanding crowd," she says:

> In *Amos Barton* and *Janet's Repentance* the movement is alternating; in *Mr. Gilfil's Love-Story* the chorus occupies the frame and the protagonist the inset story. The effect is roughly the same; we move from the shot in the dark to the truth; from the isolated creature to the diffused and comfortable warmth of the crowd; from tension to casual humor.[14]

In a general way this is sound enough, but it should be noted that the "misunderstanding crowd" which Mrs. Hardy mentions is only superficially misunderstanding. Under the crust of half-enlightened, comically quaint provincialism of the group characters, there is usually a sure grasp of what is essentially important, true, and right. Mrs. Hackit or even Mrs. Patten discussing Mr. Barton, Mr. Bates and Mrs. Sharp exchanging complacent prejudices about

[14] *The Novels of George Eliot*, p. 21.

"furriners" in Chapter III of "Mr. Gilfil's Love-Story," the villagers grieving for Mr. Gilfil in the opening chapter, or the ladies gossiping about Janet Dempster in the third chapter of "Janet's Repentance" — all express judgments which in one way or another are borne out by the events. With appropriate qualifications, the popular point of view is consistently supported in these stories. In "Mr. Gilfil's Love-Story," however, this point of view does not have to be corroborated by the narrative (though indirectly it is), since it is really incidental to it. His parishioners do not need to be convinced that Mr. Gilfil is a worthy and an interesting man; it is the reader, according to George Eliot's authorial fiction, who has to be persuaded of this.

The frame, therefore, is basic to the narrative in two different ways. The Vicar appears at first as simply one of the community, accepted and beloved by all, as provincial and dull as his flock, and, in a quaint eighteenth-century way, inefficient at his job. The love story is meant to invest the figure of Maynard Gilfil, who seems drab but really is not, with glamor and dignity. In exhibiting the strength, intelligence, and sensitivity that he showed, "with a heart full of passion and tenderness," in the romantic crisis of his life, it also explains his standing in the district. It is easy to believe that the slack and jovial parson, who "would sometimes forget to take off his spurs before putting on his surplice," who dispensed sugarplums to the village children and talked farming with informed gusto, would have been a popular man among "his bucolic parishioners." But the story of his tragic romance shows us also the qualities which, however blunted, could have inspired the farmers' respect, so that they "had not at all the less belief in him as a gentleman for his easy speech and manners." As in "Amos Barton," the parson's suffering determines his relationship with the community.[15]

In speaking of a frame structure in "Mr. Gilfil's Love-Story," it should be made clear that the components of the frame are not exactly symmetrical. The opening and closing sections both show the Vicar in his old age. But while the Epilogue consists entirely of commentary in the narrator's own voice elucidating the effects of the romance

[15] Maynard Gilfil is not the mediocrity embodied by Amos Barton. As George Eliot writes at the end of the story, "though he had something of the knotted whimsical character of the poor lopped oak, he had yet been sketched out by nature as a noble tree. The heart of him was sound, the grain was of the finest..."

on Mr. Gilfil's character, much of the first chapter is dramatic, cast in dialogue, and almost entirely concerned with his social activities and the general esteem that he enjoys. Thus there is no real symmetry in the structure of the story: the framework is incomplete and the effect is different from that of the alternating movement between the "chorus" and individual in "Amos Barton."

Only the first chapter of "Mr. Gilfil's Love-Story" shows the effect, in characterization and arrangement, of George Eliot's inclusive local interests. Here, as earlier, in "Amos Barton," the society of Shepperton is revealed through its attitude to the "hero" and through his activity and position in it. As attention moves from the community's affection for Mr. Gilfil to Mr. Gilfil himself, his nature and habits, there is even a certain alternation of perspective that resembles the overall structure of the first story. When Shepperton mourns for Mr. Gilfil we see not only the high regard which his parishioners had for him, but also something of the mentality of the parish, its quality of life. There are suggested, for example, the sense of closeness, the unspoken understanding of the initiated, as it were, together with a spirit of common values, traditions and causes. Had his nephew not arranged for the "tribute of respect" for the Vicar, "the parishioners would certainly have subscribed the necessary sum out of their own pockets." Only Mrs. Jennings, "a new-comer, and town-bred, so that she could hardly be expected to have a very clear notion of what was proper," indecorously neglects to wear mourning. This literally parochial outlook is ingrained in the provincial character, and in her regional stories George Eliot often gently exploits its humorous aspects, but she seldom if ever satirizes it or wishes to subvert it. Not only does she seem to find this rustic cliquishness quaint and appealing, but she actually sees it as an unconscious expression of the coherence and stability of rural society.

Connected with her acceptance of parochialism is the essential rightness of community opinion. Thus, quite often in the regional fiction, the provincial, old-fashioned, and native outlook is contrasted with the cosmopolitan, modern, and alien; and in spite of its narrowness and ignorance and occasional bigotry (as in "Janet's Repentance"), the provincial is in the end vindicated. The jocular scorn in "Amos Barton" for the "miserable town-bred reader" can be pertinently recalled here. Also in "Amos Barton," George Eliot mocks the coolness of the Milby ladies toward the Countess because it stems from self-righteous envy of her beauty; but however farfetched their suspicions of her are, they are at bottom quite right in treating her as an adventuress. Caroline Bridmain is an alien in the region. Her past, present, and future seem equally rootless (it is said in Chapter IV that she leads with her brother a "migratory life"), and the prolonged "visit" she is forced to pay the Bartons simply emphasizes her situation. Similarly, Mr. Barton's own recent arrival in Shepperton may in part account for the clumsiness of his efforts; in any case, it is a serious handicap in his desire to inspire and reform the community. As we have seen, he is accepted by it only after his wife's death and burial and his love and grief for her have undeniably bound him to the very soil of the village.

In "Mr. Gilfil's Love-Story," it is Tina who is the alien.[16] When she is described by the narrator, by the servants, or by Mrs. Patten years later, it is her foreignness and fragility that are stressed. Unsuccessfully transplanted from a remote, exotic land, Tina lacks the robustness of native growth. In the end, Mr. Bates's apparently wrongheaded, gloomy declaration in Chapter IV is confirmed: "it's what I shouldn't ha' looked for from Sir Cristhifer an' my ledy, to bring a furrin child into the coonthry; an' depend on't, whether you an' me lives to see 't or noo, it'll coom to soom harm."

Perhaps also implicitly upheld is the truth of Mrs. Patten's antiromantic regret that Mr. Gilfil had to fall in love with a foreigner who really "didn't care about the dairy, nor the cheeses": "It's a thousand pities as he married i' that way — a fine man like him, as might ha' had the pick o' the country an' had his grandchildren about him now." Mrs. Patten's observation — a transition to the story that explains the Vicar's "foolishness" — appropriately closes the first chapter in which her opinion of him had been concretely demonstrated. The long opening is really a comprehensive introduction to Mr. Gilfil and a further exploration, continued from "Amos Barton," of the Shepperton community, in which he is so completely at home.

His position (like that of the narrator's father in "Looking Back-

---

[16] Captain Wybrow is equally alien — in inclination, if not nationality. Even more fatally delicate than Tina, he is, in contrast to the vigorous Maynard Gilfil, clearly out of his element in the country, remote from the land and not in genuine contact with his surroundings — an incongruous heir of the energetic and imaginative Sir Christopher, as Mr. Bates remarks early in Chapter II.

ward") brings him in contact with the entire range of social life in the region. Much of this life, including some of the minor characters, is familiar from "Amos Barton," and the narrative itself harks back to the first story, in which Mr. Gilfil's "little romance" is mentioned in the preliminary description of Shepperton Church. In sketching out the background, the author relies in part on this recurrence, and there are therefore fewer leisurely introductions in "Mr. Gilfil's Love-Story" than in "Amos Barton." Instead, the social environment is built around several anecdotes and vignettes that illustrate Mr. Gilfil's character. These are executed with a rich proliferation of detail derived, often quite clearly, from fondly recollected experience. The sketch of Dame Fripp, for example, who holds, among other thriving undertakings, the unofficial post of village beggar, seems to be based on acquaintance, direct or derived rather than imagined. And the Vicar's encounter with the old woman is presented with a deliciously broad humor that, apart from anticipating Hardy's peasant comedy, suggests a cherished and often told local story:

> Such was Dame Fripp, whom Mr. Gilfil, riding leisurely in top-boots and spurs from doing duty at Knebley one warm Sunday afternoon, observed sitting in the dry ditch near her cottage, and by her side a large pig, who, with that ease and confidence belonging to perfect friendship, was lying with his head in her lap, and making no effort to play the agreeable beyond an occasional grunt.
>
> "Why, Mrs. Fripp," said the Vicar, "I didn't know you had such a fine pig. You'll have some rare flitches at Christmas!"
>
> "Eh, God forbid! My son gev him me two 'ear ago, an' he's been company to me iver sin'. I couldn't find i' my heart to part wi'm, if I niver knowed the taste o' bacon-fat again."
>
> "Why, he'll eat his head off, and yours too. How can you go on keeping a pig, and making nothing by him?"
>
> "Oh, he picks a bit hisself wi' rootin', and I dooant mind doing wi'out to gi' him summat. A bit o' coompany's meat an' drink too, an' he follers me about, and grunts when I spake to'm, just like a Christian."
>
> Mr. Gilfil laughed, and I am obliged to admit that he said good-bye to Dame Fripp without asking her why she had not been to church, or making the slightest effort for her spiritual edification. But the next day he ordered his man David to take her a great piece of bacon, with a message, saying, the parson wanted to make sure that Mrs. Fripp would know the taste of bacon-fat again.

86

His thoughtfulness and geniality are probably meant to be contrasted with Amos Barton's insensitive sternness toward Mrs. Brick. Indeed Mr. Gilfil is in many ways Mr. Barton's opposite. Without the curate's stiffness, he moves from Mrs. Fripp's company to that of the prosperous farmers, their children, and to the drawing rooms of the local gentry. Unlike Mr. Barton, whose solemn, simple-minded zeal is a source of amusement and annoyance to his parishioners, Mr. Gilfil is loved for his kindness and warmth and respected for his good sense in both practical and clerical matters. But the difference between the two may be owing as much to the periods to which they belong as to their characters. For Mr. Gilfil represents the type of easygoing, good-humored, worthy but somewhat casual and secular churchmanship of the eighteenth century. Mr. Barton, on the other hand, is caught between the Evangelical and Tractarian Movements:

> When he first came to Shepperton he was simply an evangelical clergyman, whose Christian experiences had commenced under the teaching of the Rev. Mr. Johns, of Gun Street Chapel, and had been consolidated at Cambridge under the influence of Mr. Simeon. John Newton and Thomas Scott were his doctrinal ideals . . . But by this time the effect of the Tractarian agitation was beginning to be felt in backward provincial regions . . . (Chapter II)

In response to the spirit of his time, then, Mr. Barton, as his Lending Library and the reconstruction of the church show, is intent on reform. Mr. Gilfil has no such projects, but he succeeds easily where Mr. Barton fails: in winning the trust of the community. "The Knebley farmers would as soon have thought of criticizing the moon as their pastor"; and to the Shepperton churchmen "the benefits of baptism were supposed to be somehow bound up with Mr. Gilfil's personality." But as the narrator himself points out, Mr. Gilfil did not have to face the eddies of agitation and change that were so slow in reaching Shepperton. By Mr. Barton's time the villagers had become critical of religious discourse: "they had tasted that dangerous fruit of the tree of knowledge — innovation, which is well known to open the eyes, even in an uncomfortable manner." The Evangelical Movement in Mr. Gilfil's day had not yet made the masses familiar with religious controversy.

Thus, though not to the same degree as in "Amos Barton," historical allusions are used to locate in time the regional narrative, to extend its suggestiveness and enrich its interest. But in "Mr. Gilfil's Love-Story," such allusions are briefer than in the first story and more often than not, reflecting perhaps the hero's character, they are secular rather than doctrinal. The coolness between him and Squire Old-inport, which delighted the Shepperton farmers, is an example. In the background of their quarrel is the economic situation of the country in the early nineteenth century (particularly the crisis in agriculture that followed the conclusion of the Napoleonic Wars),[17] and in the foreground are the motives that could determine the relationship between a landlord and his tenants, as well as the position of the parson — outside that relationship but in a way responsible for it. All this is suggested with great succinctness, as the knowing, ironic tone and direct, at times colloquial, language invest the passage, especially at the end, with unexpected vividness and force:

> ... Mr. Oldinport was in the worst odour as a landlord, having kept up his rents in spite of falling prices, and not being in the least stung to emulation by paragraphs in the provincial newspapers, stating that the Honourable Augustus Purwell, or Viscount Blethers, had made a return of ten percent on their last rent-day. The fact was, Mr. Oldinport had not the slightest intention of standing for Parliament, whereas he had the strongest intention of adding to his unentailed estate. Hence, to the Shepperton farmers it was as good as lemon with their grog to know that the Vicar had thrown out sarcasms against the Squire's charities, as little better than those of a man who stole a goose, and gave away the giblets in alms. (Chapter I)

Apart from Mr. Gilfil himself, only the alteration of Cheverel Manor and the figure of Sir Christopher Cheverel are, at least in part, regional in interest and function. Like Mr. Oldinport, Sir Christopher Cheverel is a landlord, but in his dealings with his tenants, which we have a chance to see directly in the interview with Mrs. Hartopp (Chapter II), he shows a rare combination of authority, shrewdness, and charity. He emerges here perhaps as a representative of the kind of enlightened feudalism — a humane, responsible, sensible relationship between master and man — that Carlyle and Ruskin made many Victorians admire. It is, however, in his role as inspired reconstructor

[17] See, for example, Asa Briggs, *The Age of Improvement* (London, 1959), pp. 171–172 and 203.

and Gothicizer that Sir Christopher is really important. The transformation of Cheverel Manor that proceeds in the background provides a kind of counterpoint to the romance: the slow but massive and orderly progress in the rebuilding, referred to every now and then through the story, unobtrusively contrasts with the crosspurposes, deceptions, and emotional confusions that slowly corrode the harmony of family ties and bring the gradual dissolution of relationships to a melodramatic climax.

The beauty of Cheverel Manor and grounds tempts George Eliot to try her hand at some rather elaborate natural descriptions; here, as in similar passages previously, the details, tone, and references suggest the extent to which her memory in these stories serves as a major creative source.[18] The Manor itself is a local landmark, a link between past and present (the narrator has himself seen and admired it), an enduring monument to Sir Christopher's "unswerving architectural purpose" and "fervour of genius." Finally, the work on the Manor also serves to remind us of the flow of history and cultural change, for we are told that Sir Christopher anticipates, "through the prompting of his individual taste, that general reaction from the insipid imitation of the Palladian style, towards a restoration of the Gothic, which marked the close of the eighteenth century" (Chapter IV).

iii

Leslie Stephen wrote of *Scenes of Clerical Life* that "it is the constant, though not obtrusive, suggestion of the depths below the surface of trivial detail which gives an impressive dignity to the work; and, in any case, marks one most distinctive characteristic of George Eliot's genius." [19] Thus, just as the commonplace Rev. Amos Barton is capable of attaining a tragic level of suffering and the amiable, prosaic Mr. Gilfil cherishes a romantic past of passion, loss, and constancy, so the backward town of Milby is in "Janet's Repentance" redeemed by its few citizens who are blessed with exceptional in-

---

[18] For the close connection between Cheverel Manor and Arbury Hall (near George Eliot's native town of Nuneaton), see the various studies of the "George Eliot Country" cited in note 30 of Chapter I, especially Lady Newdigate-Newdegate.

[19] *George Eliot*, p. 63.

tegrity and determination. By their kindness, understanding, and self-sacrifice, these persons have the power of raising the town's life out of its accustomed dull, narrow, mean, often squalid rut. As in "Amos Barton," brief glimpses of the setting are given in a way designed to support and embody the prevailing moral and social atmosphere. An early description of Milby, for example, reiterates quite explicitly the faith in hidden virtue, strength and beauty that "Janet's Repentance" as well as the two preceding stories dramatize.

> To a superficial glance, Milby was nothing but dreary prose: a dingy town, surrounded by flat fields, lopped elms, and sprawling manufacturing villages, which crept on and on with their weaving-shops, till they threatened to graft themselves on the town. But the sweet spring came to Milby notwithstanding: the elm-tops were red with buds; the church-yard was starred with daisies; the lark showered his love-music on the flat fields; the rainbows hung over the dingy town, clothing the very roofs and chimneys in a strange transfiguring beauty. And so it was with the human life there, which at first seemed a dismal mixture of griping worldliness, vanity, ostrich-feathers, and the fumes of brandy: looking closer, you found some purity, gentleness, and unselfishness, as you may have observed a scented geranium giving forth its wholesome odours amidst blasphemy and gin in a noisy pot-house. (Chapter II)

As in the other two stories, the retrospective historical point of view stresses the changes that have affected the life of the region in the quarter of a century separating the time of the narration from the events. The interval is roughly the same as in "Amos Barton," and here also the narrator is closely involved with the environment, if not with the action itself. Again the differences between past and present conditions are summarized in direct observations that are studded with personal references; and as in the first story, the tone in these comments is ironic, implying that the transformation of Milby from those benighted days is hardly as thoroughgoing as modern complacency believes. The town has acquired a new railway station, a resident rector, an enlarged church, and a reformed grammar school, but the gentlemen there still "fall into no other excesses at dinner parties than the perfectly well-bred and virtuous excess of stupidity; and though the ladies are still said to take too much upon themselves, they are never known to take too much in any other way"

(Chapter II). It is thus not at all certain that Milby is now indeed "a refined, moral, and enlightened town," any more than it is certain that the nonliterary young ladies of the earlier generation, who little dreamed "that their daughters would read a selection of German poetry, and be able to express an admiration for Schiller," were necessarily less sensitive and worthy than their culturally aspiring offspring.

The tone of personal reminiscence, without calling excessive attention to itself, invests the fairly ambitious and wide-ranging sketch of the provincial community (larger and more complex as well as less congenial than Shepperton) with a feeling of particularity, intimacy, and authenticity. The narrator's rare autobiographical digressions are never intrusive; always concerned more with the life, people, and manners remembered than with himself, his personal remarks blend smoothly into the leisurely sketch of Milby society:

> I remember blushing very much, and thinking Miss Landor was laughing at me, because I was appearing in coat-tails for the first time, when I saw her look down slyly towards where I sat, and then turn with a titter to handsome Mr. Bob Lowme, who had such beautiful whiskers meeting under his chin. But perhaps she was not thinking of me, after all; for our pew was near the pulpit, and there was almost always something funny about old Mr. Crewe. (Chapter II)

And so the description of Mr. Crewe follows. Similarly, in the account of the Confirmation in Chapter VI, when the narrator recalls kneeling next to Ned Phipps, "who . . . I am sure made me behave much worse than I should have done without him," the apparently digressive recollections incidentally give life to the portraits of the Bishop, Mr. Prendergast, and Mr. Tryan, as well as to the spirit of the occasion.

Her use of the reminiscing narrator also enables George Eliot to combine in the description of Milby an attitude of detachment and ironic tolerance with a sense of immediacy, involvement, and an occasional surge of nostalgia. The sketch of the community is designed to highlight the religious controversy (the advent of that spirit of "innovation" which Mr. Gilfil had so fortunately avoided) that looms large in the story as a whole. The abrupt opening plunges the reader into the middle of the conflict between the Dempsterites and the Tryanites; as Dempster and his companions, between drinks at the

Red Lion, urge each other on in their plot against Mr. Tryan, they are in their own words and the narrator's scathing asides effectively, if undemonstratively, condemned as an ignorant, bigoted, aggressively egoistic and hypocritically pious lot. But if Dempster's bullying, craftiness, and glibness determine from the beginning the reader's attitude to the anti-Tryanite Movement, Mr. Tryan's supporters, though treated more gently than Dempster's, do not escape the narrator's impartial clear-sightedness. Both groups embody the faults of the entire community — at the end of the second chapter Mr. Dempster, Mr. Budd, and Mr. Tomlinson are actually selected as "the three delegates representing the intellect, morality, and wealth of Milby," who carry to Mr. Prendergast the petition against Mr. Tryan — and satire, if not sarcasm, is applied also to Mr. Tryan's admirers as well as his opponents. In Chapter III, for example, which follows the dramatic introduction of Dempster and his friends and the general historical, analytical, and ironically evaluative description of Milby society, George Eliot makes amusing the mixed motives, more social than spiritual, of Mr. Tryan's lady-admirers gathered at Mrs. Linnet's. This impartiality, tinged with a considered sympathy and implicit support for Mr. Tryan's Evangelicalism, is clear in the summary of the progress he gradually makes in the town:

> The movement, like all other religious "revivals," had a mixed effect . . . It may be that some of Mr. Tryan's hearers had gained a religious vocabulary rather than religious experience; that here and there a weaver's wife, who, a few months before, had been simply a silly slattern, was converted into that more complex nuisance, a silly and sanctimonious slattern . . . Miss Eliza Pratt, listening in rapt attention to Mr. Tryan's evening lecture, no doubt found evangelical channels for vanity and egoism; but she was clearly in moral advance of Miss Phipps giggling under her feathers at old Mr. Crewe's peculiarities of enunciation. (Chapter X)

The endorsement of Mr. Tryan's efforts is subtly but deliberately prepared from the beginning, not only in the revulsion from the group at the Red Lion, but also in the apparently discursive account of the Milby community in Chapter II, which is essentially an indictment (though that may be too strong a term) of spiritual shallowness and moral callousness. In the ironic and sarcastic vignettes of the town's

leading families and their customs, George Eliot, with occasional dis-
taste and much greater vigor than she ever applies to satirizing
villages like Shepperton, criticizes the petty status-seeking, ignorant
self-satisfaction, and crude knowingness of provincial townspeople.
There is, however, no bitterness in this attack, only a resigned sense
of human imperfection, an impressively suggested familiarity with
the environment, and the ultimate faith in the presence of redeeming
virtues. (Indeed, in tone and attitude, the portrait of Milby is very
close to the descriptions of St. Ogg's and Middlemarch.

Compared with Mr. Gilfil's Shepperton, however, Milby is large,
complex, worldly, divided and almost made unmanageable by the
assertiveness of self-centered and successful citizens. The old, leisurely undemanding religion of the eighteenth century, which, through
the person of Mr. Gilfil, had been relatively effective in maintaining
a spirit of friendliness, charity, and responsibility in the village of
Shepperton, has in the town of Milby lost its power to edify and guide.
As the narrator is made to observe in Chapter II with obvious ironic
understatement, "no one is warranted in saying that old Mr. Crewe's
flock could not have been worse without any clergyman at all." The
Sunday services have degenerated into a "brilliant show of out-door
toilettes," and, among the young people especially, the "respect for
the Sabbath, manifested in this attention to costume, was unhappily
counterbalanced by considerable levity of behaviour during the pray-
ers and sermon." As in St. Ogg's, people are guided mainly by material
motives and values: "the clients are proud of their lawyer's unscrupu-
lousness," and Mr. Crewe, the curate, is "liked . . . all the better for
having scraped together a large fortune out of his school and curacy."
Because he has been "part of Milby life for half a century," the
curate is accepted and defended, but unlike Mr. Gilfil, "he was not
spoken of in terms of high respect . . . The parishioners saw no reason
at all why it should be desirable to venerate the parson or any one
else: they were much more comfortable to look down a little on their
fellow-creatures."

The indecorous and immoral slackness that prevails in the
Church infects the Chapel also: "Even the Dissent in Milby was then
of a lax and indifferent kind." The story therefore strongly implies
that "when innovation made its appearance in the person of the Rev.
Mr. Tryan," it came as a long delayed and salutary antidote to the

moral stagnation into which the town had settled. Mr. Jerome, whose judgments are given the kind of weight that Mrs. Hackit's have in "Amos Barton," affirms this when he says to Tryan: "Before you came to it, sir, Milby was a dead an' dark place: you are the fust man i' the Church to my knowledge as has brought the word o' God home to the people . . ." (Chapter VIII).

Mr. Tryan is not a conventional hero (as is made clear at the end of Chapter X), but in conception alone he is probably as heroic as any of George Eliot's protagonists. Certainly he is a far more impressive and striking figure than Amos Barton, and because of his intensity and charisma he exercises a much greater influence over the community than Mr. Barton ever could. But it is relevant that the specific reforms that Mr. Tryan introduces into Milby are essentially the same as those undertaken with such ineffective zeal by the curate of Shepperton:

> It was soon notorious in Milby that Mr. Tryan held peculiar opinions; that he preached extempore; that he was founding a religious lending library in his remote corner of the parish; that he expounded the Scriptures in cottages; and that his preaching was attracting the Dissenters, and filling the very aisles of his church. (Chapter II)

It is this religious and moral emphasis that lends focus and unity to the general account of Milby in the second chapter, but what gives the story much of its interest and effectiveness is the author's assured sense and vivid presentation of the way a provincial town functions. She is keenly aware of the interconnections between public and private issues in such a restricted community, of the way religious and moral problems affect social intercourse and professional lives, and, as in the case of Dempster, the way all such pressures can influence and operate through an individual temperament. Mr. Tryan's "innovations" threaten in particular the social prominence and self-assurance of such "sarcastic parish demagogues" as Mr. Dempster; but Dempster's violent opposition to Tryan also alienates several of his valuable clients, slowly brings out his latent pathological instability, and in the end costs him his life. And the repercussions of his hostility are felt not only by Dempster himself, his wife, and Mr. Tryan but by the entire town. Already in the opening chapter he has organized the wealthy and respectable ranks in resistance to Mr.

Tryan's plans. In Chapter IV, we see him infecting the "lower orders" with his fervor and directing a mob of town riffraff to give his delegation the appearance of massive and popular support.

As the agitation continues, its effects become increasingly extensive. In Chapter V, the division in the town has reached Miss Townley's school for young ladies. And in the next chapter, the leading "Anti-Tryanites," having lost the battle, are thinking of exerting economic pressure in order to compel the allegiance of their employees.

> "He'll not get many Milby people to go and hear his lectures after a while, I'll bet a guinea," observed Mr. Budd. "I know I'll not keep a single workman on my ground who either goes to the lecture himself or lets anybody belonging to him go."
>
> "Nor me nayther," said Mr. Tomlinson. "No Tryanite shall touch a sack or drive a waggon o' mine, that you may depend on. An' I know more besides me as are o' the same mind." (Chapter VI)

The conflict reaches its climax in Chapter IX when the two parties confront one another, and Mr. Tryan, calm and unflinching, withstands the jeers of his enemies. In Chapter X, the controversy has petered out, victory has been ceded to the innovating clergyman, and the consequences of the strife are reckoned up. Custom and practicality, it is seen, cannot remain long submerged in Milby: estranged patients return to Mr. Pilgrim and Mr. Pratt, and offended customers to merchants like Mr. Dunn. At the same time, the narrative tone, which in the intervening chapters had at times threatened to support too emphatically the Tryanite cause, regains its caustic balance and its shrewd, a little pedantic, strongly local humor:

> ... convenience, that admirable branch system from the main line of self-interest, makes us all fellow-helpers in spite of adverse resolutions. It is probable that no speculative or theological hatred would be ultimately strong enough to resist the persuasive power of convenience ... In this persuasive power ... lay Mr. Dunn's ultimate security from martyrdom. His drapery was the best in Milby; the comfortable use and wont of procuring satisfactory articles at a moment's notice proved too strong for Anti-Tryanite zeal ...

Only Mr. Dempster comes out of the fray a clear loser — and his losses multiply. After the effectiveness of Mr. Tryan's activities has been described and estimated, the focus of the story shifts abruptly to the private situation of the main figures — Dempster, Tryan, and especially Janet. This shift, in the account of Janet's "conversion," is intended in part to highlight a dramatic illustration of Tryan's ennobling influence; and the illustration, of course, provides the main narrative interest. The shift is conspicuous, however, because until this point more than a third of the story — Chapters I to X — is devoted almost entirely to a portrayal of the character and opinions of the community, with the survey alternating roughly between Dempster's party and Tryan's. Only in Chapter XI is the latter's poor health emphasized, and in Chapter XII, where he and Janet almost meet, Janet's domestic tragedy begins to usurp the stage. Dempster's decline, practically self-destruction, and prolonged death throes are described from the private and domestic point of view, albeit with a touch of inflation and melodrama. The community perspective recedes noticeably into the background, reemerging only near the end, when Janet, now openly under Mr. Tryan's spiritual guidance, begins her moral and psychological recovery and evokes the friendly concern of her neighbors.

Indeed, as Janet Dempster achieves her personal reintegration and affirms her ties with the community, the community, in turn, is shown in the process of similar self-reformation. As is suggested in Chapter X, the general impulse toward improvement is inspired by Mr. Tryan just as much as the individual: "The first condition of human goodness is something to love; the second, something to reverence. And this latter precious gift was brought to Milby by Mr. Tryan and Evangelicalism." The acceptance, sympathy, and respect shown to Janet in Chapters XXI, XXII, XXV, and XXVI, for example, and the narrator's sustained control over caustic commentary in the later parts are tacit indications of the new elevation and refinement of public morals and sensibilities:

> Janet was recovering the popularity which her beauty and sweetness of nature had won for her when she was a girl; and popularity, as every one knows, is the most complex and self-multiplying of echoes. Even anti-Tryanite prejudice could not resist the fact that Janet Dempster was a changed woman ... and that this change was due to Mr. Tryan's influence. The last lingering sneers against the Evangelical curate began to die out; and though much of the feeling that had prompted them remained

behind, there was an intimidating consciousness that the expression of such feeling would not be effective — jokes of that sort had ceased to tickle the Milby mind. Even Mr. Budd and Mr. Tomlinson, when they saw Mr. Tryan passing pale and worn along the street, had a secret sense that this man was somehow not that very natural and comprehensible thing, a humbug — that, in fact, it was impossible to explain him from the stomach-and-pocket point of view. (Chapter XXVI)

The signs of general moral improvement are even stronger at Mr. Tryan's massively attended funeral, the spirit of which is deliberately contrasted with that of Mr. Dempster's: "The faces were not hard at this funeral; the burial-service was not a hollow form" (Chapter XXVIII). But from Chapter XI on, the concern with the public condition is only sporadically evident: the emphasis is overwhelmingly private. There is here little of that sustained alternation between "choric" and individual scenes that characterize "Amos Barton," nor is there any attempt to contain the personal drama within a deliberately, if not symmetrically, arranged social frame, as in "Mr. Gilfil's Love-Story." Instead, we have here the rather awkward division in emphasis between the first third and the rest of the story. Henry James complained that "the excess of local touches" in "Janet's Repentance" diffused "the stern and tragical character" of the moral and domestic conflict.[20] But it is possible to view the story's lack of balance from another, if not the opposite, point of view: that is, not only is Janet's private drama not sufficiently integrated with the regional background, but it is itself ineffectively written. The characters of Dempster and Janet, as well as of Mr. Tryan, are fuzzily drawn, and their relationships inadequately conceived; sentimental flourishes and hysterically righteous apostrophes cloud over much of the private part of the narrative, and the precise causes of Janet's feelings of guilt and Mr. Tryan's persuasiveness are not made as clear

---

[20] See quotation on p. 5. W. J. Harvey also finds fault with "Janet's Repentance" (as well as with "Mr. Gilfil's Love-Story") because of the "large chunks of description and information, and the introduction of too many characters who tend to clutter up the story and confuse the reader" (*The Art of George Eliot*, p. 127). Since he emphasizes at this point in his study the private drama in George Eliot's work, the objection is only partly justified. His valuable perception of the unrealized comic possibilities of the minor characters in "Janet's Repentance" supports my argument, for it calls attention to yet another aspect of the imbalance in the story's structure. The same defect is noted from another point of view by Daniel P. Deneau, "Imagery in the *Scenes of Clerical Life*," *Victorian Newsletter*, no. 28 (Fall 1965), pp. 18–22.

as they could be. This tendency toward melodrama is already partially evident in the commentary describing Tina's confused feelings of betrayal, resentment, and guilt in "Mr. Gilfil's Love-Story," but in "Janet's Repentance," the forced attempts to wring the reader's heart are more frequent and heavy-handed. It is the repeated clumsiness of such passages that accentuates the division between the concrete, full, and controlled local narrative and the generally diffuse and exaggerated domestic drama.

And yet the two parts are thematically connected: each illustrates the beneficial effects of Evangelicalism and the human strength and love that can be called forth out of squalid circumstances, public or private. As later in *Daniel Deronda*, it is the execution, the lack of control and authentic feeling for the reality of characters and psychological situations, that impairs the intellectually conceived unity between personal and social issues. For contrast, it is valuable to refer back to George Eliot's first story, in which she successfully maintains such a unity, mainly through an effective blending of local and private matters and a deliberate avoidance of melodrama and sentimentality. The potentially most exotic elements in the story, the past of the Countess and Mr. Barton's relationship with her, are deflated at the very outset. And the account of Milly's death, though the narrator's tone falters at points, is generally unmarred by forced, gushing pathos. Leslie Stephen's comment on this scene is altogether just: "we are never crossed by the thought which disturbs so many deathbeds in fiction, that she is somehow conscious of an audience applauding her excellence in the part." [21] At her best in *Scenes of Clerical Life*, George Eliot is able to subdue her tendency toward pathos and melodrama, even as she strives to win our sympathy for her characters; at her best, too, she depicts concretely, authentically the interaction between private and public lives. She goes on to express these interests and talents with far greater consistency and fullness in *Adam Bede*.

[21] *George Eliot*, p. 62.

98

5 The Speech of the Landscape: *Adam Bede*

Altogether, my father's England seemed to me lovable,
laudable, full of good men, and having good rulers . . .
— "Looking Backward"

i

George Eliot's first novel, which she began almost directly after completing *Scenes of Clerical Life*, is surprisingly free from the faults of the novice — the want of balance and lapses of tone, the abrupt transitions and awkward structure — that mar her first work of fiction, particularly "Janet's Repentance." *Adam Bede*, with its thoroughgoing care for unity and reliance on a network of emphases, parallelisms, contrasts, and cross-references, is aesthetically a sophisticated and "modern" book. Edmund Gosse, who concurred in the critical disapproval, general in his day, of George Eliot's late novels because in them she has "turned away from passive acts of memory to a strenuous exercise of intellect," [1] must have passed over, together with most readers, the many signs of a designing intelligence at work in the early ones. *Adam Bede* may not be precisely Jamesian in structure, but neither is it one of those "loose baggy monsters" of Victorian fiction that James deplored. As W. J. Harvey points out, George Eliot's novels are "built around a balance or conflict of a number of centres of interest" rather than one dominant figure.[2] It is only recently that the rich unity of these centers of interest has been acknowledged and defined.

Thus, in evidence of the complexity of organization of *Adam Bede*, many striking interconnections have been cited. Several critics have noted and interpreted the patterns of imagery that sustain the progress of the plot and the development of moral vision, especially in Adam's growth through suffering. The author's deliberate attention to time and the seasonal cycle, the symbolic contrast between the two counties in which the action mainly occurs, the thematic links and suggestive differences between consecutive chapters, and the coherence of the underlying ideological design have all received due recognition. Other links have been found in the consistency with which certain characters are paired and contrasted with one another (for example, Adam and Arthur, Hetty and Dinah, Hetty and Bess Cranage, Arthur and Hetty, Adam and Hetty, Adam and Dinah) and in the juxtaposition of the principal households (the Bede cottage, the Rectory, the Hall Farm, and Donnithorne Chase).[3] Even the two

[1] Edmund Gosse, "George Eliot," *The London Mercury*, I (1918–19), 36.
[2] *The Art of George Eliot*, p. 27.
[3] See especially the studies by Reva Stump, Barbara Hardy, Harvey, Paris,

apparently random references to Dr. John Moore's story *Zeluco* have been investigated and shown to cast light on Arthur's character and to foreshadow his seduction of Hetty.[4]

In this line of analysis, several critics have also written about the symbolic or suggestive quality of the physical descriptions in *Adam Bede*.[5] Now it is interesting that *Adam Bede*, though it derives much less from memory and personal experience than *Scenes of Clerical Life* and is not even set in George Eliot's native Warwickshire, should be so much more pictorial than its predecessor. For in spite of Harvey's objections to excessive physical detail in *Scenes of Clerical Life*, with the exception of the two or three isolated passages, that book is not taken up with descriptions. Apart from Cheverel Manor in "Mr. Gilfil's Love-Story," there are no unusually precise or concrete visual impressions of the settings in which the stories are located. What distinguishes the landscapes and interiors in *Scenes of Clerical Life* from those in *Adam Bede* is a matter of quality, not quantity: it is the narrator's obtrusive, openly autobiographical feeling of personal acquaintance with the region. Often the background in the stories is more factual than functional; it does not have the suggestive power, the sense of latent significance, that the setting in *Adam Bede* radiates. As Harvey rightly notes, *Scenes of Clerical Life* shows "an over-reliance on memory, on actual facts and situations already known to the novelist. It is significant that those interested in the local history behind George Eliot's fiction find their richest

---

and Knoepflmacher; also the essays by Creeger and Foakes as well as the following: Dorothy Van Ghent, "On *Adam Bede*," *The English Novel: Form and Function* (New York, 1953); Martin Hussey, "Structure and Imagery in *Adam Bede*," *Nineteenth-Century Fiction*, X (1955–56), 115–129, and Clyde de L. Ryals, "The Thorn Imagery in the Novels of George Eliot," *Victorian Newsletter*, no. 22 (Fall 1962), pp. 12–13. Without pursuing at any length these much discussed topics, I would simply like to point out yet another linking device in the novel: the contrast and parallelism in the arrangement of events and titles of chapters in the first and last Books of the novel. These superficial connections support the novel's underlying movement toward balance and completeness.

[4] Jerome Thale, "*Adam Bede*: Arthur Donnithorne and *Zeluco*," *Modern Language Notes*, LXX (1955), 263–265 and Irving A. Buchen, "Arthur Donnithorne and *Zeluco*: Characterization via Literary Allusion in *Adam Bede*," *Victorian Newsletter*, no. 22 (Fall 1962), pp. 18–19.

[5] Among them, Hussey, Creeger, Foakes, Casson, F. W. Willey, and James H. Wheatley in his unpublished doctoral dissertation "George Eliot and the Art of Thought: Studies in the Early Novels" (Harvard University, 1960). Because he is concerned with other issues, Wheatley does not follow up his observation that in *Adam Bede* George Eliot "begins to think morally and artistically in terms of modes of visualization" (p. 130).

source in *Scenes of Clerical Life* rather than in the most personal of her novels, *The Mill on the Floss*." [6]

Adam Bede, of course, is quasi-biographical rather than autobiographical. It is based, according to George Eliot's own testimony, on family history and her father's background, not her own.

> As to my indebtedness to facts of locale, and personal history of a small kind, connected with Staffordshire and Derbyshire — you may imagine of what kind that is, when I tell you that I never remained in either of those counties more than a few days together, and of only two such visits have I more than a shadowy, interrupted recollection. The details which I knew as facts and have made use of for my picture were gathered from such imperfect allusion and narrative as I heard from my father, in his occasional talk about old times. (*Letters*, III, 176)

In *Adam Bede*, George Eliot's sense of the locale is intimately imagined rather than intimate. It may be that it was the absence of strong personal involvement with the region as well as her newly acquired experience and confidence as an author that set her free to manipulate and deploy physical descriptions in acordance with her general design. She uses these descriptions to provide a rich and credible setting for the narrative and to bring out the distinctiveness, the individual character of the setting. It is felt to be not only an authentic place in which people live, but a particular place to which the characters are bound by ties almost of instinct, of family tradition, community coherence, memory, work, residence, and affection. Finally, George Eliot uses landscape to define, reinforce, and foreshadow the events of the plot and the moral situation.

Something of this multiple use of setting is suggested in the opening vignette — the first of many in the novel — of the workshop in which the bare facts of time and place are vitalized by the warmly observed sensory details. The warmth of the sun, the scent of pinewood and elder-bushes, the light of the sunbeams striking the flying shavings of wood and reflected in the oak paneling, and Adam's baritone voice establish a satisfying, concrete background for the revealing argument and implicit characterizations that follow. The atmosphere of sunny, harmonious, energetic rusticity is complicated but not shattered by the diversity of personalities and underlying

[6] *The Art of George Eliot*, p. 131.

tensions. This dual strain of physical harmony and psychological restiveness is to be explored in the rest of the novel, just as Adam's nature, as it is compactly suggested in this scene (even the song he is given to sing is in character), is to be tested and developed.

Still richer in suggestion and oblique, tentative anticipations of the narrative is the extended description of the village and countryside of Hayslope near the beginning of the second chapter. The landscape is detailed and orderly, observed with a gradually narrowing perspective but built on the somewhat ominous contrast between the abundant, undulating district of Loamshire, in which Hayslope lies, and the "grim outskirt of Stonyshire" visible not far away. Although the description is general, it is focused in the village green from which the awkwardly conceived "traveller" regards his surroundings. Because of this precise and firmly centered observation and the coherent description, the reader easily imagines and retains the scene; yet what carries over most resonantly into the rest of the book is the sense of the intangible influences that the landscape suggests.

Indeed what seems at first only an orderly and objective account of the appearance of the countryside can be read also as an emblematic vision of moral realities. The way in which the abundance, comfort, charm, and color of Loamshire operate symbolically in conjunction with the rugged barrenness and austerity of Stonyshire has been already examined by some of the critics I have mentioned earlier; here I may perhaps simply call attention to the vague sense of threat which undercuts, though ever so slightly, the congeniality of the scene.

> High up against the horizon were the huge conical masses of hill, like giant mounds intended to fortify this region of corn and grass against the keen and hungry winds of the north; not distant enough to be clothed in purple mystery, but with sombre greenish sides visibly specked with sheep, whose motion was only revealed by memory, not detected by sight; wooed from day to day by the changing hours, but responding with no change in themselves . . . (Chapter II)

Although it is set in the middle of predominantly pleasant description, the passage qualifies the reassurance of the account as a whole. In its ostensible concern with agricultural cultivation, it also contains the as yet hesitant suggestion that the control over their lives for which men aspire (as Arthur, Adam, and Hetty, for example, do) is at best precarious in achievement and always exposed to the ravages of irresistible forces. To infer from an apparently innocuous and straightforward landscape a whole *Weltanschauung* (one gloomy and perhaps even banal enough to evoke the German term) may seem unjustified and heavy-handed. But the deliberate arrangement of the novel should be remembered here, for what follows the description of the setting and the survey of the villagers collected on the Green is Dinah's sermon, which is a fervent Christian appeal to the pleasantly complacent people of Hayslope to remember the uncertainty of their position in this life. Thus the preaching translates into religious and human terms the pregnant hints of the landscape, and anticipates, especially in Dinah's effect on Bess Cranage, the moral movement of the novel.[7]

Dinah is the right person to bring this lesson home to Hayslope. A native of Stonyshire and the one "alien" among the book's leading characters, she repeatedly refers in conversation to the differences between her county and Loamshire, differences which are recognized by the other characters (such as Mr. Irwine, Adam, Lisbeth, Mrs. Poyser) but not from exactly the same perspective as hers. In Chapter VIII, for example, she tells Mr. Irwine: "I've noticed that in these villages where the people lead a quiet life among the green pastures and the still waters, tilling the ground and tending the cattle, there's a strange deadness to the Word . . . the soul gets more hungry when the body is ill at ease." Such remarks, whether made by Dinah or by someone else in the book, develop in precise local terms the Ruskinian idea of interaction between the face of the land and the nature of the people that is first suggested in the juxtaposition of landscape and sermon in Chapter II. Gradually, the stark and cold country of Stonyshire comes to be associated with the austerity of truth. It is in Stonyshire that the trial takes place, it is here that both Hetty and Adam fully recognize and accept the burden of past delusions, and it is also here, in the cooler, crisper, clearer atmosphere, that Dinah at last acknowledges her need of Adam (and Loamshire) and that they are united.

At that point, Adam's impression of Stonyshire differs significantly from the bleakness ("the town lay grim, stony, and un-

[7] In "From Abstract to Concrete in *Adam Bede*," *College English*, XVII (1955–56), 88–89, William F. Jones regards the entire novel as an extended *exemplum* of Dinah's sermon.

sheltered") stressed in Chapter XXXVIII, when he first approached Snowfield in search of Hetty. In Chapter LIV, as he is waiting at the same spot for Dinah, the earlier impression is deliberately recalled.

> The scene looked less harsh in the soft October sunshine than it had done in the eager time of early spring; and the one grand charm it possessed in common with all wide-stretching wood-less regions — that it filled you with a new consciousness of the overarching sky — had a milder, more soothing influence than usual, on this almost cloudless day. Adam's doubts and fears melted under this influence as the delicate web-like clouds had gradually melted away into the clear blue above him. He seemed to see Dinah's gentle face assuring him, with its looks alone, of all he longed to know.

The threat of "the keen and hungry winds of the north" from which Hayslope is protected by the Stonyshire hills is like the threat of reality — complex, inescapable, hard but bracing — that impinges on the sheltered, pleasant, and well-ordered lives of the people. Materializing in a rising sequence of shocks, this threat disturbs the self-assurance and complacency expressed at the outset by such diverse figures as Adam, Arthur, Hetty, even in a way, Mr. Irwine, but above all Mrs. Poyser. When Mrs. Poyser speaks, especially in her arguments with Dinah about Methodism, we hear in her inflection and idioms as well as in her principles the quintessential voice of Loamshire: [8]

[8] There is certainly no clear attempt in the novel to satirize or deprecate Mrs. Poyser's position any more than there is an obvious preference, moral or other, for Stonyshire over Loamshire. The movement of the novel is perhaps designed to show up the incompleteness of the practical values of provincial common sense, but it does not question its validity. Thus, although Hussey writes in his essay that "if more were heard of Snowfield ... one might be justified in pressing the Shakespearian parallel of Sicilia and Bohemia, for Hayslope's limitations are exactly those of Bohemia," he nevertheless regards Mrs. Poyser as "the genuine voice of farming life," "the true voice of tradition," and the one really vital person in the novel of "Lawrentian force" (*Nineteenth-Century Fiction*, X, 122, 125, 129). George Creeger makes a related point, though with some exaggeration: "both Loamshire and Stonyshire are so stringently qualified that it is impossible to say of one that it is a positive, or the other a negative symbol." Creeger also contrasts Adam's two visits to Stonyshire, noting of the second that "Adam sees Stonyshire now through Dinah's eyes, as it were, and if his vision includes the barren land, it also includes the wonderful flooding light and the large embracing sky" (*ELH*, XXIII, 219, 237). R. A. Foakes, who objects to Creeger's overemphatic attention to Stonyshire, believes (rightly, I think) that the function of Stonyshire "is to establish that there is a world of poverty and suffering outside the self-sufficing community of Hayslope, a harsher world to set against the paradisal image. But the main values and perspectives remain

"But, for the matter o' that, if everybody was to do like you, the world must come to a standstill; for if everybody tried to do without house and home, and with poor eating and drinking, and was allays talking as we must despise the things o' the world, as you say, I should like to know where the pick o' the stock, and the corn, and the best new-milk cheeses 'ud have to go. Everybody 'ud be wanting bread made o' tail ends, and everybody 'ud be running after everybody else to preach to 'em, istead o' bringing up their families, and laying by against a bad harvest. It stands to sense as that can't be the right religion." (Chapter VI)

ii

Physical setting in *Adam Bede* is used in several other ways than that suggested by the emblematic general sketch at the opening of the second chapter. Most often, however, as before, the descriptions of environment or allusions to it tend to perform the at least triple function of establishing setting and atmosphere, building up a sense of the distinctness of the locale, and advancing the action. One of these effects may be emphasized in a particular case and made to overshadow the other two, but almost always a scene, viewed as a whole, is imbued with a greater significance than the sum of its details.[9] This is not to say, however, that George Eliot indulges in the pathetic fallacy. Usually it is in the interpretive commentary, not in the depiction itself of scenery or weather, that the correspondence between human and natural events is dwelt on. The opening of Book Three (Chapter XXII), for example, with its picture of a lush, expectant landscape and its air of suspension and hovering crisis is designed precisely to prefigure the situation of the story and cast a glance backward in appraisal of what has gone before. But it is essentially the author's explanation of the natural setting and atmosphere that suggests, however tacitly, this connection: "the sweet time of early growth and vague hopes is past; and yet the time of

___

fixed in Loamshire, and to these everything returns" (*English*, XII, 174). About Mrs. Poyser's role in *Adam Bede*, W. J. Harvey echoes Hussey's judgment: "She is the mouthpiece of the community, the articulation of a way of life. Into her witty aphorisms are compressed the wisdom of a tradition, a compassion, honesty and an acceptance of all the facts of life, so that we are not really surprised when she is so quick to forgive Hetty. Hers is a limited way of life but it is a good one" (*The Art of George Eliot*, pp. 157–158).
  [9] Cf. Harvey, pp. 228–230, on the use of natural description in *Adam Bede*.

harvest and ingathering is not come, and we tremble at the possible storms that may ruin the precious fruit in the moment of its ripeness." [10] George Eliot has characteristically selected here the natural details that suit her general purpose and deployed them in such a way as to give her work an extensive and substantial sense of artistic coherence.[11]

Philosophically committed as she was to a belief in Nature's indifference to human fate, she would hardly have been likely to impose on the world of her novel for the sake of heightened emotional effect the kind of factitious correlation between natural and human experience that Ruskin meant by the pathetic fallacy.[12] What she relies on instead is the entirely credible and natural appropriateness between human activity and the physical environment in which that activity, particularly in the form of rural occupations, is carried on. The harmony thus suggested between work and landscape is inherent in the pattern of agricultural life itself, with its responsiveness to weather and the seasonal cycle. Men are related to their environment mainly through their work: through work they make their impression on it, create it, and are in turn molded by it. And it is to George Eliot's profound sense of this interaction, and not simply to poetic license, that we must look to affirm the realistic consistency of her natural descriptions while recognizing at the same time their symbolic meaning.

She is herself conscious of this problem and, by casually bringing it into the open, seems to imply that the occasional oblique reflec-

---

[10] Hussey cites this passage as well as others in the book that hint at nature's responsiveness to the human situation, but he seems to want to have it both ways. Of the description of Snowfield in Chapter XXXVIII ("The town lay, grim, stony, and unsheltered, up the side of a steep hill . . ."), he remarks cryptically that it "has behind it not only positivism but also the Victorian belief in the pathetic fallacy." Recalling, however, passages of different import, he adds at once that "George Eliot did not believe that Nature necessarily mirrored human situations" (*Nineteenth-Century Fiction*, X, 118).

[11] Reva Stump's analysis brings out the numerous clusters of symbols and images that crowd the novel.

[12] See especially Paris, pp. 245–250. The whole question of the relation between man and nature in the novels of George Eliot is a vexing one, particularly when defined rather flexibly and applied to *Silas Marner* or *Daniel Deronda*, where the reliance on coincidence and poetic justice is so pronounced as to imply and at times unequivocally assert the controlling presence of a supernatural agency and order. See, for example, Thomson on the fairy-tale quality of *Silas Marner* and, on the occult and visionary aspects of *Daniel Deronda*, the essays already cited by Carroll and Pryer, and Ian W. Adam, "Character and Destiny in George Eliot's Fiction," *Nineteenth-Century Fiction*, XX (1965), 127–143.

tion of human events in the natural world which her novel shows is not much more than perfectly common coincidence. Thus the scene for the crucial moment of Adam's disenchantment is set in the description that begins Book Four, with its suggestion of remote disaster, local instability, and restlessness amid the prevailing beauty and gladness, and the slight hint of human delusion: "the grown-up people, too, were in good spirits, inclined to believe in yet finer days, when the wind had fallen. If only the corn were not ripe enough to be blown out of the husk and scattered as untimely seed!" But she chooses next to emphasize the merriment of the occasion and comments on the incongruity between nature and human destiny: "For if it be true that Nature at certain moments seems charged with a presentiment of one individual lot, must it not also be true that she seems unmindful, unconscious of another? . . . There are so many of us, and our lots are so different: what wonder that Nature's mood is often in harsh contrast with the great crisis of our lives?" There is a comparable paradoxical suggestion of appropriateness and disjunction between man and nature near the end of Book Four, when Hetty, now beset by her "Hidden Dread," is wretchedly walking to Treddleston; and the author makes an elaborate and somewhat sentimental comment on the hidden anguish that is often "strangely out of place in the midst of this joyous nature."

By indicating in this way that she is aware of her technique, that she has considered it in relation to the realistic tone and atmosphere that she has been carefully building up, George Eliot succeeds in maintaining the even flow and credibility of the novel. Her realism, however, is qualified, if not by the pathetic fallacy, then by other equally pastoral elements. Indeed a number of critics have tried to show that *Adam Bede* is not at all realistic in the style of the Dutch painters whom George Eliot, in the famous apology for realism in Chapter XVII, professes to admire, but is idealized in the manner of a pastoral romance. In a perceptive essay, R. A. Foakes observes that the world of *Adam Bede* "is partly analogous with that of pastoral, offering a frame of values for a way of life seen to be good, but simplified, and with the harshness of real life absent." He notes that in the novel work is "simply ennobling" and that "we get little sense of the sweat and filth of labour." [13]

[13] R. A. Foakes, *English*, XII, 174–175. Opposed to Foakes is Ian Milner's view that "there are few such feeling eulogies of the dignity and social worth of the

Ian Gregor, in "The Two Worlds of *Adam Bede*," when he attacks
the novel itself and V. S. Pritchett's estimation of it as "our supreme
novel of pastoral life," [14] takes a more extreme position than Foakes.
He too remarks that if "there is toil here, it is the idealized toil of
Goldsmith's *Deserted Village* or Gray's *Elegy*." But his principal objection to the novel is the unreconciled disjunction which he finds between the predominantly pastoral and, as he sees them, idealized and
unrealistic elements in the book and Hetty's tragedy. Whereas Pritchett has defined the limitations of *Adam Bede* in terms of Victorian
reticence about sexual matters, Gregor believes the whole book fails
because "George Eliot is extremely uncertain about the *kind* of novel
she is writing. She describes the situation and she resolves its conflict
by an appeal to a pastoral art; she develops the situation and brings
it to a climax by an appeal to the fiction of moral and psychological
enquiry." [15]

Apart from the arbitrary categories which he applies here to the
novel, Gregor throughout his essay exaggerates to the point of distortion its pastoral aspects. Assuming without offering evidence that it

---

working man in all English literature," in "The Structure of Values in *Adam
Bede*," *Philologica Pragensia*, IX (1966), 283.

[14] In *The Living Novel*, p. 82. Although I differ with Pritchett on several
points (specifically, his objections to George Eliot's treatment of Hetty, which
he thinks simply cruel and false and for which he accounts by some unpersua-
sive psychoanalysis, and his comments about the neglect of sexual feeling and
jealousy in the marriage of Adam and Dinah), he writes with perception and
eloquence about her local attachments and the strengths of *Adam Bede* — particularly its social sense, which he rightly sees as being both pastoral and realistic: "*Adam Bede* is animated by the majestic sense of destiny which is fitting
to novels of work and the soil . . . When she wrote of the peasants, the craftsmen,
the yeomen, the clergy and squires of Warwickshire, George Eliot was writing
out of childhood, from that part of her life which never betrayed her or any
of the Victorians. The untutored sermons of Dinah have the same pastoral quality
as the poutings of Hetty at the butter churn, the harangues of Mrs. Poyser at
her cooking, or the remonstrances of Adam Bede at his carpenter's bench . . . We
seem to be looking at one of Morland's pictures, at any of those domestic or
rustic paintings of the Dutch school, where every leaf on the elm trees or the
limes is painted, every gnarl of the bark inscribed, every rut followed with
fidelity. We follow the people out of the hedgerows and the lanes into the
kitchen. We see the endless meals, the eternal cup of tea; and the dog rests his
head on our boot or flies barking to the yard, while young children toddle in
and out of the drama at the least convenient moments. Some critics have gibed
at the dialect, and dialect is an obstacle; but when the great moments come,
when Mrs. Poyser has her 'say out' to the Squire who is going to evict her; or,
better still, when Mrs. Bede laments the drowning of her drunken husband, these
people speak out of life" (pp. 84–85).

[15] Ian Gregor and Brian Nichols, *The Moral and the Story* (London, 1962),
p. 29.

is Hetty's tragedy that is central, he develops the notion that Hetty, the pretty Arcadian dairymaid, is in the course of the book transferred from an idyllic to a sternly moral world. This is of course true, but he does not consider the possibility that George Eliot is undercutting the idealized frivolity of "Hetty's World"; that it is Hetty's assumptions and aspirations (as well as Arthur's) that are Arcadian, unreal, and incongruous in Hayslope. He ignores also the psychologically acute and penetrating characterizations which, in spite of the moral determinism that does intrude at several important points, are wholly credible.

Because others have already performed this task, it seems unnecessary to try to establish here the status of *Adam Bede* as a satisfactory novel, to define in detail the successful blending of pastoral and realistic elements, or to defend at great length its genuine, if selective, realism.[16] There are, however, a numbr of minor points relevant to the problems of realism as well as regionalism that have usually been neglected by critics. Gregor thinks that work and the relations between landlord and tenant are idealized in the novel, purified, as it were, of all unpleasantness and oppressiveness. But toil is not the less real for being relished; after all, to the Poysers, to Adam, even to Lisbeth and, in her different way, to Dinah, work is their calling, their vocation; itself dependent on the local environment, it in turn becomes a way of life for the people, affecting their status, their character, and their speech. And this cross-pattern of connections and influences George Eliot shows with an authoritative fullness of detail and subtlety of presentation.

It has long been recognized that the characters in *Adam Bede* not only have their distinctive ways of speaking, but also reveal their métier in their language. Lisbeth Bede takes her idioms and similes from housekeeping with the same consistency, if not vigor, as Mrs. Poyser; and Adam, of course, relies on carpentry, building, and

[16] See especially the dissertations by Casson, Wheatley, and F. W. Willey. Casson entitles his Chapter III "*Adam Bede*: Realism and Romance," and while noting elements of romance in the book, he affirms its realism: "It is a work of a middle-class author who takes her characters seriously; its attitude toward society is democratic, its characters 'mixed,' its action probable; hard facts (including the importance of money) are squarely faced; the value of work is hymned, and all this is done with 'breadth and detail, in other words, at some length'" (p. 114). Willey discusses the novel from a similar perspective in a chapter entitled "The Two Worlds of *Adam Bede*: A Happy Synthesis of the Novel and the Romance."

mechanics to provide him with metaphors and images, just as Mr. Poyser draws on his farming. Similarly, the language that Dinah speaks, in its lilt and diction, is suitably and unmistakably Biblical. Such appropriateness, though it may be at times monotonous, emphasizes the extent to which their daily work is imbedded in the personalities of these people. When Adam privately makes his plans for marrying Hetty, what he considers first and most of all is his working status, on which economic and social standing depends; the Poysers also have this in mind when they encourage his wooing of Hetty. The precision with which Adam's professional situation and ambition are delineated makes us feel all the personal and social implications and possibilities that are held in suspense:

> ...at the beginning of November, Jonathan Burge, finding it impossible to replace Adam, had at last made up his mind to offer him a share in the business, without further condition than that he should continue to give his energies to it, and renounce all thought of having a separate business of his own. Son-in-law or no son-in-law, Adam had made himself too necessary to be parted with, and his headwork was so much more important to Burge than his skill in handicraft, that his having the management of the woods made little difference in the value of his services; and as to bargains about the Squire's timber, it would be easy to call in a third person. Adam saw here an opening into a broadening path of prosperous work, such as he had thought of with ambitious longing ever since he was a lad ... and went home with his mind full of happy visions, in which ... the image of Hetty hovered, and smiled over plans for seasoning timber at a trifling expense, calculations as to the cheapening of bricks per thousand by water-carriage, and a favourite scheme for the strengthening of roofs and walls with a peculiar form of iron girder." [17] (Chapter XXXIII)

Not only is Adam firmly placed in his locale, but the locale itself, with its small but fairly complicated economy, interdependent relations, and overlapping of personal and business affairs, is amply realized and brought to life. It will be noted that the emphasis in this passage (as well as others concerned with occupation and ambition) is personal rather than technical, but it is not imprecise. The book is full of brief descriptions of doors, cabinets, and barns that Adam is constructing as well as of extended allusions to the variety of jobs

---

[17] Such passages notwithstanding, Gregor writes that in *Adam Bede* "We do not think of work in economic terms at all" (p. 16).

and problems that compose the daily routine of the Poyser farm. These solidify the realistic texture of the novel without obtruding unduly into the narrative. Occasionally, George Eliot even uses a kind of technical minuteness, though never for its own sake. The story that Adam tells Bartle Massey in Chapter XXI about the frame for a screen which he had made for Lydia Donnithorne is an instance of this. The anecdote is meant to illustrate the characters and relations of the Squire, his daughter, and Adam rather than Adam's workmanship; it does both, but the noteworthy thing is that it is not really necessary to the general design of the novel. Equally needless is the discussion Mr. and Mrs. Poyser have on their way to church about Sally, the short-horned cow. Yet such scenes are not unfunctional: they are a part, rather, of that prolific, deliberate accumulation of details — many of them, like Mr. Irwine's sisters or Squire Donnithorne's rheumatism, equally gratuitous — through which the communal life of the region is abundantly realized.

Adam Bede is also full of minute observations of rustic behavior and peasant mentality and consciousness of rank that contribute to the realistic level of presentation. The gathering in the church for Thias Bede's funeral, like the birthday, brings all the segments of the community together but at the same time shows the local social gradations in action: the farmers, laborers, and craftsmen form distinct little groups, united in restrained deference to the Squire and Mr. Irwine and in their participation in the service. Class, of course, plays a central part in the plot; as we are repeatedly told, the naïveté and irresponsibility of Arthur and Hetty reside precisely in their violation of the social distance between them and reluctance, especially Hetty's, to admit the impossibility of the liaison. Class also colors the relation between landlord and tenant and, as is the case with Arthur and Adam, between patron and craftsman. As the tensions underlying these relations are gradually made clear, the relations themselves and the social context are fully examined. The rumors about the mysterious new tenant, the apprehensive irritation with which Mrs. Poyser keeps alluding to the Squire, and the comments that Arthur makes about his grandfather and his own squirarchal aims — all these reach a climax in the old Squire's visit to the Hall Farm and the energy with which Mrs. Poyser rejects his shrewd proposition.

Adam Bede may not have "the sense of struggle, the grasping for security and social status, the frank acceptance of material values, the occasional note of protest"[18] that occur in the later novels, but its social medium, however tinged with a sympathetic rural haze, is presented with informed and satisfying complexity. By the time Mr. Donnithorne comes to the Hall Farm, Adam, having caught Arthur with Hetty, has already lost the affection and feudal deference with which he had regarded the young Squire. The two conflicts — between Adam and Arthur and between the Poysers and Mr. Donnithorne — are then skillfully intertwined in the aftermath of Hetty's imprisonment. The Poysers, feeling dishonored by Hetty and abused by Arthur, determine to leave Hayslope, and Adam, together with his mother and brother, plans to accompany them.

The life of the lower ranks in this rural setting is not integrated into the plot as fully as are the social realities of class, status, and occupation, but it does support and enrich the authenticity of the background. George Eliot's peasants and laborers, as we see them at the preaching, the birthday feast, the harvest supper, and similar occasions, are based on no Arcadian model, but are rather somewhat coarse and primitive figures. Slow of thought, speech, and movement, amiably crude and naive, they are seen as shaped by their environment; and their outlook, language, and appearance reflect regional characteristics. This treatment follows, as others have suggested, George Eliot's own prescription in "The Natural History of German Life" for a true-to-life account of the English working classes.[19] It is in these passages that the hardship and unpleasantness of toil are implied. Adam's disgusted remark at the very beginning of the novel that he "can't abide to see men throw away their tools i' that way, the minute the clock begins to strike, as if they took no pleasure i' their work, and was afraid o' doing a stroke too much" is only a casual and indirect sign of her unidealized presentation of labor. Other indications of this are found mainly in agricultural situations, as in the allusion to the coarseness of haymakers (Chapter XIX) that echoes a longer but similar passage in the review of Riehl, or in the description of the worn, weather-beaten, rough-mannered, taciturn, and frequently surly laborers at the Hall Farm.

[18] Bissell, *ELH*, XVIII, 231.
[19] See Hussey, p. 123, Casson, pp. 109, 111, and Pinney's note in *Essays*, p. 266.

Two other elements contributing to the impression of realism, which George Eliot clearly wishes to maintain, may be mentioned here: the full, fairly exact, and persistent location in time and the precise location in space.[20] Almost every chapter begins with a notation of the weather, season, month, date, day, or time of day. The story opens on 18 June 1799 and closes near the end of November 1801; the Epilogue is set at the end of June 1807. The first two books cover in great detail and at a leisurely pace a very short time: Book One spans four consecutive days, 18–21 June, and Book Two takes up two days, Sunday and Monday, 23–24 June. With Book Three, all of which is set on Arthur's birthday, 30 July 1799, the slow preparation of the setting, characters and relations is concluded; as Adam discovers Hetty's treasured locket, the tragic sequence of events is set in motion, and from now on the pace of the story picks up considerably, with much telescoping of time.

Supporting these usually definite and explicit datings are a great many temporal and historical allusions that range from the *Lyrical Ballads* to the Napoleonic Wars, Methodism, Arthur Young's agricultural studies, and so on. These names, dropped casually in conversation, call our attention to genuine and familiar historical events, and the fictional situations, by being linked with these, share in their "actuality," or rather our acceptance of that actuality. The effect of the geographical location is similar. Not only is the description of Loamshire and Stonyshire a recognizable account of northeastern Staffordshire and southwestern Derbyshire, but the fictional places like Hayslope, Oakbourne, and Snowfield closely resemble in location, appearance, and relative situation the real places that in 1859 were quickly identified as their prototypes. This resemblance is naturally not something that influences our impression of the book, but the geographical and descriptive exactitude and consistency with which the fictional region is treated are striking in themselves and obviously instrumental in the creation of a realistic atmosphere.

The realism of the setting and its distinctness are heightened by the fidelity to actual geography that marks the itinerary of Hetty's journey to Windsor. Hetty's ignorance makes places like Stoke, Ashby,

---

[20] See Hussey on these points and Daniel P. Deneau's note on "Inconsistencies and Inaccuracies in *Adam Bede*," *Nineteenth-Century Fiction*, XIV (1959–60), 71–75.

Leicester, and Stratford seem like new worlds to her and perhaps also to the reader; this effect is in part supported by the equally parochial attitudes that she encounters on her way. At the same time, however, our sense of the contiguity of the "fictional" counties of Loamshire and Stonyshire and the real counties around them is brought out by the mention of the connecting coach routes which the characters, particularly Hetty, follow, the easy recognition and acceptance during her journey of Hetty's distinctly "northern" speech and identity, and the scattered wide-ranging allusions to places and events outside the action and region of the novel. Loamshire and Stonyshire, then, clearly do not represent some idealized or fabulous land but are firmly and precisely fixed in the provincial England of the eighteenth century. *Adam Bede* is a pastoral novel, not a pastoral romance. If it is justly thought of as pastoral, it is because of the full, authentic, and affectionate attention, not any falsely refined coloring, with which it presents rural life.

iii

The sympathy and nostalgic attachment to rural life and "old Leisure" that modify the realism, if not the authenticity, with which George Eliot depicts the world of *Adam Bede* are clearly apparent in the landscapes and interiors of the novel. In many scenes taken up with natural description, she succeeds, by her selection of details and her interpretive comments, in directing the reader's attitude to the setting, in tacitly encouraging him to connect his impressions of the way the setting looks with the underlying moral realities of the story. The account of the Hall Farm in Chapter VI, for example, which follows the narrator's "visits" to the Bedes' cottage and the Rectory, is controlled by such suggestiveness. If Mrs. Poyser is built up in the course of the book as the voice of rural tradition and authority, her home, judging by the tone and emphasis with which it is described and referred to (as well as by the frequency with which it serves as a setting), is clearly the physical and dramatic center. It provides Mrs. Poyser with a background that illustrates without her asperity the values so pungently reiterated in her talk; it embodies vividly and winningly the satisfactions and beauty of ordinary existence, the attainable virtues and available advantages of real life — orderliness, energy, love, comfort, security, sociality, and peace of mind — which all the characters but Hetty recognize and accept. Even Arthur regards the Hall Farm as a kind of local landmark and compliments Mrs. Poyser for keeping it "in better order than any within ten miles of us; and as for the kitchen . . . I don't believe there's one in the kingdom to beat it" (Chapter VI).

The characters in *Adam Bede* are not alone in their enthusiasm about the Hall Farm, for the author is herself deeply fond of it and lingers lovingly over its appearance. She delights in the light, color, and din of the yard and in the purposeful bustle in the barn, but most of all she relishes the bright, comfortable, well-worn domesticity of the house (especially the kitchen) and the calm efficiency of Mrs. Poyser and Dinah. Her enjoyment runs through the description. It is evident even in the way she playfully gives the reader a first peek through the gate at the house as a whole and then, through the back window, into the now-abandoned parlor. In a warm, confiding tone, she interprets what she observes; the precision of the details and the particularly distinctive history of the house suggest that she is drawing from life and memory, but her approach, her selectivity and stress, tend to color and soften the sharpness of the picture, idealizing it without dulling or distorting.

As in the initial sketch of the workshop — it is still the same day — sunshine lights up the scene and this, together with other positive details, all concretely observed and admiringly commented on, directs the reader's responses. The focus of life at the erstwhile Hall, has shifted from the parlor to the yard:

> Plenty of life there! though this is the drowsiest time of the year, just before hay-harvest; and it is the drowsiest time of the day too, for it is close upon three by the sun, and it is half-past three by Mrs. Poyser's handsome eight-day clock. But there is always a stronger sense of life when the sun is brilliant after rain; and now he is pouring down his beams, and making sparkles among the wet straw, and lighting up every patch of vivid green moss on the red tiles of the cow-shed, and turning even the muddy water that is hurrying along the channel to the drain into a mirror for the yellow-billed ducks, who are seizing the opportunity of getting a drink with as much body in it as possible. There is quite a concert of noises . . . and, under all, a fine ear discerns the continuous hum of human voices.

The kitchen, the other focus of activity, is also sunlit: "Everything was looking at its brightest at this moment, for the sun shone right on the pewter dishes, and from their reflecting surfaces pleasant jets of light were thrown on mellow oak and bright brass . . ." Although it is calculated to bring the scene to life and charm the reader, this is fairly straightforward description. But the similar passage connecting the two excerpts just cited and introducing the interior of the house ends with a seemingly casual comment, in which the setting is made to play a part in the plot and the moral design of the book:

> Surely nowhere else could an oak clock-case and an oak table have got to such a polish by the hand: genuine "elbow polish," as Mrs. Poyser called it, for she thanked God she never had any of your varnished rubbish in her house. Hetty Sorrel often took the opportunity, when her aunt's back was turned, of looking at the pleasing reflection of herself in those polished surfaces, for the oak table was usually turned up like a screen, and was more for ornament than for use; and she could see herself sometimes in the great round pewter dishes that were ranged on the shelves above the long deal dinner-table, or in the hobs of the grate, which always shone like jasper.

Here the shallowness and self-love that determine Hetty's character and fate are first laid down, apparently quite innocuously, but actually with definitive force. For this image of Hetty is soon taken up: repeatedly we see her lost in self-admiration, almost wholly absorbed in romantic fancies. In her vanity she is like Arthur, who is something of a coxcomb. He struts before a mirror, savoring the dashing effect of his militia uniform, and rides through the country in a daze of complacent anticipation of his role as the wise, able, and popular squire.

George Eliot, who regards a lack of interest in reality as symptomatic of egoism, illustrates the nature of her characters in *Adam Bede* by the way they respond to their surroundings. Hetty and Arthur, like all her villains, sinners, and victims, are egoists. And we see this not only in their dim superficial awareness of the moral and social laws that govern life, but also in their impercipience of the environment. Thus Hetty does not simply take the Hall Farm, with its congenial vitality and harmony, for granted but is wholly blind to it until fear, remorse, and suffering teach her to see. To begin with, she is aware of the closely knit, energetic routine just enough to resent it and the duties it involves for her. Her emotional life is shallow and fanciful, sealing her off from the real life around her, from the atmosphere of fruitful, well-ordered activity, contentment, and love that prevails at the farm.

Hetty's self-enclosed condition is especially evident in the unseeing way she walks through the countryside. In Chapter XIII, for example, on the way home from the Chase and excited by the hope of meeting Arthur, she thinks "nothing of the evening light that lay gently in the grassy alleys between the fern, and made the beauty of their living green more visible than it had been in the overpowering flood of noon: she thought of nothing that was present." A little earlier, Arthur had passed through the Grove in similar absorption, intent on intercepting Hetty. His imagination is not as limited as hers — he is articulate, literate, and lively — but it too is whimsical, self-indulgent, and therefore unreal. Thus he too does not see his actual surroundings but transforms them mentally into a romantic landscape that reflects his amorous feverishness:

> It was a wood of beeches and limes, with here and there a light, silver-stemmed birch — just the sort of wood most haunted by the nymphs: you see their white sunlit limbs gleaming athwart the boughs, or peeping from behind the smooth-sweeping outline of a tall lime; you hear their soft liquid laughter — but if you look with a too curious sacrilegious eye, they vanish behind the silvery beeches, they make you believe that their voice was only a running brooklet, perhaps they metamorphose themselves into a tawny squirrel that scampers away and mocks you from the topmost bough.[21] (Chapter XII)

By contrast, Adam and Dinah are always responsive to their environment, sensitive to the presence of others, in thoughtful contact with the life around them. In the explicit juxtaposition of Chapter XV, "The Two Bed-Chambers," for example, Dinah and Hetty are shown just before retiring. While Hetty sits before her mirror, religiously "bent on her peculiar form of worship," trying on her trinkets and cherishing her beauty, Dinah is in almost a trance of religious contemplation, "enclosed by the Divine Presence," concerned about Hetty's future. Significantly, she is not in front of a mirror but looks outward:

> Dinah delighted in her bedroom window. Being on the second story of that tall house, it gave her a wide view over the fields.

[21] For a close analysis of this passage see Reva Stump, pp. 16–19.

The thickness of the wall formed a broad step about a yard below the window, where she could place her chair. And now the first thing she did on entering her room, was to seat herself in this chair, and look out on the peaceful fields beyond which the large moon was rising, just above the hedgerow elms. She liked the pasture best where the milch cows were lying, and next to that the meadow where the grass was half mown, and lay in silvered sweeping lines. Her heart was very full, for there was to be only one more night on which she would look out on those fields for a long time to come; but she thought little of leaving the mere scene, for, to her, bleak Snowfield had just as many charms: she thought of all the dear people whom she had learned to care for among these peaceful fields, and who would now have a place in her loving remembrance for ever.[22]

Thus the symbolic use of setting, without undermining at all its precisely realized concreteness, serves to embody vividly the central contrast between Hetty's self-enclosed blindness and Dinah's expansive vision. The contrast itself is far from simple, for it involves not the opposition of single qualities but of two characters. Dinah's reflections about leaving Hayslope, for example, reveal not only her openness to impressions and contacts but her rootedness, her mature sense of human attachments, memory, and continuity. This is meant to be placed against the heavily loaded analysis of Hetty that occurs a page or two earlier. Hetty is delightedly envisioning a vague but idyllic life with Arthur, and the narrator comments:

Does any sweet or sad memory mingle with this dream of the future — any loving thought of her second parents — of the children she had helped to tend — of any youthful companion, any pet animal, any relic of her own childhood even? Not one. There are some plants that have hardly any roots: you may tear them from their native nook of rock or wall, and just lay them over your ornamental flower-pot, and they blossom none the worse. Hetty could have cast all her past life behind her, and never cared to be reminded of it again. I think she had no feeling at all towards the old house, and did not like the Jacob's Ladder and the long row of hollyhocks in the garden better than other flowers — perhaps not so well.

If Dinah, a visitor in Hayslope, is superficially an alien, Hetty, who has grown up there, is an alien at heart. She is rootless because

[22] Reva Stump (p. 25) refers briefly to this passage as she contrasts the attitudes of Hetty and Dinah to their environment; F. W. Willey (pp. 121-122) and Harvey (p. 141) also cite it in illustration of the same comparison.

of her lack of sympathy and awareness, her petty but all-consuming vanity. Her (and Arthur's) difference from Adam as well as from Dinah is repeatedly dwelt on, often through a similar use of landscape and setting. Thus in the beginning of Chapter XIX, Adam is on his way to work and, like Arthur earlier, he is thinking of Hetty, but unlike Arthur, he is keenly aware of his real environment, and his thoughts of Hetty blend comfortably with the pleasure he derives from the countryside, the job to which he looks forward, and his plans for the future. Similarly, in the preceding chapter, set in the affectionately described little church during the Sunday service, while Hetty is fervently storing up her grievances against Arthur, who has failed to appear, Adam responds to the ritual with a full heart. He finds in worship a ready expression for his mingled emotions, his habitual reverence and attachment to the familiar church, his grief and remorse for his father, and his love for Hetty.

> . . . Adam's thoughts of Hetty did not deafen him to the service; they rather blended with all the other deep feelings for which the church service was a channel to him this afternoon, as a certain consciousness of our entire past and our imagined future blends itself with all our moments of keen sensibility . . . The secret of our emotions never lies in the bare object, but in its subtle relations to our own past . . . (Chapter XVIII)

iv

Since that passage immediately follows the account of Hetty's furtive tears and peevish anger that make her oblivious of the service, the contrast between her and Adam is practically explicit. And the point of the contrast, as Barbara Hardy briefly indicates, is the importance of local roots, of psychological, social, moral, and almost physical ties: "Adam's response to the ritual underlines the strength of his rootedness — Hetty has no roots . . ." Linking this scene with the preaching and the birthday festivities (all are communal events),[23] Mrs. Hardy writes:

[23] Foakes notes four such events: "The rhythm and order of Hayslope life are established in relation to the four points at which all the villagers assemble — to hear Dinah preach on the village green (Chapter 2); at the church to witness the funeral of Thias Bede (Chapter 18); at the Hall for the festivities of Arthur's twenty-first birthday (Chapters 23–26); and at the harvest supper on the farm (Chapter 53). The locations are symbolic of the strength of the com-

These scenes present the community as something reaching back in time as well as actively joined in social life. This sense of time is very necessary here because George Eliot is going to show Hetty's tragedy, in part coming from her casual unattachment, as a social disaster which shakes the tenacious life of the whole village, sending Arthur into exile and nearly tearing the Poysers and Adam from their strong roots.[24]

Because she is really interested in George Eliot's delineation of Adam and uses the scene in the church only to chart the tragic process of the novel and Adam's evolution as a heroic figure, Mrs. Hardy does not elaborate on this remark or clarify the connection between the "sense of time" in the communal scenes and the social repercussions of Hetty's misfortune. The sense of time, however, is nothing more arcane than an aspect of the depth and fullness with which George Eliot, true to her critical principles, describes the locale of *Adam Bede*, the physical, social, and moral "medium." Owing to this fullness, we have a concrete, well-defined awareness of the prevailing moral values in the district, the hierarchy and coherence of social life, the economic situation, and the various factors affecting status. The local roots of the people are embodied in such manifestations, and it is because of the way individual lives depend on these things for definition and satisfaction and are through them made dependent on each other that Hetty's disaster can cause so much social as well as private disruption.

The sense of time which pervades the depiction of the community is in a way a social factor of this kind, for it is a fundamental expression of rootedness and is built up not only by means of the numerous notations of the seasons, months, days, and hours, but also through the frequent retrospective remarks which both the author and

---

munity, and help to bring out the bonds linking its members, the ties of loyalty, duty, responsibility between labourer, farmer, clergyman, and squire, which form a moral framework that is seen as strong, good, and enduring" (174). To these ceremonial points should be added a fifth, the final communal scene in which the villagers who had gathered in church for Thias Bede's funeral are seen together again, about two and a half years later, to witness his son's wedding; cf. Reva Stump, p. 65.

[24] *The Novels of George Eliot*, p. 40. For yet another interpretation of the community's role in *Adam Bede*, see also Dorothy Van Ghent's essay in which she goes so far as to affirm that "it is the community that is the protagonist of this novel" (p. 177). This view has been taken up by others, and especially, with some distortion of emphasis, by the two Marxist critics of George Eliot, Anna Katona and Ian Milner.

the characters make. These remarks are always proper and natural to the occasion, so that they do not call attention to themselves but rather create cumulatively an indelible sense of the extension in time of the lives of the characters and the community. When Lisbeth recalls that "her old man come from that Stonyshire side, but left it when he war a young un," when Kester Bale, "having begun his career by frightening away the crows under the last Martin Poyser but one," calls Mr. Poyser "the young master," or when Mr. Irwine reminds his parishioners, as he thanks them for the toast in his honor, that "it is twenty-three years since I first came among you," the impact at the time is not great, but as such comments accumulate, a sense of temporal perspective and dimension is created. Through the characters' (as well as the author's) consciousness of their past, the actuality of their presence is brought out with a distinctive fullness and a feeling of the continuity of communal existence is delicately suggested.

Memory, as one of the chief means by which the continuity of individual lives is sustained, is of recurrent thematic importance in George Eliot's work. It is bound up with all manifestations of unity, with psychological wholeness, moral integrity, and social traditions. In *The Mill on the Floss*, memory, especially the memory of dramatic instants of recognition and insight, acts as a guide to action; and in *Adam Bede*, too, it appears in such moments of impressibility and responsiveness as well as in the recollections of the characters. It is through these moments that the psychological and moral development of the novel's leading figures can be charted, but quite often the setting also is included in the emotion and in this way becomes imbued with meaning. In such instants of crisis, perception, or joy, just as it is linked, through the frequency and regularity of habit and routine with a whole way of life, landscape becomes associated with personal experience; and in these associations and meanings are embodied the regional ties of the characters. The tree in the Grove near which he discovers Arthur and Hetty thus comes to have particular significance for Adam:

> For the rest of his life he remembered that moment when he was calmly examining the beech, as a man remembers his last glimpse of the home where his youth was passed, before the road turned, and he saw it no more. The beech stood at the last

turning before the Grove ended in an archway of boughs that let in the eastern light; and as Adam stepped away from the tree to continue his walk, his eyes fell on two figures about twenty yards before him. (Chapter XXVII)

Later, after the trial, in Chapter XLVIII, which is entitled "Another Meeting in the Wood" in order to help us recall this incident, Adam again stops before the same tree, and the meaning of the original encounter is now elaborated and its consequences illustrated.

> Adam had on his working-dress again, now, — for he had thrown off the other with a sense of relief as soon as he came home; and if he had had the basket of tools over his shoulder, he might have been taken, with his pale wasted face, for the spectre of the Adam Bede who entered the Grove on that August evening eight months ago. But he had no basket of tools, and he was not walking with the old erectness, looking keenly round him; his hands were thrust in his side pockets, and his eyes rested chiefly on the ground. He had not long entered the Grove, and now he paused before a beech. He knew that tree well; it was the boundary mark of his youth — the sign, to him, of the time when some of his earliest, strongest feelings had left him.

The first time, Adam had stopped by the beech out of strictly professional interest, but with the shock which he then suffered, the tree became an inextricable part of his emotional life, and when he looks at it again, it is to him a symbol of his lost youth. His reflections near the end of the book as he rides to Snowfield to claim Dinah show a similar connectedness with landscape, though in a somewhat different key:

> What keen memories went along the road with him! He had often been to Oakbourne and back since that first journey to Snowfield, but beyond Oakbourne the grey stone walls, the broken country, the meagre trees, seemed to be telling him afresh the story of that painful past which he knew so well by heart. But no story is the same to us after a lapse of time; or rather, we who read it are no longer the same interpreters: and Adam this morning brought with him new thoughts through that grey country — thoughts which gave an altered significance to its story of the past. (Chapter LIV)

Adam's responsiveness to his surroundings is an index of his rootedness, just as the sentimental allegiances of Lisbeth and the hard-working complacency of the Poysers indicate theirs. It is made emphatically clear in the novel that these people are strongly connected with the land and the community. To illustrate the tenacity of their local attachments by citing additional passages in which rootedness is discussed explicitly would be a simple matter. But this is something that requires no verbal corroboration. The treatment of landscape, work, character, and community is designed to suggest the interdependence of all four, so that it comes as no surprise to us when Mr. Poyser tells his wife after her outburst to the Squire, "I should be loath to leave th' old place, and the parish where I was bred and born, and father afore me. We should leave our roots behind us, I doubt, and niver thrive again" (Chapter XXXII).

We have been amply made to feel the nature and force of Mr. Poyser's roots in the district and can understand his fear; no explanation or emphasis is necessary. But to find Arthur attaching a comparable significance to local ties is at least unexpected. From the beginning, George Eliot presents Arthur as a sympathetic but spoiled young gentleman, as vain, romantic, and frivolous in his literate and sophisticated way as the naive and ignorant Hetty. Where Adam is striking and exceptional in appearance, bearing, and character, Arthur is attractive but quite ordinary — typical, in fact, as the author implies, of his class and age: "If you want to know more particularly how he looked, call to your remembrance some tawny-whiskered, brown-locked, clear-complexioned young Englishman whom you have met with in a foreign town, and been proud of as a fellow-countryman . . ." (Chapter V).

Again, unlike Adam, whose thoughts, when they turn, as they constantly do, to his work and plans, are precise, concrete, and practical, Arthur is charmed by a vision of himself as the adored and competent squire, a vision which is only a little less naive than Hetty's dream of a glamorous marriage to him. We see this clearly in the boyish enthusiasm and rather gushing vagueness with which he describes his plans: "there's nothing I should like better than to . . . set improvements on foot, and gallop about from one place to another and overlook them. I should like to know all the labourers, and see them touching their hats to me with a look of goodwill" (Chapter XVI). Such a tone seems to suggest that Arthur has only a flimsy, if idealistic, conception of the nature and obligations of the position to which he aspires. Despite his zest for the country, despite his wish to be well informed about community affairs and to be widely liked, at the dance he does not know Ben Cranage's name; it is Mr. Irwine, always close to local life, who has to remind him and "place" Ben in the community.

The impression of Arthur's immaturity is also supported by his self-indulgent, pettish behavior at home and vacillating resolutions about Hetty, and it is tragically confirmed, of course, by his seduction of her. At one point, as if to emphasize his adolescent thoughtlessness, George Eliot, by means of imagery, equates him with Hetty, who is consistently described in diminutive terms, whether of pettiness, pathos, or sweetness:

> Such young unfurrowed souls roll to meet each other like two velvet peaches that touch softly and are at rest; they mingle as easily as two brooklets that ask for nothing but to entwine themselves and ripple with ever-interlacing curves in the leafiest hiding-places. While Arthur gazed into Hetty's dark beseeching eyes, it made no difference to him what sort of English she spoke; and even if hoops and powder had been in fashion, he would very likely not have been sensible just then that Hetty wanted those signs of high breeding. (Chapter XII)

Thus, while she suggests with understanding Arthur's weakness, George Eliot manages almost at the same time to indicate subtly the social barriers that separate him from Hetty and that should have exacted greater discretion from him. And yet in spite of his deficiencies, Arthur remains an attractive character and is in the end, through recognition and suffering, redeemed. This is, no doubt, partly owing to George Eliot's compassionate, if at times patronizing, analysis of his character, partly to the sense she manages to impart (largely through his own lurking awareness of what is right as well as Mr. Irwine's grieved but constant affection for him) that Arthur is potentially a finer man than his behavior toward Hetty indicates, and partly through the sincerity of his attachment to Hayslope, the tenants, and the local values. His sincerity is apparent even in the superficial but consistent way in which he dreams of his role as the young squire; it is clearer still, together with his genuine good will and enthusiasm (as well as the less commendable rationalizations), in the reflections and resolutions that pass through his mind as he is returning to assume the estate and position which at last, on his grandfather's death, are his.

> He would show the Loamshire people what a fine country gentleman was; he would not exchange that career for any other under the sun. He felt himself riding over the hills in the breezy autumn days, looking after favourite plans of drainage and enclosure; then admired on sombre mornings as the best rider on the best horse in the hunt; spoken well of on market-days as a first-rate landlord; by-and-by making speeches at election dinners, and showing a wonderful knowledge of agriculture; the patron of new ploughs and drills, the severe upbraider of negligent landowners, and withal a jolly fellow that everybody must like, — happy faces greeting him everywhere on his own estate, and the neighbouring families on the best terms with him. (Chapter XLIV)

And as his coach passes a village, Arthur thinks: "What a much prettier village Hayslope was! And it should not be neglected like this place: vigorous repairs should go on everywhere among farm-buildings and cottages, and travellers in post-chaises, coming along the Rosseter road, should do nothing but admire as they went."

For the reader, Arthur's idyllic ambitions at this point are severely undercut by the echo of the verdict that has been read to Hetty a page or two before, in the preceding chapter. Of this, Arthur is ignorant as yet, but when he and Adam meet again in the wood, he shows the same signs of suffering that we have seen in Adam. It is then that Arthur, largely, if not entirely, matured by the harrowing experience of guilt and misery, shows a keen sensitivity to the feelings of the Poysers and of Adam and seriously recognizes for the first time the significance of local roots for himself as well as for them. As he pleads with Adam to remain in Hayslope and to persuade the Poysers to remain also, it is clear that he is sacrificing his own happiness to preserve as far as possible the stable, cohesive, and semi-feudal order which he had hoped to perpetuate and improve but which he has instead frivolously violated. That the Poysers should "leave the place where they have lived for so many years — for generations," seems to Arthur not only unjust but repugnant and unnatural. He understands how impossible it is for the Poysers to stay on as his tenants and recognizes too that his dreams of squirarchal distinction have been shattered by his own essentially anti-social and subversive action. Thus he decides, so "that no one else may leave Hayslope," so that the social wound may be allowed to heal, to leave himself.

v

Hetty, whose egoism and rootlessness, emotional superficiality and meagre intelligence are much more cruelly insisted upon than Arthur's defects, undergoes in the course of her fear, bewilderment, and misery a pattern of redemption more limited than his but also more dramatic. For her too the process involves a realization of the significance of local and domestic attachments, and she begins to acquire this realization fairly early in her ordeal. During her first night from home, Hetty misses the warmth, security, and social acceptance of Hayslope, and in her regret for what she has lost she gets a glimpse of the moral realities of which she has not before been conscious.

> Now for the first time . . . she felt that her home had been a happy one, that her uncle had been very good to her, that her quiet lot at Hayslope, among the things and people she knew, with her little pride in her one best gown and bonnet, and nothing to hide from anyone, was what she would like to wake up to as a reality, and find that all the feverish life she had known besides was a short nightmare. (Chapter XXXVI)

Her plight opens her eyes to a certain extent not only to her past but also to the world presently around her. In need of sympathy and attention, she becomes herself, though only a little, more sympathetic and attentive. "Through the new susceptibility that suffering had awakened in her," Hetty notices and responds to the small frightened dog she meets on her way: "she felt as if the helpless timid creature had some fellowship with her" (Chapter XXXVI). As Reva Stump writes, "though Hetty is still a novice in the school of suffering, this journey has helped prepare her for the hardship which is to come." [25]

Through the small perceptions and stirrings that begin with a growing consciousness of the home she has left behind, Hetty comes gradually to rely for guidelines on the values of her class and region.

[25] *Movement and Vision in George Eliot's Novels*, p. 30. On Hetty's regeneration, see especially Ian W. Adam, "Restoration through Feeling in George Eliot's Fiction: A New Look at Hetty Sorrel," *Victorian Newsletter*, no. 22 (Fall 1962), pp. 9–12.

Thus when the elder Poyser bitterly disowns her in Chapter XL ("Pity?" . . . "I ne'er wanted folks's pity i' *my* life afore . . ."), he really echoes Hetty's abhorrence of public charity in Chapters XXXVI and XXXVII. It is clear then how incomplete and superficial is her rejection of her background; and as she becomes more aware of that background and desperately clings to her remembrance of it, her feeling of confusion and guilt becomes more oppressive. Even in her wretchedness as an outcast she is guided by her grandfather's outlook, by the rugged sense of independence and self-righteousness "of people who were somewhat hard in their feelings even towards poverty, who lived among the fields, and had little pity for want and rags as a cruel inevitable fate such as they sometimes seem in cities, but held them a mark of idleness and vice" (Chapter XXXVII). Thus at Windsor, with "the pride not only of a proud nature but of a proud class — the class that pays the most poor-rates, and most shudders at the idea of profiting by a poor-rate" (Chapter XXXVI), Hetty flashes out angrily at the innkeeper's slight insinuation. "I belong to respectable folks . . . I'm not a thief" (Chapter XXXVII).

Hetty's tragic development and regeneration culminate in the prison, in her reunion with Dinah and reconciliation with Adam. When she responds to the affection and sympathy they hold out to her, she is at last able to utter her unhappiness and break out of her isolation. But although she does find relief in giving expression to her feelings, in winning forgiveness and renewing personal contacts, she can never regain her old place in the community. Her disgrace, misfortune, and banishment are the natural consequences, as George Eliot sees it, of the frivolous egoism and indifference that had originally set her apart from the life around her. But even in the beginning Hetty's disconnection from her environment is not complete, for she is always anxious, in her daydreams of romance, luxury, and distinction, to be admired and envied by her family and neighbors: "she would have borne anything rather than be laughed at, or pointed at with any other feeling than admiration" (Chapter XVIII). When she is oppressed by the dread of pregnancy, it is the thought of public discovery of her shame that keeps her from suicide. She tries, on the way to Windsor, to be as furtive as she had been at home, but now her attempts at concealment are pitifully ineffectual. As she thinks more and more, among strangers, of the lost comforts of home, and identifies and judges herself according to the standards of her family and village, Hetty shrinks from the idea of returning to Hayslope, rejecting it as fiercely as her uncle and grandfather later reject her. And behind this self-banishment is the horror of public disgrace: "she could never endure that shame before her uncle and aunt, before Mary Burge, and the servants at the Chase, and the people at Broxton, and everybody who knew her" (Chapter XXXVII).

Hetty is thus seen as bound to the community by ties of which, in her ignorance of herself and her blindness to her environment, she is for a long time unaware. Arthur's somewhat similar dependence on popular sentiments must by now also be abundantly clear. We are told directly that he "lived a great deal in other people's opinions and feelings concerning himself" (Chapter XVI), and his ambitions reflect this concern. The tenants and neighbors indeed do like him and expect much from his elevation to the estate, but sincere as his aspirations for local popularity and accomplishment are, they are vitiated, like Hetty's reveries, by vanity, thoughtlessness, and self-indulgence. Community opinion, however — a pervasive and crucial fact of existence in Hayslope as much as in Shepperton — affects and defines also other lives than Arthur's and Hetty's. Although people like Mr. Irwine and the Poysers do not deliberately set out to be highly regarded, they owe their stature as social figures and as characters in the novel to what is said and thought about them in the district. This is particularly clear in the toasts and responses in Chapter XXIV.

The texture of opinion formed out of the accumulation of diverse individual judgments complements the physical descriptions, social commentary, and scenes of more or less formal gatherings in providing a detailed and inclusive picture of regional life. We hear the voice of local opinion for the first time near the beginning of the novel, when Mr. Casson talks with the stranger about Hayslope. With an amusing irony of which he is unconscious, the conceited but knowing landlord of the Donnithorne Arms lays stress on the distinctiveness of the community.

> "They're cur'ous talkers i' this country, sir; the gentry's hard work to hunderstand 'em. I was brought hup among the gentry, sir, an' got the turn o' their tongue when I was a bye. Why, what do you think the folks here says for 'hevn't you?' — the gentry, you know, says, 'hevn't you' — well, the people about here says

'hanna yey.' It's what they call the dileck as is spoke here about, sir. That's what I've heard Squire Donnithorne say many a time; it's the dileck, says he." (Chapter II)

He goes on in this gossipy fashion to suggest something of the economic life and religious divisions in the district. By the way, he also introduces us to the Poyser establishment, mentions the general anticipation of Arthur's coming of age ("we shall hev fine doin's"), and indicates Adam Bede's reputation in the village:

"... everybody knows him hereabout. He's an uncommon clever stiddy fellow, an' wonderful strong. Lord bless you, sir — if you'll hexcuse me for saying so — he can walk forty mile a-day, an' lift a matter o' sixty ston'. He's an uncommon favourite wi' the gentry, sir: Captain Donnithorne and Parson Irwine meks a fine fuss wi' him. But he's a little lifted up an' peppery-like."

The hint of reservation with which Mr. Casson winds up his account confirms the impression Adam makes in the argument with Ben Cranage (Chapter I) and is supported in turn by the feelings that some of the people waiting for Dinah express about him. As they chat, they also fill out the innkeeper's brief allusions to Dinah and the Poysers, and thus advance the plot. Throughout the book, George Eliot continues in this way to refer to the general attitudes toward the leading characters as well as to mention unobtrusively the views that these characters have of one another. She is able by means of such references to create a convincing and vital atmosphere in which real people are involved in real relations with each other and with their society. And this air of authenticity probably owes much to the fact that she presents the various attitudes in motion, as it were, so that we can see them developing, even shifting, and extending in time. Thus the beginning of Mr. and Mrs. Poyser's regard for Adam antedates the opening of the novel, as does also Arthur's first infatuation with Hetty.

One of the effects, then, of George Eliot's attention to local opinion is to strengthen the illusion of the *presence* of the setting, of the actuality of its existence. She can also turn this attention to gain a comparable result in characterization: by modifying and showing through the narrative the inadequacy of the personal reputation of her figures, she endows them with a sense of depth. Mr. Irwine's surprise, after he has brought the news of Hetty's tragedy and disgrace, that "Mrs. Poyser was less severe than her husband" is a minor but effective instance of the characters' flexibility. The old Squire's ability, in spite of his widespread unpopularity, to retain his stature and dignity is another. But the most obvious and dramatic illustration of the working of opinion and its fluctuation is Arthur's fall from public favor and his consequent transformation. The birthday festivities, particularly the enthusiastic toasts in his honor, represent a kind of formal climax in his progress toward realizing his impatient yearning for authority and esteem. Immediately after the celebration, the crisis occurs during which Adam revises sharply his respect for Arthur as "one of those gentlemen as wishes to do the right thing, and to leave the world a bit better than he found it." Having caught Hetty and Arthur in an embrace, he brusquely rejects Arthur's pose of innocence.

> "... instead of acting like th' upright, honourable man we've all believed you to be, you've been acting the part of a selfish light-minded scoundrel ... though it cuts me to th' heart to say so, and I'd rather ha' lost my right hand ... You know it couldn't be made public as you've behaved to Hetty as y' have done without her losing her character, and bringing shame and trouble on her and her relations. What if you meant nothing by your kissing and your presents? Other folks won't believe as you've meant nothing; and don't tell me about her not deceiving herself ... you're not the man I took you for ..." (Chapter XXVII)

When Mr. Poyser later echoes Adam's disenchantment with Arthur, we hear again the same sense of betrayal, the same resentment of the idolized young Squire's duplicity, and the same anxiety about public opinion:

> "Ah, there's no staying i' this country for us now," said Mr. Poyser, and the hard tears trickled slowly down his round cheeks ... "An' me, as thought him such a good upright young man, as I should be glad when he come to be our landlord. I'll ne'er lift my hat to him again, nor sit i' the same church wi' him ... a man as has brought shame on respectable folks ... an' pretended to be such a friend t' everybody ... Poor Adam there ... a fine friend he's been t' Adam, making speeches an' talking so fine, an' all the while poisoning the lad's life, as it's much if he can stay i' this country any more nor we can." (Chapter XL)

Now though the community shares the feeling of disappointment with Arthur and anger against him, George Eliot chooses to stress at this point the compassion extended to the Poysers. She mentions the widespread indignation only in passing (though with an ironic understatement of some sting), when she describes the reactions of the servants at the Chase to the disclosure:

> They had the partisanship of household servants who like their places, and were not inclined to go to the full length of the severe indignation felt against [Arthur] by the farming tenants, but rather to make excuses for him; nevertheless, the upper servants, who had been on terms of neighbourly intercourse with the Poysers for many years, could not help feeling that the longed-for event of the young Squire's coming into the estate had been robbed of all its pleasantness. (Chapter XLIV)

Behind this passage, as in many similar ones in *Adam Bede* surveying local opinion, are implicit the closeness of social intercourse, the interconnections linking families and classes, and the interdependence of private and public actions. The social structure and coherence of local life are most elaborately dramatized in the communal and institutional scenes — the preaching, the night-school, the church, the birthday celebrations, the harvest supper, and the wedding — but something of the intimacy and warmth and mutuality of the small rural community is apparent in the way the news of Hetty's tragedy and Arthur's disgrace flies through the district and the way it is received:

> On leaving Lisbeth, Mr. Irwine had gone to Jonathan Burge, who had also a claim to be acquainted with what was likely to keep Adam away from business for some time; and before six o'clock that evening there were few people in Broxton and Hayslope who had not heard the sad news. Mr. Irwine had not mentioned Arthur's name to Burge, and yet the story of his conduct towards Hetty, with all the dark shadows cast upon it by its terrible consequences, was presently as well known as that his grandfather was dead, and that he was come into the estate. For Martin Poyser felt no motive to keep silence towards the one or two neighbours who ventured to come and shake him sorrowfully by the hand on the first day of his trouble; and Carroll, who kept his ears open to all that passed at the Rectory, had framed an inferential version of the story, and found early opportunities of communicating it. (Chapter XL)

The climate of overlapping interests and communal concerns

brought out in this account, the high regard and sympathy which their neighbors show to the Poysers, all prepare the way for their eventual decision to remain in their native parish. The sense of dishonor and shame which oppresses both father and son turns out to be somewhat exaggerated, especially when placated by Arthur's perceptive and genuinely courageous offer. His remorseful self-banishment serves also as a tacit but public acknowledgement of responsibility for Hetty's catastrophe and the consequent wider distress. The healing aftermath of the disruption is traced in the last Book: though effects of emotional affliction remain, harmony and wholeness are gradually being restored. The purposeful activity at the farm goes on in the old fashion, and the harvest supper, though it celebrates the natural continuity and agricultural routine that have been constantly in the background, now indicates also the reintegration of the Poyser household. Actually, the reintegration is still proceeding at that stage and is not complete until the marriage of Dinah and Adam. The growth of their love — which had been anticipated, however slightly, in Book One [26] — provides the central subject matter here and reaches its sacramental celebration in the wedding. The ceremony is sacramental also in a broad social sense, for it solemnizes not simply the union of Adam and Dinah but, with a glance backward to the beginning of the book, the renewed integrity of the community.

> It was an event much thought of in the village. All Mr. Burge's men had a holiday, and all Mr. Poyser's . . . I think there was hardly an inhabitant of Hayslope specially mentioned in this history and still resident in the parish on this November morning, who was not either in church to see Adam and Dinah married, or near the church door to greet them as they came forth . . . The churchyard walk was quite lined with familiar faces, many of them faces that had first looked at Dinah when she preached on the Green; and no wonder they showed this eager interest on her marriage morning, for nothing like Dinah and the history which had brought her and Adam Bede together had been known at Hayslope within the memory of man. (Chapter LV)

[26] Not all critics are equally disturbed by the marriage of Adam and Dinah. Despite the fact that it is prepared for with some care from the beginning, many critics have expressed dissatisfaction with the marriage. See, for example, J. S. Diekhoff, "The Happy Ending of *Adam Bede*," *ELH*, III (1936), 221–227, Foakes, p. 176, and Harvey, pp. 180–181.

6 The Landscape of Memory:
The Mill on the Floss

Never trust the artist. Trust the tale.
— D. H. Lawrence

i

The great popularity of *Adam Bede* sharpened George Eliot's natural concern about the fate of her next book, *The Mill on the Floss*. She communicated her anxiety to the ever-solicitous Lewes and to her publishers, and no doubt their increasingly enthusiastic reactions to each manuscript instalment served to reassure her about her ability to equal the success of her first novel. But the sense of pressure under which she worked (and which Lewes and the Blackwoods shared with her from the beginning) was not simply a burden, for it helped her to define with some precision the differences between the two novels and, therefore, the nature of each novel. On 21 April 1859, fairly early in the writing of *The Mill on the Floss* (when the identity of "George Eliot" was still a secret), Lewes, as her spokesman, described the new book to John Blackwood by contrasting it with its predecessor: "You must prepare for a surprise with the new story G.E. is writing. It is *totally* unlike anything he has written yet. The novel will be a companion picture to Adam Bede; but this story is of an imaginative philosophical kind, quite new and piquant" (*Letters*, III, 55). Eleven months later, Blackwood was congratulating "Mrs. M. E. Lewes" on the completion of her novel: "No words of mine can convey the greatness of the success you have achieved . . . This book is a greater triumph even than Adam and you may make your mind easy about all Critics. Any mean creature that may venture to carp will only dispute himself" (*Letters*, III, 277).

The reviews of *The Mill on the Floss* were indeed generally favorable, but the enthusiasm of many critics was checked somewhat by their recollection of *Adam Bede*, which they found to be an altogether more delightful, if less ambitious, work.[1] Even Lewes seems to have

---

[1] See, for example, *Athenaeum*, 7 April 1860, pp. 467–468; *Atlantic Monthly*, V (1860), 756–757; *Macmillan's Magazine*, III (1861), 441–448; and *Westminster Review*, XVIII n.s. (1860), 24–33. About three months after publication, Blackwood reported to George Eliot (who, with Lewes, had just left Italy for Switzerland) on the London reception of *The Mill on the Floss*: "There is a great deal of balancing as to the merits of the two books, and I think generally Adam is the most popular but there are quite enough supporters of the Mill to make the verdict a close divided one, and I have heard nobody worth a farthing who did not think the last book fully worthy of the author of the other" (*Letters*, III, 305). To this the author herself, bolstered perhaps by advancing sales as well as such critical encouragement, replied: "As for 'The Mill' I am in repose about it now I know it has found its way to the great public. Its comparative rank can only be decided after some years have passed, when the judgment upon it

shared this opinion, for in commenting on the new book's initial reception he wrote in his Journal: ". . . I doubt whether it is intrinsically so interesting as 'Adam.' Neither the story nor the characters take so profound a hold of the sympathies" (*Letters*, III, 292). George Eliot herself, although she had put so much of herself into the novel — especially into Maggie — that she wrote the ending in tears,[2] came close to agreeing with Lewes's analysis, if not with his implied evaluation. Still during the early stage of the composition, she told John Blackwood in a letter: "I'm glad my story cleaves to you. At present, I have no hope that it will affect people as strongly as Adam has done. The characters are on a lower level generally, and the environment less romantic" (*Letters*, III, 133). Having herself anticipated it, she agreed also with Bulwer-Lytton's criticism that the tragic conclusion of the novel was not adequately prepared.[3] In a letter to D'Albert-Durade (who had translated *Adam Bede* into French and was now engaged in translating *The Mill on the Floss*), she compared the two novels on the basis of structure, and though she found *Adam Bede* better proportioned, her emphasis and peculiarly reticent tone seem to betray a preference for the later novel:

---

is no longer influenced by the recent enthusiasm about 'Adam,' and by the fact that it has the misfortune to be written by me instead of by Mr. Liggins" (*Letters*, III, 307).

[2] See *Letters*, III, 269 and also George Eliot's note of relief at the conclusion of her task: "I think Rome will at last chase away Maggie and the Mill from my thoughts: I hope it will, for she and her sorrows have clung to me painfully" (*Letters*, III, 285).

[3] Sir Edward Bulwer-Lytton's long letter, containing a little carping, some valuable criticism, and much praise, was addressed to John Blackwood, who sent it on to George Eliot. In returning it, she wrote on 9 July 1860: "On two points I recognize the justice of his criticism. First, that Maggie is made to appear too passive in the scene of quarrel in the Red Deeps. If my book were still in MS., I should — now that the defect is suggested to me — alter, or rather expand that scene. Secondly, that the tragedy is not adequately prepared. This is a defect which I felt even while writing the third volume, and have felt ever since the MS. left me. The '*epische Breite*' into which I was beguiled by love of my subject in the two first volumes, caused a want of proportionate fullness in the treatment of the third, which I shall always regret" (*Letters*, III, 317). *The Mill on the Floss* was published on 4 April 1860; a day earlier, George Eliot had written to Blackwood from Rome: "As for the book, I can see nothing in it just now but the absence of things that might have been there. In fact, the third volume has the material of a novel compressed into it" (*Letters*, III, 285). While the work was still in progress, John Blackwood had observed in a letter to his brother William that it showed a "want of the hurrying on interest of a taking narrative . . . when at the middle of the second volume the hero and heroine are not above 16" (*Letters*, III, 233).

I see that you think there are many [French] readers who will prefer "The Mill" to "Adam." To my feeling, there is more thought and a profounder veracity in "The Mill" than in "Adam"; but "Adam" is more complete and better balanced. My love of the childhood scenes made me linger over them; so that I could not develop as fully as I wished the concluding "Book" in which the tragedy occurs, and which I had looked forward to with much attention and premeditation from the beginning.[4] (*Letters*, III, 374)

In seizing on the disproportionate concision of the ending as the novel's major fault and in vigorously rejecting the complaints of critics about "Maggie's position toward Stephen" (*Letters*, III, 317), George Eliot showed sound and authoritative judgment. For in the critical controversy that has grown up around the questions of her handling of Maggie and Stephen, her attitude to them and their passion, and the validity of Maggie's moral dilemma, it is usual to blame the uneasy execution of the concluding scenes on the author's imperception or lack of detachment. But as several critics have suggested, it may be more accurate to attribute the failure in presenting these issues, at least partly, to abbreviated and hasty exposition.[5]

[4] This is an expansion of a comment in an earlier letter to the same correspondent (*Letters*, III, 362) and echoes her explanation to Blackwood of the disproportion that Bulwer-Lytton had noted.

[5] Swinburne's enraged outburst against Maggie's lover ("He should be horsewhipped!") and Leslie Stephen's more decorous complaints are well known, but it is Leavis's objection to George Eliot's handling of the affair that is most cogent and interesting. Noting the strong autobiographical nature of the novel and the "feminine presentment of Stephen Guest," he finds in the depiction of the lovers and their entanglement "an element of self-idealization" and "an element of self-pity." He believes that Stephen is "sufficiently 'there' " but that he is realized uncritically, and that the author's emotional involvement in Maggie's character "represents an immaturity that George Eliot never leaves safely behind her" (*The Great Tradition*, pp. 39–46). Joan Bennett, however, agrees with George Eliot's own judgment and attributes the uneasiness with which Stephen affects the reader to the lack of space: "some defect in the drawing of Stephen is a contributory cause of dissatisfaction with the end of the book, and this defect is a probable result of the relative brevity with which this part of the composition is treated." In opposition to Leavis, Mrs. Bennett insists that George Eliot *intends* Stephen "to be disagreeable ... a vulgarian ... a coxcomb and an insensitive egotist" (*George Eliot*, pp. 116–117). W. J. Harvey supports this explanation, noting (in contrast to Leavis) that "even as a worthless popinjay Stephen isn't adequately realized, he isn't really there as a force in the novel at all ... And the simple truth of the matter is that George Eliot had no *time* to portray him; given the space left at her disposal, she could do no more than sketch in a few gestures" (*The Art of George Eliot*, pp. 123–124). On the question of self-identification and idealization, he acknowledges that it is impossible "to demolish Leavis's diagnosis completely," but he does effectively call attention to the "intermittent attempt [that] is made to 'place' Maggie by the comments

There is a very real disparity in treatment and mood between the first five Books of *The Mill on the Floss* and the last two, and it is marked mainly by the change of locale at the beginning of Book Six and the abruptness with which the story of the Tulliver family is then resumed after a lapse of two years. The difference in emphasis is supported also by the clear predominance from this point on of the book's "imaginative philosophical" quality. The focus of attention, which had been centered in Maggie's growth in a domestic and narrowly social context, is shifted almost entirely to the inner life of her mind and feelings. Now it is her conscience much more than the mill or St. Ogg's that serves as the arena for action and struggle; and the novel's sense of disharmony is intensified by the cloudy, somewhat theoretical, arbitrary, and sentimental way in which that struggle is at times described and in the end resolved.[6]

---

and views of other characters, notably Philip and Tom" and to the author's "cool recognition of Maggie's naïveté . . . and . . . inexperience . . ." (pp. 187–188). As is generally recognized, the same problems arise in the relationship between Dorothea and Will Ladislaw in *Middlemarch*.

[6] Of the ending, Joan Bennett has remarked that "this poetic justice at the culminating point of a long, serious, naturalistic novel, is a dishonest contrivance . . . [George Eliot] has let [Maggie] choose and then she has refused to imagine the results of her choice . . . the inflated, melodramatic style of the close is a symptom of the relaxation of the author's serious concern with her characters." But she goes on to add that "the imperfect fraction of the novel, Book VI, has within it the seed of a new development in English fiction which will ultimately come to rich fruition in the works of Conrad and Henry James and which was to prosper better in some of George Eliot's later work than it did in her second novel" (*George Eliot*, p. 130). Mrs. Bennett is presumably referring here to the subjective emphasis and psychological and moral exploration of the final section. W. J. Harvey echoes her view of the ending and backs it up with an intelligent analysis of a crucial passage near the end of the novel: "Romance, though still tempting, is again and finally rejected, and Maggie in agony falls on her knees in prayer: ' "Oh God, if my life is to be long, let me live to bless and comfort" — At that moment, Maggie felt a startling sensation of sudden cold about her knees and feet; it was water flowing under her. She started up; the stream was flowing under the door that led into the passage. She was not bewildered for an instant — she knew it was the flood!' At this climactic moment one cannot but feel that the novel comes perilously close to the ludicrous, so promptly is Maggie's prayer answered, so pat upon its cue does the river enter. And the disquiet we feel is mainly the result of enforced speed. This over-compression may also give rise to more serious doubts; to the view, for instance, that the catastrophe is really an evasion by George Eliot of the moral problem she has posed in the rest of the book, rather than a true and satisfying conclusion" (*The Art of George Eliot*, pp. 125–126). Both critics imply that the mismanagement of the ending can be explained as a result not only of the lack of space but also of the yoking together of naturalistic with symbolic technique which disintegrates as the latter comes more and more to dominate the author's vision.

The subjective quality of *The Mill on the Floss*, which represents one of its chief points of difference from *Adam Bede*, is not of course suddenly intruded into the closing sections but is apparent from the very first in the remarks about intelligence and heredity, the contrast between Maggie and Tom, and the discussions of education, memory, and the nature of childhood. Indeed the psychological and moral interest in growth and shaping influences is so pronounced that, if categories have to be drawn, *The Mill on the Floss* is described more appropriately as a *Bildungsroman* than a regional novel. Such regional touches as are present in it — and there are enough to justify the inclusion of the book in this study — are on the whole subsumed in the theme of the development of Maggie and Tom. But whereas in the opening and major portion of the novel the country, the society, the home, and the family are firmly, if not always minutely, painted, in the last two Books they are indicated briefly through the pressures acting on Maggie, or rapidly sketched in, as in the introduction of the Guests and their circle — whose existence, rank, and manners reveal a more complex social structure than the earlier account of St. Ogg's had hinted at.[7] The depiction of the environment and community is an important source of the novel's vitality. But in the conclusion that depiction is not maintained, and the weight of psychological and ethical analysis, inadequately rooted in the background, contributes to the sense of disequilibrium that harms *The Mill on the Floss*.

ii

That the strength of *The Mill on the Floss* is to be found in its early parts is not an uncommon judgment. It has been most aptly expressed, from the point of view of my present concerns, by Joan Bennett.

> *The Mill on the Floss* is among the major English novels, but it holds its position in spite of great defects. It owes it to the invention and the masterly presentation of the Tulliver family and the Dodson aunts, to the story of Maggie's childhood and adolescence in the world they inhabit, and to the humour and

---

[7] By this I do not mean to advocate what Harvey, in reference to *The Mill on the Floss*, criticizes as "the over-leisurely beginning" and its counterpart, "the rushed and crowded ending" (*The Art of George Eliot*, p. 126).

compassion with which the author conceives and presents that world.[8]

Because of the tendency in some recent analyses of *The Mill on the Floss* to blame society for the death of Maggie and Tom, Mrs. Bennett's reminder of "the humour and compassion" with which the world of St. Ogg's is presented is extremely useful. To be sure, the novel differs from *Adam Bede* not only in its "imaginative philosophical" quality and the relative subordination of the social perspective which follows from that quality, but also in the nature of the society which it depicts. George Eliot must have had this difference in mind when she referred in Book Four, Chapter I, to the lack in the "sordid life . . . of the Tullivers and Dodsons" of "that primitive rough simplicity of wants, that hard, submissive, ill-paid toil, that child-like spelling-out of what nature has written, which gives its poetry to peasant life."

The Mill on the Floss is thus quite clearly devoid of the pastoral atmosphere that contributes so much substance and color to *Adam Bede*. The past is not as remote or quite as congenial, and the location is not as vividly exploited or used with comparable precision and suggestiveness. On the other hand, the thrust of individual needs and demands is much more urgent in *The Mill on the Floss* and, as a result, the perspective through which provincial life is viewed is as often satirical as it is humorous or compassionate. Sometimes, as in the chapter just referred to ("A Variation of Protestantism Unknown to Bossuet"), the tone is philosophically detached, if not disillusioned, and at one point (the account of the condemnation by "the world" and "the world's wife" of Maggie's entanglement with Stephen), it is sarcastic, though not actually ill-tempered or hostile.

F. R. Leavis has briefly but acutely noted this essential difference in social climate between the two books:

> . . . if "charm" prevails in *Adam Bede* . . . there should be another word for what we find in *The Mill on the Floss*. The fresh directness of a child's vision that we have there, in the autobiographical parts, is something very different from the "afternoon light" of reminiscence . . . Instead of Mrs. Poyser and her setting we have the uncles and aunts . . . [who] associate not with the frequenters of Mrs. Poyser's kitchen, but with the tribe that forgathers at Stone Court waiting for Peter Featherstone to die.[9]

[8] *George Eliot*, p. 130.
[9] *The Great Tradition*, p. 38.

142

What Leavis is getting at here, of course, is the aggressive material-
ism that determines the social atmosphere of *The Mill on the Floss*.
Whereas Adam's world had been richly pastoral — organic and stable
in structure, shrewdly practical but amiable in daily intercourse, and
in moral attitudes upright, naturally devout, but sensible and tolerant
— Maggie's world is provincial rather than rural, constricting rather
than coherent, ignorant and superstitious rather than naïve or Christian. As the references to money, property, and advancement that
stud the book's pages make clear, St. Ogg's is almost exclusively concerned with economic gain and social position. It makes its moral and
personal judgments according to worldly success alone.

This aspect of the novel has been cogently and suggestively
defined by Claude Bissell, whose remarks are essentially an elaboration of Leavis's sense of the difference between *Adam Bede* and *The
Mill on the Floss*. Bissell writes:

> Completely absent from *Adam Bede* are the sense of strug-
> gle, the grasping for security and social status, the frank ac-
> ceptance of material values, the occasional note of protest that
> characterize the increasingly middle-class society of Victorian
> England. *The Mill on the Floss* ushers us immediately into
> such a world . . . a society where a certain measure of equality
> is within the grasp of all, provided one has a comfortable balance
> in the bank and the assurance of a good return on investments.[10]

It would be easy to document Bissell's comments and document
them profusely, but they are so obviously apt and pertinent and expressed with such trenchant precision that to do so would be over-
punctilious and pedantic. It should be recognized, however, that
George Eliot's satiric treatment of the Philistine world of St. Ogg's
stops short of the kind of indictment that Bissell expresses:

> With a few exceptions, the good citizens of St. Oggs — inde-
> pendent farmers, merchants, professional men — subscribe to
> the gospel of success whose characteristic virtues are diligence,
> frugality, and if circumstances permit, honesty . . . We are
> now in a world that is dominated by the pursuit of financial
> security, a world that is to become increasingly familiar to us
> in English fiction. The passion for money runs through the story
> like a repulsive disease; the history of the Tulliver family, for
> instance, is charted in a series of financial crises.

[10] *ELH*, XVIII (1951), 232.

By likening the concern with money to "a repulsive disease" and by accusing St. Ogg's of dishonesty, Bissell attributes to George Eliot a harsher view of the community than the novel itself shows her to hold. For one thing, she makes clear repeatedly that the people of St. Ogg's, especially as they are represented by the Dodsons, are fiercely, self-righteously honest.

> A Dodson would not be taxed with the omission of anything that was becoming, or that belonged to that eternal fitness of things which was plainly indicated in the practice of the most substantial parishioners, and in the family traditions — such as, obedience to parents, faithfulness to kindred, industry, rigid honesty, thrift . . . The Dodsons were a very proud race, and their pride lay in the utter frustration of all desire to tax them with a breach of traditional duty or propriety. A wholesome pride in many respects, since it identified honour with perfect integrity, thoroughness of work, and faithfulness to admitted rules: and society owes some worthy qualities in many of her members to mothers of the Dodson class, who made their butter and their fromenty well, and would have felt disgraced to make it otherwise. (Book Four, Chapter I)

The analysis is amply demonstrated in the story. In prosperity as well as disaster, Mr. Tulliver proudly and sincerely proclaims his honesty and is vindicated when his creditors are paid through Tom's exertions. Mr. Deane, in his two talks with Tom, is the voice of shrewd, if somewhat sanctimonious and complacent, commercial pride and probity. And Tom (who "takes after his mother's side") proves his kinship with the Dodsons by obeying their most cherished principles in order to save the family from disgrace and restore materially as well as socially its position in the community.

Not that there are no dishonest men in St. Ogg's. Mr. Wakem, after all, is a "raskil" in the town's eyes as well as Mr. Tulliver's. Unlike Mr. Tulliver, however, who hates the lawyer as an agent of "Old Harry" and his own particular enemy, "the majority of substantial men . . . were perfectly content with the fact that 'Wakem was Wakem'" (Book Three, Chapter VII). Wakem himself is "too acute not to believe in the existence of honesty . . . no one knew better than he that all men were not like himself." The cynical lawyer's ethic of expediency is treated not so much as an isolated case in the community but as an irregular and unorthodox one. It is the integrity of the Dodsons and Tullivers, aggressive and parsimonious though it may be, that embodies the prevailing social morality. Their "sense of honour and rectitude," conceived mainly in terms of family loyalty and material obligations, is seen as "the tradition which has been the salt of our provincial society" (Book One, Chapter XIII).

iii

The question of honesty would not need to be labored at all if it were not part of the larger problem of George Eliot's attitude to the environment in which Maggie and Tom live and die. Bleak and narrow as that environment appears to be, to regard her portrayal of it as hostile is to misrepresent her feelings in this particular case as well as her characteristic pose of thoughtful and balanced compassion. The society of St. Ogg's being what it is, however, it is easy to overlook the qualifying comments and events that accompany her analysis and to impute to the author a dislike which she does not feel. Such imputations are not new, even though some recent discussions of *The Mill on the Floss* are constructed around them. They go back a long way, as do George Eliot's protests against them. On completing the third volume of the book, she wrote to John Blackwood that she was "grateful and yet rather sad to have finished — sad that I shall live with my people on the banks of the Floss no longer" (*Letters*, III, 279). When the first reviews regretted what they took to be the author's antagonism toward Tom and the Dodsons, she had occasion to reiterate her objectivity as well as her attachment to the world of *The Mill on the Floss*.

> I have certainly fulfilled my intention very badly if I have made the Dodson honesty appear "mean and uninteresting," or made the payment of one's debts appear a contemptible virtue in comparison with any sort of "Bohemian" qualities. So far as my own feelings and intentions are concerned, no one class of persons or form of character is held up to reprobation or to exclusive admiration. Tom is painted with as much love and pity as Maggie, and I am so far from hating the Dodsons myself, that I am rather aghast to find them ticketed with such very ugly adjectives. (*Letters*, III, 299; cf. 397)

It is useful to keep such declarations in mind when discussing George Eliot's attitude to the society of *The Mill on the Floss*, for they

145

express something of the penetrating and comprehensive intelligence, the judicious sympathy, with which she regards humanity and through which she seeks to avoid a melodramatic simplification of life. Simply to condemn St. Ogg's, to make it responsible for what happens to Maggie, would constitute a drastic departure from that large-minded understanding and tolerance. This is not to say that in *The Mill on the Floss* she succeeds always in doing justice to the complexity of experience she has made us feel: in the often disparaged ending she seems beset by confusion and irresolution, and distorts and evades through melodrama the issues that the book raises.

To understand George Eliot's feelings toward provincial society at its most depressing, and to demonstrate convincingly the lack of animosity in her treatment of St. Ogg's, we must turn to the novel itself; it will be convenient, however, at the same time to refer to interpretations of *The Mill on the Floss* that are most obviously opposed to my own view. As several critics have noted, there are in the book many animal images. These have been taken to denote "those elements in the society of St. Ogg's which are destructive in the sense that they narrowly restrict the imagination and partially destroy the capacity for adequate emotional response." [11] Now though George Eliot in her commentary and narrative explicitly shows St. Ogg's to be provincial in the worst sense of the word — its intellectual atmosphere is benighted, its emotional life bleak, it is almost entirely lacking in sensitivity, warmth, and generosity — to call it destructive is to overstate the case. It must be clear, after all, that while Maggie's imagination does not find scope or encouragement in her environment, it is certainly not starved by it or even exceptionally restricted. If anything, her imagination and "capacity for emotional response" continue to grow; reacting to domestic circumstances, she becomes more tender toward her family and at the same time more dissatisfied with her lot. Her imagination and responsiveness, expressing themselves as impetuousness, plunge her as a child into one minor crisis after another; near the end they bring about her climactic dilemma. Society is responsible for Maggie's distress mainly as its values operate through her consciousness, and these values are as much her own as the desires and aspirations with which they come into conflict. And since the novel does not put forward with any emphasis or delibera-

[11] Reva Stump, *Movement and Vision in George Eliot's Novels*, p. 76.

tion a more enlightened environment as an alternative to St. Ogg's, there is little encouragement to believe that Maggie would have fared better in a different society.

Critics who see *The Mill on the Floss* as an indictment of St. Ogg's usually point to a passage in Book Four, Chapter I, where a somewhat over-elaborate and curiously exotic comparison of ruins on the banks of the Rhine with those on the Rhone introduces a direct and full examination of the values of Maggie's people. In contrast to the glamor and romance suggested by the Rhine castles, says George Eliot, "these dead-tinted, hollow-eyed, angular skeletons of villages on the Rhone oppress me with the feeling that human life — very much of it — is a narrow, ugly, grovelling existence . . ." Then, completing the comparison, she apologizes to the reader, in a tone rather different from the half-jocular intrusions in *Scenes of Clerical Life* and *Adam Bede* but with the same notion of realism in mind, for the sort of world she has to present in her story:

> Perhaps something akin to this oppressive feeling may have weighed upon you in watching this old-fashioned family life on the banks of the Floss, which even sorrow hardly suffices to lift above the level of the tragi-comic. It is a sordid life, you say, this of the Tullivers and Dodsons — irradiated by no sublime principles, no romantic visions, no active, self-renouncing faith . . . Here, one has conventional worldly notions and habits without instruction and without polish — surely the most prosaic form of human life: proud respectability in a gig of unfashionable build: worldiness without side-dishes.

Now although George Eliot goes on to say "I share with you this sense of oppressive narrowness," she does not actually equate St. Ogg's with the abandoned villages on the Rhone. Rather, she compares, always speculatively and with much hesitation, reactions to two kinds (and stages) of provincial sordidness. First she is concerned with the "effect produced on us by these dismal remnants of commonplace houses, which in their best days were but the sign of a sordid life, belonging in all its details to our own vulgar era." Then to this impression she likens the annoyance that she supposes the reader to feel with "these dull men and women" of St. Ogg's, who could be seen "as a kind of population out of keeping with the earth on which they live — with this rich plain where the great river flows forever onward, and links the small pulse of the old English town with the beatings of the world's mighty heart." [12] Now if the tie between the French and English setting were not sufficiently loosened by the involved way in which it is made, the sense of vitality and significance, however hedged, that is attached in this passage to the English setting surely qualifies it seriously.

The qualification of the tentatively suggested similarity between the Rhone remnants and St. Ogg's is strengthened by the tone and bias of the account of "the religious and moral ideas of the Dodsons and Tullivers" that immediately follows the passage just cited. George Eliot writes:

> I share with you this sense of oppressive narrowness; but it is necessary that we should feel it, if we care to understand how it acted on the lives of Tom and Maggie — how it has acted on young natures in many generations, that in the onward tendency of human things have risen above the mental level of the generation before them, to which they have been nevertheless tied by the strongest fibres of their hearts . . . In natural science, I have understood, there is nothing petty to the mind that has a large vision of relations, and to which every single object suggests a vast sum of conditions. It is surely the same with the observation of human life.

There is much here that is characteristic of George Eliot: the qualified belief in social progress, the recognition of familial affections and the ties of the past, the sense of an almost cosmic interconnectedness of phenomena, the scientific allusion and the philosophic stance. But what we should particularly notice is that all these things (and especially the reminder of the scientific respect for apparent trivia) act to dignify the life of the Dodsons and Tullivers. As the description of their life continues, it becomes a little more clearly sympathetic. Though it is always mocking and humorous, the account is not unamiable and certainly not intolerant.

> Their theory of life had its core of soundness, as all theories must have on which decent and prosperous families have been reared and have flourished; but it had the very slightest tincture of theology . . . Their religion was of a simple, semi-pagan kind,

[12] The last phrase, referring, one must suppose, to London, is a direct echo of the concluding lines of Wordsworth's sonnet "Composed upon Westminster Bridge, Sept. 3, 1802": "Dear God! the very houses seem asleep/And all that mighty heart is lying still!"

but there was no heresy in it — if heresy properly means choice — for they didn't know there was any other religion, except that of chapel-goers, which appeared to run in families like asthma . . . To be honest and poor was never a Dodson motto, still less to seem rich though being poor; rather the family badge was to be honest and rich; and not only rich, but richer than was supposed.

Here there is clearly no admiration for the Dodsons or idealization of them, and yet the passage radiates with the warmth of understanding and familiarity, a warmth that a critical emphasis on "these emmet-like Dodsons and Tullivers" misses altogether. We must not ignore the reservations that make the link between the ruined villages on the Rhone and the thriving town on the Floss, at the very least, hesitant (and, at most, unsustained, infelicitous, and confusing). That in spite of this comparison, in spite of the "sense of oppressive narrowness" with which the village remnants affect George Eliot, the "obscure vitality" they suggest has its own interest, significance, and dignity, she goes on directly to indicate. Even in her wry description of the parochialism of St. Ogg's there is evident, as I have already suggested, the belief in the mixed nature of things. She is as skeptical about the existence of consistent and purposeful malignity as she is about the existence of perfect goodness, and in her portrait of provincial culture she steers carefully away from an impression of unredeemed moral squalor. She repeatedly cautions the reader against melodramatic interpretations of the motives of the characters. Mr. Riley promotes Mr. Stelling's interests not from "far-sighted designs" but "small promptings," for "plotting covetousness and deliberate contrivance, in order to compass a selfish end, are nowhere abundant but in the world of the dramatist . . ." (Book One, Chapter III). In his superstitious paranoia, Mr. Tulliver attributes to Mr. Wakem "deliberate contrivance" and infernally directed viciousness, but Wakem's hostility toward him is merely "parenthetic" and aroused by his own fierce and insulting antagonism toward the lawyer. Similarly, the rich historic past and pleasant appearance of St. Ogg's as well as the staunchness and integrity of the Dodsons and Tullivers indicate that life here is not made up of unrelieved opportunism. When Maggie ultimately affirms her allegiance to familial, personal, and social ties, she expresses in an individually revitalized way the values of her environment at its best.

When the entire picture of the community is thus recalled, the ambiguous irony of the intricate comparison at the beginning of Book Four seems less elusive than at first reading. It becomes clear that in deploring the oppressive narrowness of St. Ogg's George Eliot has not abandoned her faith in hidden beauties, redeeming virtues, and the potential heroism of the obscure and mundane. Bound up with the doctrine of all-embracing sympathy, this faith characterizes all of her writings. We have already seen it dramatized in *Scenes of Clerical Life* and in *Adam Bede*; in her last published work, *Impressions of Theophrastus Such* (1879), she still affirms it.

> But every age since the golden may be made more or less prosaic by minds that attend only to its vulgar and sordid elements, of which there was always an abundance even in Greece and Italy, the favourite realms of the retrospective optimists. To be quite fair to the ages, a little ugliness as well as beauty must be allowed to each of them, a little implicit poetry even to those which echoed loudest with servile, pompous, and trivial prose. ("Looking Backward")

iv

In missing the poetry that is more than implicit in Maggie's life, critics run the risk of distorting the novel. Reva Stump, for example, sees the society of St. Ogg's as being almost unredeemed in its animalism; as a result, she is led to describe it in terms of somewhat incongruous perversions — effeminacy as well as crudeness, mechanization as well as brutality.[13] For her, Tom's drowning foreshadows the "symbolic drowning" of the Dodson way of life, while Maggie's prefigures "the total destruction to which this way of life is leading." [14] She goes on to observe that the "river is only the second cause of

[13] *Movement and Vision in George Eliot's Novels*, pp. 79–100. On p. 98, for example, she cites what she calls an "incidental image" in the novel: "Mr. Moss who, when he married Miss Tulliver, had been regarded as the *buck* of Basset, now ... had the depressed, unexpectant air of a *machine-horse*" [Miss Stump's italics]. In this passage, she writes, "the partially suppressed meaning implies ... that the men have somehow become submissively less than men and that the women have become both aggressively more and submissively less than women." But with the possible exception of Lucy Deane, no figure in *The Mill on the Floss* is less aggressive than the plaintive and good-hearted Mrs. Moss. And to regard the entire society of St. Ogg's as effeminate or dominated by women is to forget that one of the novel's compelling concerns, after all, has to do with the restrictions imposed on women by provincial traditions.

[14] *Ibid.*, p. 115.

Maggie and Tom's death. The first cause is the society itself"; it is "the *machinery* of St. Ogg's, symbolized in general by the mill, which crushes Maggie and Tom." [15] But there are no indications in the text that St. Ogg's is machine-ridden — even when writing of the England of her own day George Eliot seems undisturbed by the Victorian bogey of "machinery" and industrialism — or that the mill is to be identified with St. Ogg's and regarded as injurious.

There are at issue here two important and closely related points; with the first of these — the town's implication in Maggie and Tom's death — I have already to some extent dealt, but I shall need to return to it presently. The second point has to do not only with the author's attitude to St. Ogg's and provincial society in general but also with her ideas about social evolution. This is the view, not wholly eccentric or unfounded, that in *The Mill on the Floss* George Eliot tries through commentary, action, and symbol to suggest the movement and direction of old-fashioned provincial consciousness as well as to describe a primitive stage of social development and the dilemma of the individual at odds with her time and place. Thus George Levine regards the society of St. Ogg's as being decadent as well as backward. Interested in the novel's ideological framework, he finds both "in its personal drama and in its vividly imagined period of social transition . . . many of Comte's and Feuerbach's notions of social and moral growth." Making no reference to Miss Stump's work, he also cites in evidence of the primitive nature of the community "the frequency with which all the characters are compared to insects and animals." [16] Although his judgment of the people of St. Ogg's is a good deal less harsh than hers, Levine also believes that their fate is anticipated in the drowning of the heroine: "It is likely that George Eliot sees Maggie's death by water as a preparation for the condition in which the society would be prepared [for the higher sacrament]." [17] The hint of hesitation here is entirely justified, for *The Mill on The Floss* simply does not have the sustained and inclusive network of connections, comments, and events that can convincingly demonstrate the desired correlation between private and public life. If George Eliot intended to chart a stage of social development accord-

[15] *Ibid.*, pp. 132–133.
[16] George Levine, "Intelligence as Deception: *The Mill on the Floss*," PMLA, LXXX (September 1965), 403.
[17] *Ibid.*, 408.

ing to the teachings of Comte and Feuerbach and to symbolize it in the personal fate of Maggie and Tom, she has not, as Levine himself acknowledges, realized this intention with any completeness. And her failure in this respect is attested to by the precipitancy and irresoluteness of the novel's conclusion and the comparative lack of attention in the final parts to the general life of the town.

In the attempt to relate the thematic content of *The Mill on the Floss* to the philosophies of Comte and Feuerbach, Levine's criticism is still too much at the service of his ideological interests to allow him to deal adequately with the problems raised by the book, in particular by the ending. Claude Bissell, on whose remarks most subsequent interpretations of St. Ogg's seem to depend, has also neglected to discuss these issues. Had he done so, he would probably have found it necessary to amplify and qualify his contrast between *Adam Bede* and *The Mill on the Floss*:

> . . . the analysis of social forces is here bound up closely with the working out of the theme. Whereas in *Adam Bede* society is simply framework or background, in *The Mill on the Floss* it is an active agent. Not merely must the heroine subdue the tumult in her own soul; she must fight against the collective prejudices of a society for which the greatest good can be reckoned only in terms of material success.[18]

But, as some later critics have argued, society in *Adam Bede*, in spite of its rustic charm and simplicity, is more than "simply framework or background." As for *The Mill on the Floss*, its social environment does indeed interact with the plot but not in the complete and organic way that Bissell claims. For society is here "bound up with the working out of the theme" largely through the heroine's inner conflict rather than through her resistance to any external pressure. Maggie is not grossly oppressed or threatened by social forces; nor does she seem unduly disturbed by "the collective prejudices" of her society. The "tumult in her own soul" results from the clash of her private aspirations with her stubborn sense of responsibility and attachment to family, friends, society, and environment.

In spite of her rebelliousness as a child, in spite of the town's final rejection of her, Maggie is not depicted as a conscious and wilful outcast. Unlike Philip, for example, who from the beginning despises

[18] *ELH*, XVIII, 234.

the provincialism of St. Ogg's and is consistently spurned by the town, Maggie feels completely at home in the region. Indeed Philip, when he argues against her "narrow asceticism," attempts almost to turn her dissatisfaction with life against what he calls "the dead level of provincial existence" but without much success, for that is not the real source of her unhappiness. Maggie's ardent nature makes her glow with a nobler vision and higher goals than her milieu can apparently satisfy, but her local ties nevertheless remain strong. She is fond of St. Ogg's and loves the mill. It is only after Mr. Tulliver's bankruptcy and illness, with her home pervaded by a spirit of obstinate gloom, vindictiveness, and single-minded determination to satisfy the creditors, that Maggie becomes genuinely discontented and restive. The depressing unresponsiveness of her father and Tom, the total absence of warmth and tenderness in the home, the cramping demands of family loyalty — all thwart her impulse for happiness, for emotional fulfillment and spiritual and intellectual enlightenment.

Caused as it is, then, by exceptional domestic misfortunes, Maggie's alienation from her environment is highly ambiguous. That she becomes near the novel's close an outsider cannot reasonably be denied, but she is ostracized rather than alienated, rejected rather than rejecting. And as she herself recognizes, it is her own rashness and passionate self-indulgence, however misunderstood in the town, that lead to her condemnation:

> Maggie . . . was too entirely filled with a more agonising anxiety to spend any thought on the view that was being taken of her conduct by the world of St. Ogg's . . . The idea of ever recovering happiness never glimmered in her mind for a moment . . . Life stretched before her as one act of penitence, and all she craved, as she dwelt on her future lot, was something to guarantee her from more falling: her own weakness haunted her like a vision of hideous possibilities, that made no peace conceivable except such as lay in the sense of a sure refuge. (Book Seven, Chapter II)

Because Maggie's divided self is to some extent at least a product of her environment, it is impossible to absolve the culture of St. Ogg's of some responsibility for her predicament, but the main source of her distress, as the passage just quoted makes clear, is deeply personal. By tracing through similar passages the development of

Maggie's unhappiness, it is possible to define better the nature of her alienation and at the same time to shed some light on George Eliot's attitude toward the world of St. Ogg's, on the question of social involvement in the final deaths, and the relation between plot and background.

v

Maggie's darkest reflections about social life occur not near the end of the book but in the aftermath of her father's stroke and financial ruin. Rebuffed by Tom's harshness, Maggie feels that the "world outside of the books was not a happy one . . . it seemed to be a world where people behaved the best to those they did not pretend to love, and that did not belong to them. And if life had no love in it, what else was there for Maggie?" (Book Three, Chapter V). But this feeling does not make her turn with contempt or hatred against the world: if she recoils it is only against the misery of her immediate situation. Made by necessity more and more aware "of conflict between the inward impulse and the outward fact, which is the lot of every imaginative and passionate nature," she turns inward in search of intellectual and moral bulwarks, of an outlook to help her understand and bear the wretchedness so unjustly, as she feels, imposed on her. The escape promised by literature ("all Scott's novels and all Byron's poems") she perceives to be profitless:

> She could make dream-worlds of her own — but no dream-world would satisfy her now. She wanted some explanation of this hard, real life: the unhappy-looking father, seated at the dull breakfast-table; the childish, bewildered mother; the little sordid tasks that filled the hours, or the more oppressive emptiness of weary, joyless leisure; the need of some tender, demonstrative love; the cruel sense that Tom didn't mind what she thought or felt, and that they were no longer playfellows together; the privation of all pleasant things that had come to *her* more than to others: she wanted some key that would enable her to understand, and, in understanding, endure, the heavy weight that had fallen on her young heart. (Book Four, Chapter III)

It is thus made clear that her unhappiness is caused not by an uncongenial society or a perverted morality but by the barrenness of her domestic circumstances. These circumstances, as we see later in Maggie's exhilarated response to the comparative wealth, ease, and refinement at Lucy's house, are not a full reflection of the social spirit; her resentment turns against a private, peculiar situation:

> She rebelled against her lot, she fainted under its loneliness, and fits even of anger and hatred towards her father and mother, who were so unlike what she would have them be — towards Tom, who checked her, and met her thought or feeling always by some thwarting difference — would flow out over her affections and conscience . . . (Book Four, Chapter III)

The key to existence for which Maggie casts about comes to her in the form of the doctrine of self-renunciation of Thomas à Kempis: "here was a sublime height to be reached without the help of outward things — here was insight, and strength, and conquest, to be won by means entirely within her own soul . . ." As with eager desperation she grasps this key and its promise of relief, of emotional independence and moral direction, Maggie rises for the time being above her circumstances as well as above the spiritual level of her society. For if provincial culture is at fault in *The Mill on the Floss*, it is so, as this chapter implies, in its lack of guiding values of any vitality, of dynamic and inspiring principles to which Maggie could have instinctively turned. The account of her "conversion" ends, interestingly, with one of George Eliot's ironic apologies to the reader which develops into a somewhat labored digression about the nature of social structure and inequalities (and which gives a hint of her Ruskinian awareness of industrial toil and exploitation). The refined reader of good society, she fears, may be puzzled by her emphasis on the heroine's spiritual crisis and queer resolution of it:

> But then, good society has its claret and its velvet carpets, its dinner-engagements six weeks deep, its opera and its faëry ball-rooms . . . and [gets] its religion [done] by the superior clergy who are to be met in the best houses: how should it have time or need for belief and emphasis? But good society, floated on gossamer wings of light irony, is of very expensive production; requiring nothing less than a wide and arduous national life condensed in unfragrant deafening factories, cramping itself in mines, sweating at furnaces, grinding, hammering, weaving under more or less oppression of carbonic acid — or else, spread over sheepwalks, and scattered in lonely houses and

huts on the clayey or chalky corn-lands, where the rainy days look dreary. This wide national life is based entirely on emphasis — the emphasis of want, which urges it into all the activities necessary for the maintenance of good society and light irony: it spends its heavy years often in a chill, uncarpeted fashion, amidst family discord unsoftened by long corridors. Under such circumstances, there are many among its myriads of souls who have absolutely needed an emphatic belief . . . Some have an emphatic belief in alcohol, and seek their *ekstasis* or outside standing-ground in gin; but the rest require something that good society calls "enthusiasm," something that will present motives in an entire absence of high prizes . . . (Book Four, Chapter III)

This disquisition obviously extends the perspective of the novel and, by mocking the refined delusions of advanced, sophisticated society and viewing in a heroic light the spiritual promptings of obscure individuals, once again invests "the history of unfashionable families" with dignity and wide significance. It serves also as a kind of coda to the analysis of St. Ogg's which occurs two chapters earlier. There the author concluded the description of the moral life of Maggie's family with a rueful stress on the ineffectuality of the church as an edifying institution: "If such were the views of life on which the Dodsons and Tullivers had been reared in the praiseworthy past of Pitt and high prices, you will infer from what you already know concerning the state of society in St. Ogg's, that there had been no modifying influence to act on them in their maturer life." Now, in justifying Maggie's "enthusiasm" and placing it in the context of general spiritual need, George Eliot can define with some precision the intellectual and moral deprivations which the exceptional individual in a provincial environment has to endure. (The wryly depreciatory tone of the comments on good society implies, however, that spiritually it has not progressed much beyond the backward state of St. Ogg's — indeed its refinements may seduce and stifle inspired appetites like Maggie's.) If we thus link these two passages of social analysis, we will understand clearly Maggie's need of guidance and inspiration, the genuine worth of the doctrine she clings to (as well as her extravagant application of it), and the barrenness of the moral climate that forces her into withdrawal and self-reliance.

Since the society's "sin" is one of omission, Maggie is essentially struggling for a personal answer to a personal problem. In her worn copy of *The Imitation of Christ* she finds a response to her "enthusiasm" and the nearest equivalent available to her of the kind of intimate and inspired moral direction and sustenance that Janet Dempster, as well as the town of Milby in general, had derived from Mr. Tryan. But if St. Ogg's lacks a redeeming presence of a forcefulness comparable to Mr. Tryan's, it is less desperately in need of redemption than Milby. Although its citizens are narrow, parochial, and acquisitive, they are also more placid and responsible than the people of Milby, and show little of that gross crudity of manners and violence of spirit that characterize Dempster's gang. As Mr. Deane's expositions of his sturdily principled, if not exactly enlightened, business ethic show, St. Ogg's is not guided to the same extent as Milby by mindless expediency. In spite of its lack of awareness, "fine old St. Ogg's" is "venerable," "quaint," and "mellow" (Book One, Chapter XII) and therefore a pleasant contrast with the cramped and dingy ugliness of Milby. If we are to have an accurate picture of the atmosphere in which Maggie grows up, we must keep such saving features in mind, together with the deficiencies, which are admittedly rather more in evidence.

vi

Maggie's attachment to St. Ogg's, although it does not play a part of any importance in the first five Books (where the mill is the physical and emotional focus), is assumed throughout. It becomes explicit in Book Six, in which Maggie, now nineteen, returns to the town after two years as an assistant in an apparently remote school. Not only does she feel no rebellious scorn then for the "state of society in St. Ogg's" or even an urge to reform it — she positively enjoys it. Her delight, however, is not unmixed. As Lucy's cousin and guest, she can participate in the life of St. Ogg's from a position of unaccustomed privilege and graciousness; at the same time she responds keenly to the associations which the familiar surroundings awaken in her. The impact of these, mingling itself with her delight in a life of ease and elegance, makes her thoughtful and suspicious:

. . . her eyes wandered to the window, where she could see the sunshine falling on the rich clumps of spring flowers and on the long hedge of laurels — and beyond, the silvery breadth of the dear old Floss, that at this distance seemed to be sleeping in a morning holiday. The sweet fresh garden-scent came through the open window, and the birds were busy flitting and alighting, gurgling and singing. Yet Maggie's eyes began to fill with tears. The sight of the old scenes had made the rush of memories so painful, that even yesterday she had only been able to rejoice in her mother's restored comfort and Tom's brotherly friendliness as we rejoice in good news of friends at a distance, rather than in the presence of a happiness which we share. Memory and imagination urged upon her a sense of privation too keen to let her taste what was offered in the transient present: her future, she thought, was likely to be worse than her past, for after her years of contented renunciation, she had slipped back into desire and longing: she found joyless days of distasteful occupation harder and harder — she found the image of the intense and varied life she yearned for, and despaired of, becoming more and more importunate. (Book Six, Chapter II)

Once again we see that Maggie's dissatisfaction springs from her private situation, from both "her burden of larger wants than others seemed to feel" (Book Four, Chapter III) and her impoverished economic and social circumstances. Here arises a crucial difficulty in the novel. For Maggie's aspirations, which had been described mainly in terms of vague grandeur, intensity, and restless idealism, are from this point on defined not with increased precision but in a different light altogether. The comfort, luxury, and admiration that she finds at Lucy's house, together with the temptation of love and sexual passion, not only exercise a fatal attraction on Maggie but seem (with the apparent sympathy and concurrence of the author) entirely to meet the reach of her desires.

It was not that she thought distinctly of Mr. Stephen Guest, or dwelt on the indications that he looked at her with admiration; it was rather that she felt the half-remote presence of a world of love and beauty and delight, made up of vague, mingled images from all the poetry and romance she had ever read, or had ever woven in her dreamy reveries. Her mind glanced back once or twice to the time when she had courted privation, when she had thought all longing, all impatience was subdued;

but that condition seemed irrecoverably gone, and she recoiled
from the remembrance of it. No prayer, no striving now, would
bring back that negative peace: the battle of her life, it seemed,
was not to be decided in that short and easy way — by perfect
renunciation at the very threshold of her youth. (Book Six,
Chapter III)

The "tumult" is still located strictly in Maggie's own soul, but
the stakes of the conflict seem to have been reduced: her desires
appear now not too vast but, by comparison with what we had been
led to think, somewhat ignoble. This impression is confirmed and the
resulting confusion compounded when we see her struggling with
herself to renounce Stephen.

There were moments in which a cruel selfishness seemed to be
getting possession of her: why should not Lucy — why should
not Philip suffer? *She* had had to suffer through many years
of her life; and who had renounced anything for her? And
when something like that fulness of existence — love, wealth,
ease, and refinement, all that her nature craved — was brought
within her reach, why was she to forego it, that another might
have it — another, who perhaps needed it less? (Book Six,
Chapter XIII)

Now, although she is even at this point aware of higher claims,
of moral aspirations to which she ultimately proves true, there is no
indication that her "selfish" promptings, apart from their selfishness,
are unworthy of her. Nor, it appears, would they clash with her moral
idealism were the interests of others not involved. There is a strong
suggestion that only the previous claims that Lucy and Philip have
on her loyalty stand in the way of Maggie's complete happiness and
fulfillment with Stephen:

Was that existence which tempted her the full existence she
dreamed? Where, then, would be all the memories of early
striving — all the deep pity for another's pain, which had been
nurtured in her through years of affection and hardship — all
the divine presentiment of something higher than mere personal
enjoyment, which had made the sacredness of life? She might
as well hope to enjoy walking by maiming her feet, as hope to
enjoy an existence in which she set out by maiming the faith
and sympathy that were the best organs of her soul. (Book
Six, Chapter XIII)

Later, on board the ship where she finds herself with Stephen, Maggie is startled out of her stupor by a dream in which she recognizes with terrible clarity the full meaning of her situation. We note that at this crucial moment of vision she recoils against her weakness in having yielded to Stephen's entreaties and blames herself alone for her alienation:

> . . . she was alone with her own memory and her own dread. The irrevocable wrong that must blot her life had been committed: she had brought sorrow into the lives of others — into the lives that were knit up with hers by trust and love. The feeling of a few short weeks had hurried her into the sins her nature had most recoiled from — breach of faith and cruel selfishness; she had rent the ties that had given meaning to duty, and had made herself an outlawed soul, with no guide but the wayward choice of her own passion . . . Her life with Stephen could have no sacredness: she must for ever sink and wander vaguely, driven by uncertain impulse; for she had let go the clue of life — that clue which once in the far-off years her young need had clutched so strongly. (Book Six, Chapter XIV)

Thus, as she works out this moral calculus, Maggie's sense of personal responsibility, which does not allow her to blame anyone but herself for her predicament, now compels her to leave Stephen. Affirming the primacy of her obligations to Lucy and Philip with a new-found assurance, she nevertheless makes it clear that only the existence of those ties and her sense of their inviolability keep her from going away with him:

> "I cannot marry you: I cannot take a good for myself that has been wrung out of [Philip and Lucy's] misery . . . it would rend me away from all that my past life has made dear and holy to me. I can't set out on a fresh life, and forget that: I must go back to it, and cling to it, else I shall feel as if there were nothing firm beneath my feet."

Maggie clearly believes (and the author never decidedly differs from her) that Stephen and the life he offers her represent a genuine "good." There is nothing really mean or contemptible in this, in Maggie's wishing simply for "love, wealth, ease, and refinement," but we are led to believe that she is really after something nobler and grander when, for example, she tells Philip much earlier of her desire for "a full life" (Book Five, Chapter I). Without any warning from the author — unless we accept as clues the indications of Maggie's impetuosity and emotional egoism — the heroine's great expectations are suddenly transformed and, in their new mundaneness, diminished. It thus becomes even more difficult than it would otherwise have been to regard her as the victim of a destructively materialistic society.

If the change in Maggie's aspirations is unsettling, the tragic or, more precisely, pathetic ending of the novel increases the confusion. For the author takes pains to present Maggie's death as a release and fulfillment: Maggie has nothing left to live for — or so we are meant to think. But it is difficult to feel this. Not only does her death seem unnecessary, arbitrary, and evasive, but if regarded as a release from an unbearably oppressive life, it inevitably undercuts to a large extent the moral victory that Maggie gains when she rejects Stephen and returns to St. Ogg's. The melancholy vision of an empty life that frightens her just before she becomes conscious of the flood seems to suggest that of the two alternatives between which she has had to decide it was the elopement with Stephen, not the affirmation of firm moral principles and enduring personal ties, that offered true richness and fulfillment. Philip's letter, on the other hand, as well as the reconciliation with Lucy, the reunion with Tom, and Tom's final perception of her heroic constancy, all tend to vindicate the rightness of her choice. The vindication, however, is subverted by her death, which simply does not feel like the resolution it is obviously intended to be; instead, by the lurking suggestion that in giving up Stephen Maggie has lost her one chance for "a full life," the death runs counter to the visible and conscious impulse of the book.

vii

At the time of her decision on board ship to leave Stephen, the fact that Maggie is powerfully drawn to him and the sexual, emotional, and material gratifications that he represents is necessary to make her temptation genuine and her triumph almost perverse and agonizingly poignant. The motive force of the triumph is her individually deduced and felt moral vision. Although she arrives at her ethic without the aid of her family or society, it is nevertheless centered, through its emphasis on sympathy, wholeness, stability, and continuity, around personal relations and the responsibility as well as the holiness of the heart's affections. When she goes from Stephen she has only one thought: "Home — where her mother and brother were — Philip — Lucy — the scene of her very cares and trials — was the haven towards which her mind tended — the sanctuary where sacred relics lay — where she would be rescued from more falling" (Book Six, Chapter XIV).

Oppressed by a sense of personal failure and of betrayed responsibility (to those she has hurt or disgraced: Philip, Lucy, Stephen, Tom, and her mother), Maggie is at first unaware of the town's condemnation of her. Her remorsefulness springs from her violation of her own values rather than society's; penitent and bent on atonement, she resigns herself to a bleak but resolute life, which she is determined to spend in her native environment: "somehow or other she would maintain herself at St. Ogg's" (Book Seven, Chapter II). Even after she realizes the meaning of the cool disdain and insulting familiarity with which the townspeople regard her, she remains too deeply immersed in the inner repercussions of her rashness to be greatly disturbed by their manner. Her own judgment of herself anticipates and overshadows the judgment of the town and gives her the determination she needs to remain there.

But Maggie's decision to stay in St. Ogg's is based not only on her wish to be near the people she loves and has hurt and her resolve to make amends to them, to restore the ties she has broken. She stays also because she has to, because of an instinct for self-preservation: "Oh, if I could but stop here!" she exclaims to Dr. Kenn. "I have no heart to begin a strange life again. I should have no stay. I should feel like a lonely wanderer — cut off from the past" (Book Seven, Chapter II). Her attachment to her milieu remains unshaken even in the face of the antagonism which she meets. When Dr. Kenn, having taken Maggie into his home as a governess, finally bows to social pressure and offers dejectedly to find a similar position for her away from St. Ogg's, Maggie can barely contain her heart-wrenching unhappiness.

> Poor Maggie listened with a trembling lip: she could say nothing but a faint "thank you — I shall be grateful;" and she walked back to her lodgings, through the driving rain, with a

new sense of desolation. She must be a lonely wanderer; she must go out among fresh faces . . . she must begin a new life, in which she would have to rouse herself to receive new impressions — and she was so unspeakably, sickeningly weary! There was no home, no help for the erring: even those who pitied were constrained to hardness. (Book Seven, Chapter V)

Clearly there is nothing in Maggie's pathetic reflections to support the notion that she is alienated from her society, in the sense of antipathy and disaffection that the term usually means. On the contrary, to leave behind the world in which her past is lodged and her affections are rooted is a painful exile for her, and insofar as death preserves her from the fate of estrangement and rootlessness, it comes as an escape, if not quite convincingly as a redemption. There is virtually nothing in the account of the flood to indicate that George Eliot intends it as a foreshadowing of social destruction, a culmination of tendencies inherent in the world of St. Ogg's, or a representation of righteous vengeance, whether supernatural or natural. But there is a great deal to show that she uses the flood as an *ex machina* device to impose on the novel an ending of tragic triumph. As Harvey says, "Maggie has to be brought into a final relationship with Philip, Lucy, Stephen, and Tom, in that order." [19] The final relationship involves a kind of moral reinstatement of Maggie. Through the understanding, forgiveness, and reassuring admiration that Philip communicates in his letter and that Lucy expresses in her brief visit, and through her own victory over the temptation of Stephen's letter, Maggie is emphatically vindicated.

But it is the flood that provides her with an opportunity for the ultimate self-exoneration, for it enables her dramatically to convince Tom of her abiding love and loyalty, to demonstrate to him what she has already proved to herself and the reader — that in her passionate, romantic, fitfully visionary idealism she has struggled to absorb and preserve the personal integrity and responsibility that ennoble the otherwise drab moral order of the Tullivers and Dodsons. Partly arbitrariness and evasion, partly irresolution, and partly the lack of space prevent George Eliot from fully achieving her purpose, but that purpose is by now fairly clear: it is to present Maggie, a victim of circumstances and even more of her own character, triumphing over

[19] *The Art of George Eliot*, p. 125.

those circumstances by virtue of her character, and attaining in death the wholeness, unity, and heroic stature for which she has always yearned. At the cost of being weak, the ending is sincere: there is no ironic or accusing side glance at St. Ogg's either in the final embrace of brother and sister or in the inscription on their tomb, "In their death they were not divided."

viii

By now the implausibility of viewing the drowning of Maggie and Tom as a result of the destructive tendencies of their society should be amply clear. Not only do the reflections about the heroine's situation (her own as well as the author's) emphasize the solitary and psychological aspect of her dilemma, but the society that is examined in so leisurely a fashion in the early parts of the book receives scant attention near the end. The resulting imbalance also makes it difficult to regard the death of the protagonists as a symbolic anticipation of the fate of St. Ogg's. For while allusions to social change, especially in the opening sections, are quite numerous in *The Mill on the Floss*, they are not unified in a coherent, climactic vision, nor do they systematically insist that the changes to which they point are decadent in nature.

The sense of change that is built up in the course of the novel is primarily centered around economic matters and, to a lesser extent, social ones. Mr. Tulliver sounds the keynote of the spirit of the time at the beginning of the second chapter: "What I want . . . is to give Tom a good eddication; an eddication as'll be a bread to him . . . all the learnin' *my* father ever paid for was a bit o' birch at one end and the alphabet at th'other." In one way or another, the idea implicit in this declaration is repeated again and again: it is a time of economic flux, of opportunities for self-advancement and, for the unwary and unadaptable, of bewildering traps. Mr. Tulliver is an old-fashioned man, as the narrator keeps observing, one of the "people of the old school" whom Mr. Riley loves to patronize. As the book progresses and things prove too "puzzlin'" for him, he grows more and more irritable, plaintive, and depressed about his lack of sophistication; he yearns for a simpler time in which articulateness and cunning did not threaten to dispossess simple, hard-working, honest folk:

". . . if the world had been left as God made it, I could ha'
seen my way, and held my own wi' the best of 'em; but things
have got so twisted round and wrapped up i' unreasonable words,
as aren't a bit like 'em, as I'm clean at fault, often an' often.
Everything winds about so — the more straightforard you are,
the more you're puzzled." (Book One, Chapter III)

The political and religious developments of the day strengthen
and justify Mr. Tulliver's worry about his immediate circumstances.
Current events are not referred to as frequently or as skillfully in
The Mill on the Floss as they are in *Middlemarch*, but in Mr. Tulliver's
talk with his brother-in-law, Mr. Deane, the historical context of the
story is quickly but vividly sketched in. The amused detachment of
the narrative tone and the somewhat self-satisfied but amiable narrowness of the two men give the conversation its distinctly provincial
perspective. "They would exchange their views concerning the Duke
of Wellington, whose conduct in the Catholic Question had thrown
such an entirely new light on his character." Mr. Tulliver, obviously
soured by the frustrations besetting his own affairs, expresses the
fear "that the country could never again be what it used to be; but
Mr. Deane, attached to a firm of which the returns were on the in-
crease, naturally took a more lively view of the present" (Book One,
Chapter VII).

Mr. Deane's buoyancy derives not only from his firm's success
but his own. His climb to wealth and status is earnest, purposeful,
energetic as well as honest, and it is still in progress during the course
of the story. It is to Mr. Deane that Tom turns for a job and for
inspiration: "he would be like his uncle Deane — get a situation in
some great house of business and rise fast" (Book Three, Chapter V).
Applying himself industriously with the characteristic Dodson single-
ness of purpose, Tom does indeed realize his ambition; as Mr. Deane
tells him, his advancement is much more rapid than it could have
been a generation ago: "You see, Tom . . . the world goes on at a
smarter pace than it did when I was a young fellow . . . Everything
was on a lower scale . . . It's this steam, you see, that has made the
difference: it drives on every wheel double pace, and the wheel of
fortune along with 'em, as our Mr. Stephen Guest said at the anni-
versary dinner . . ." (Book Six, Chapter V). Both Mr. Deane and Tom
are obviously far more adaptable than Mr. Tulliver had been. "I don't

find fault with change, as some people do," says Mr. Deane with the complacent but far from contemptible self-confidence of the successful businessman. He expresses, echoing Macaulay's assertive faith in material progress, the optimism of the beginning of the Victorian era:

> "Trade, sir, opens a man's eyes; and if the population is to get thicker upon the ground, as it's doing, the world must use its wits at inventions of one sort or other. I know I've done my share as an ordinary man of business. Somebody has said it's a fine thing to make two ears of corn grow where there only grew one before; but, sir, it's a fine thing, too, to further the exchange of commodities, and bring the grains of corn to the mouths that are hungry. And that's our line of business; and I consider it as honourable a position as a man can hold, to be connected with it." (Book Six, Chapter V)

The narrator's frequent digressions and asides, made from the "modern" point of view of 1861, support and enlarge the consciousness, however dim or partial, that the characters themselves have of their position in history. As in *Scenes of Clerical Life* and *Adam Bede*, such allusions to change and improvement tend to have an ironic slant, teasing the reader's sense of superiority over past crudities, questioning the extent and quality of the enlightenment that is supposed to have been achieved since the provincial heyday treated in the novel. Historical irony of this sort underlies the description of Mrs. Glegg's superstitions (Book One, Chapter XII), the account of Tom's haphazard education (Book Two), or the contrast between "our instructed vagrancy" and the attachment of "an old-fashioned man like Tulliver" to his native place (Book Three, Chapter IX). In such passages the cultural distance between past and present is decreased, and there is very little to urge on us the view that St. Ogg's is a decadent society, corrupting or actually destroying the individuals who seek to rise above the general norm. What may, however, be a symptom of social dissolution and disease (although the text does not insist on this diagnosis) is the emergence, or rather the prevalence, of individualism. I hesitate to say emergence because in spite of all the signs of social flux it is not really clear that individualism is a new phenomenon. But new or not, it abounds and affects seriously moral conduct as well as material existence. Individualism as the idea of single struggle against hereditary and environmental *données*, as the notion of self-dependence, defines, for example, the theme of personal growth. We have already seen this in Maggie's case, but even Tom, the staunch family man, moves in his rigid way towards a well-defined separatism. In spite of his automatic allegiance to the code of the Dodson clan, he is never at his ease among even his closest relatives. The harshness with which he treats Maggie stems from private rather than familial chagrin, for his is "a nature in which family feeling had lost the character of clanship, in taking on a double deep dye of personal pride" (Book Seven, Chapter III).

Individualism as a social and economic manifestation is implicit in the background of self-advancement, business enterprise, and litigation against which the narrative is placed. The strongest and most serious suggestion, however, that presents it as a general ailment of the culture occurs near the end of the novel, where Dr. Kenn deplores the fragmentation corroding the communal coherence of St. Ogg's. The passage comes as the culmination of one of the few examples of extended social analysis in the closing parts of *The Mill on the Floss*. Regretting the town's self-righteous condemnation of Maggie, Dr. Kenn attributes it to the eroding of communal spirit and connections — an erosion with which he contrasts Maggie's almost compulsive sense of local roots and personal ties:

> "Your prompting to go to your nearest friends — to remain where all the ties of your life have been formed — is a true prompting, to which the Church in its original constitution and discipline responds . . . And the Church ought to represent the feeling of the community, so that every parish should be a family knit together by Christian brotherhood under a spiritual father. But the ideas of discipline and Christian fraternity are entirely relaxed — they can hardly be said to exist in the public mind: they hardly survive except in the partial, contradictory form they have taken in the narrow communities of schismatics." (Book Seven, Chapter II)

Dr. Kenn's speech might seem somewhat pompous if it were not for the genuine importance of his observations and their broad relevance to the narrative. But the attention that his words excite in the reader is not exploited and soon lapses. By this time, the subjective quality of the novel is so dominant that social commentary, however pertinent, seems almost digressive. Even though the Rector's judgment of the situation is accurate, even though his words hark back to the narrator's analysis in Book One of the religious life of St. Ogg's ("The days were gone when people could be greatly wrought upon by their faith"), at this moment he is not really responding to the urgency of Maggie's spiritual need. In the context of her fervent concern with the state of her own conscience, his declamation seems somewhat intrusive and stark.

But since "there is no private life untouched by a wider public life," as George Eliot writes in *Felix Holt*, Dr. Kenn's social comments, in spite of their anticlimactic effect, are not beside the point. For Maggie's ethical self-reliance may be seen as a necessary answer to the fragmentation and mundane wilfulness with which he is preoccupied. Her affirmation of duty, renunciation, and human ties constitutes an individualistic groping after "the ideas of discipline and Christian fraternity." Thus, when Dr. Kenn, carrying out his principal function in the novel, provides an explicit and authoritative vindication of Maggie's conduct, he dwells on the contrast between her moral stringency and the prevailing laxness. "At present everything seems tending towards the relaxation of ties — towards the substitution of wayward choice for the adherence to obligation, which has its roots in the past. Your conscience and your heart have given you true light on this point, Miss Tulliver" (Book Seven, Chapter II).

Compared to the emphasis with which Dr. Kenn sanctions Maggie's behavior, his dejection over the increasing dissolution of social bonds and the ineffectuality of the Church seems incidental. His comments about the state of society, which exist mainly to heighten our sense of the singularity of Maggie's moral sensibility, are weakened by their subservient role. The lack of development, dramatic illustration, or sustained emphasis also qualifies the effectiveness of his social criticism and renders questionable its validity. In spite of scattered instances that separately support the notion, the erosion of social coherence does not exist in *The Mill on the Floss* as an elaborately developed theme. Nor is there any strong impression that the provincial society depicted here is a degenerate descendant of a nobler and better world. In Book One, to be sure, a vision of the spiritually heroic past of St. Ogg's is conjured up — a past which the town characteristically ignores — and the unshaken faith, religious passions, and enthusiastic dedication of legendary times and of the seventeenth century are contrasted with the uninspired ordinariness of the nineteenth century. But there is no attempt to trace the historical evolution connecting these periods, so that we do not regard St. Ogg's as an emblem of a decadent civilization, but rather as a provincial town without the inspired dedication that the narrator attributes to the two earlier eras. For much of the novel's action the idealized past is almost as remote from the reader's mind as it is from the mind of the town. The enduring tradition, the real sense of continuity, is that of the Dodsons.

ix

For ardent and idealistic souls like Maggie's the lack of the sort of spirituality and fiery commitment that George Eliot attributes in passing to the Puritans and Cavaliers creates a moral and psychological void. Because the religious life of her environment cannot meet her need for what "good society calls 'enthusiasm,'" she resorts at first to literature but ultimately comes to rely on herself, on privately cultivated moral instincts, for support in personal crises. In the scrupulous moral introspection that this process involves, memory plays a crucial part. When Maggie yields to Stephen and, against her painfully formed resolve, accompanies him in the boat, her memory, we are told, is "excluded" (Book Six, Chapter XIII). But when she decides to return to St. Ogg's, it is because she lets herself be guided by her memory — the memory of her affection for Philip and Lucy and of her moral ideals. When she is tempted for the last time, it is memory that helps her resist the reproaches and importunings of Stephen's letter. Just as she is about impulsively to give in once again to his appeal, "her mind recoiled; and the sense of contradiction with her past self in her moments of strength and clearness, came upon her like a pang of conscious degradation" (Book Seven, Chapter V).

The echo of Wordsworth at this point in the novel can hardly be accidental. His influence is probably more obvious in *The Mill on the Floss* than in any other of George Eliot's novels (with the possible exception of *Silas Marner*), and the lines that are closest in meaning to the words she uses about Maggie are underscored in her copy of *The Prelude*: [20]

[20] See Pinney, "George Eliot's Reading of Wordsworth: The Record," *Victorian Newsletter*, no. 24 (Fall 1963), pp. 20–22. I owe this particular connec-

> So feeling comes in aid
> Of feeling, and diversity of strength
> Attends us, if but once we have been strong.
> (XII, 269-271)

Of all the Wordsworthian elements in the novel — the heroine's moral fervor and struggle for wholeness and continuity, the author's love of the countryside and emphasis on duty and endurance — the role of memory is the most prominent. Without relying to the same extent as Wordsworth on "emotion recollected in tranquillity," [21] George Eliot does cast *The Mill on the Floss* in a strongly autobiographical and self-exploratory mold. It is the subjective element into which she is led by her autobiographical interest that accounts in part for the incomplete development of the social theme and for the peculiarly elusive regionalism of the novel.

In *The Mill on the Floss*, the locale and incidents are not simply recalled and thinly disguised for narrative ends, as in *Scenes of Clerical Life*, nor are they imagined with significant objectivity and thoughtful selectivity, as in *Adam Bede*. Instead, perhaps with a view toward masking her strong personal involvement with the story, George Eliot shifts the setting from Warwickshire to Lincolnshire — though the reader, of course, does not need to be aware of this — and

---

tion between *The Mill on the Floss* and *The Prelude* to Professor J. H. Buckley. Pinney, in the article cited earlier, "The Authority of the Past in George Eliot's Novels," writes perceptively of the significance of memory in the work and thought of George Eliot and of Wordsworth. Though his direction is different from mine, he recognizes and deals briefly but effectively with what I am most concerned with here: the profound attachment, in experience and in memory, of George Eliot's characters to their native environment, and the ways in which this attachment shapes the structure of her work. I came to his essay some time after this study was completed. Perhaps I should add that I am not entirely persuaded by the way in which Pinney employs his acute insight into the central quality of the early novels to define *Daniel Deronda* as a radical shift of direction in George Eliot's work.

[21] For Wordsworth's exploitation of memory, see, for example, Basil Willey's familiar essay, "On Wordsworth and the Locke Tradition" in *The Seventeenth Century Background: Studies in the Thought of the Age in Relation to Poetry and Religion* (London, 1934), pp. 296-309, reprinted in M. H. Abrams, ed., *English Romantic Poets: Modern Essays in Criticism* (Galaxy Books, 1960), pp. 84-94; and Basil Willey's more extended treatment of the subject in " 'Nature' in Wordsworth," *The Eighteenth Century Background: Studies in the Idea of Nature in the Thought of the Period* (London, 1946), pp. 253-293. For George Eliot's influence on Proust and a comparison of the two novelists' use of memory, see Franklin Gary, "In Search of George Eliot: An Approach through Marcel Proust," *Symposium*, IV (1933), 182-206, and L. A. Bisson, "Proust, Bergson, and George Eliot," *Modern Language Review*, XL (1945), 104-114.

changes the Arbury Farm of her childhood into Dorlcote Mill. (At a fairly early point in the novel she also departs almost entirely from the factual story of her youth, though never altogether from her own character.) But more important than the geographical shift in locale is the transformation that the locale undergoes because of the quality of vision with which it is presented. The vision springs from memory, but it is the memory of emotions associated with a place rather than of the place itself. Natural description is not abundant in *The Mill on the Floss*, and when it does occur it is almost always general and attached to a mood or feeling being recalled.

The opening scene of the novel, for example, presents an expansive landscape; in spite of the threatening clouds and a suggestion of duskiness, the impression is one of orderly beauty. But the mistily nostalgic tone of the description introduces a note of sadness — sadness for the world of youth that only memory can recapture. The narrator insists that she is visualizing a scene she remembers, and her thrill of recollection invests the landscape with particular poignance.[22] As the background recedes and the view focuses on the mill, both the center of interest and the feeling generated by the personal tone of the description become connected with the little girl, who is observing the mill with the same intensity as the narrator. It is almost as if for the only time in the book the author and the heroine who represents her (however indirectly or equivocally) were confronting each other. Would it be fanciful to suggest here that this opening "snapshot," in which the writer "Maggie" grew up to be faces her young self, betrays the speciousness of the heroine's death in the ending? Though the little girl is not said to be Maggie, there is every reason to suppose that she is; on the other hand, there is no reason to suppose that the narrator is anyone else but the author. The scene as a whole does not so much set the atmosphere as it evokes a mood — a mood in both the narrator and reader. It is hardly necessary to the action of the novel; it is static and, since the relation of the narrator to the little girl and to the scene remains unexplained, since the narrator's presence there is never located in the time scheme, it may be said to be timeless. It is possible, however, to explain this awkward

[22] It is not made clear whether the narrator is male or female, but since George Eliot's identity was already known at the time of publication and since the book is strongly autobiographical in content, tone, and involvement, it seems reasonable to think of the narrator as a woman.

structural device by viewing it as a dark hint, conscious or not, of the relation between the narrator and the heroine, and certainly as an indication, both teasing and emphatic, of the author's presence in the book and the retrospective nature of the story.

Intriguing as I find this speculation, I cannot pursue it here, but it seems to me to be supported by the importance that memory comes to have in the novel, both in the author's perspective and emphasis and in the consciousness of the characters. Just as Wordsworth imbibed strong and formative impressions among the Cumberland hills he loved, the heroine of *The Mill on the Floss* draws from the country around Dorlcote Mill and from treasured moments of affection and tenderness many of the influences that shape her nature and direct her life. Thus, in Book One, near the end of Chapter V, George Eliot, in describing Maggie and Tom's exploratory ramblings and fishing expeditions, their attachment to their surroundings, and their childish assumption of stability, observes that "Life did change for Tom and Maggie; and yet they were not wrong in believing that the thoughts and loves of these first years would always make part of their lives." Almost imperceptibly she begins to generalize from the experience of her two youthful protagonists ("We could never have loved the earth so well if we had had no childhood in it ... What novelty is worth that sweet monotony where everything is known, and *loved* because it is known?"). But to illustrate the idea of impressibility and continuity in growth, she turns to her own experience, thus revealing once again her deep involvement in the narrative.

> The wood I walk in on this mild May day, with the young yellow-brown foliage of the oaks between me and the blue sky, the white star-flowers and the blue-eyed speedwell and the ground ivy at my feet — what grove of tropic palms, what strange ferns or splendid broad-petalled blossoms, could ever thrill such deep and delicate fibres within me as this home scene? These familiar flowers, these well-remembered bird-notes, this sky, with its fitful brightness, these furrowed and grassy fields, each with a sort of personality given to it by the capricious hedgerows — such things as these are the mother tongue of our imagination, and the language that is laden with all the subtle inextricable associations the fleeting hours of our childhood left behind them.

Memory's way of binding one's affections to familiar places and people is evident in Maggie's enduring local roots and personal affections or in Tom's determined effort to reclaim the mill, but it is most vividly suggested in Mr. Tulliver's almost organic attachment to the mill. His love for the place stems from causes identical with those working on his children. In Book Three, Chapter IX, Mr. Tulliver, still recuperating from his stroke, is considering whether to leave the mill or stay on as Wakem's manager; all but Tom have advised him to stay.

> But the strongest influence of all was the love of the old premises where he had run about when he was a boy, just as Tom had done after him. The Tullivers had lived on this spot for generations, and he had sat listening on a low stool on winter evenings while his father talked of the old half-timbered mill that had been there before the last great floods which damaged it so that his grandfather pulled it down and built the new one. It was when he got able to walk about and look at all the old objects, that he felt the strain of this clinging affection for the old home as part of his life, part of himself. He couldn't bear to think of himself living on any other spot than this, where he knew the sound of every gate and door, and felt that the shape and colour of every roof and weather-stain and broken hillock was good, because his growing senses had been fed on them. Our instructed vagrancy, which has hardly time to linger by the hedgerows, but runs away early to the tropics, and is at home with palms and banyans . . . can hardly get a dim notion of what an old-fashioned man like Tulliver felt for this spot, where all his memories centred, and where life seemed like a familiar smooth-handled tool that the fingers clutch with loving ease.

The thrill of homecoming that Maggie feels on returning to St. Ogg's after an absence of two years springs from a "clinging affection" similar to her father's, but her attachment at that point is made poignant by her sense of her own homelessness, poverty, and restless aspiration for a fuller life. The aspiration strains drastically her personal and regional ties; promptings of passion "exclude" the steady force of memory underpinning her moral judgment — but this exclusion is only temporary. Once, when Philip had complained that she would never love him as well as she loved her brother, Maggie answered: "Perhaps not . . . but then, you know, the first thing I ever remember in my life is standing with Tom by the side of the Floss, while he held my hand: everything before that is dark to me" (Book Five, Chapter I). Near the end, having reaffirmed the holiness of her heart's affections and the unity of her life in the face of Stephen's desperate fervor and the town's hostility, Maggie contemplates in solitude a bleak future. At the same time, however, she draws strength from "the long past" with its "fountains of self-renouncing pity and affection, of faithfulness and resolve." The flood comes as if in answer to her prayer, and her first thought, after making sure of the safety of Bob Jakin and his family, is of Tom and the mill.

As she paddles her boat toward "the old home" and "the long-loved faces," she regards the flood almost consciously as her special chance to restore her original and tenacious affections: "Along with the sense of danger and possible rescue for those long-remembered beings at the old home, there was an undefined sense of reconcilement with her brother . . . that swept away all the later impressions of hard, cruel offence and misunderstanding, and left only the deep, underlying, unshakable memories of early union" (Book Seven, Chapter V). Maggie thus recovers that very first memory of which she speaks to Philip; in the recovery of that memory she prepares to return to her old relation with Tom, while in the actual return, on the river, to the mill and to Tom she recaptures the experience itself. The experience is essentially emblematic of a distilled, unreservedly happy version of her childhood, in which she and Tom are never to separate, either from each other or from their native surroundings. As day dawns and she approaches the mill, Maggie feels the thrill of homecoming:". . . she could discern the tints of the trees — could see the old Scotch firs far to the right, and the home chestnuts . . ." "With panting joy that she was there at last," she recaptures the past. Her death and Tom's, unsatisfying and frustrating though the reader may find it, is meant to enshrine the heroic restoration she accomplishes — a restoration that could not be maintained in life, since in life "you can't go home again." Although George Eliot lapses here into sentimentality and falseness of tone, she clearly wishes to see the drowning as a tragic fulfillment of Maggie's "clinging affection" for the world of her childhood: "brother and sister had gone down in an embrace never to be parted; living through again in one supreme moment the days when they had clasped their little hands in love, and roamed the daisied fields together."

7 Toward the Literature of Displacement: *Silas Marner*

The remedial influences of pure,
natural human relations.
— Letters

i

Silas Marner is George Eliot's last strongly regional novel. Compared with *The Mill on the Floss*, it is a fully realized and controlled work, which shows in the bold stylized simplicity of its theme and structure the hand of a writer with a complete mastery over her craft and materials. In *Silas Marner* George Eliot always knows what she is doing and attempts only what she is certain she can do. Since her range is wide, the story is not impoverished by the author's technical self-awareness, and it is certainly not without daring. There is perceptible, however, even in its clear-sighted, smoothly achieved purposefulness, a recognition of the limitations of her chosen setting and society — a growing impatience, perhaps, with the familiar subjects she has mastered so easily and is about to relinquish.[1] Raveloe as a particular place in the Midlands still figures significantly in the narrative but without the nostalgia, enchantment, or even the exasperated affection which she had attached in turn to Shepperton, Hayslope, and St. Ogg's. It is presented with a cool, discerning humor and in a perspective that calmly balances the shortcomings of old-fashioned village life against its compensations. The rustic charm of the earlier books is profusely undercut here, but not, as in *The Mill on the Floss*, by the confining rigidity of provincial morals or the economic and social problems of a stirring society. In *Silas Marner* the dominant characteristics of the country are grossness, laxness, and dullness of mind and spirit. The emphasis, which in its consistency, assurance, and deliberateness marks a departure for George Eliot, derives as much from a fully developed sense of independence, emotional and intellectual, of the provincial milieu as from a pose of detachment cultivated for purely aesthetic reasons.

Silas Marner is not as ambitious a work as *The Mill on the Floss*: it does not strive as urgently for profound truths or raise for both author and reader issues as complicated and elusive. Above all, it

[1] Cf. Thomson, "The Theme of Alienation in *Silas Marner*," *Nineteenth-Century Fiction*, XX (June 1965): "To convey a more genuinely tragic vision of life, George Eliot had to suggest vaster, less easily discernible or accessible sanctions and powers than Maggie's conscience or the petty tyranny of St. Ogg's society. She had to find a way of portraying characters ill-attuned to the ruling conditions of the world, a way of putting more inscrutability into the operation of human destinies" (p. 71); "In *Silas Marner*, George Eliot succeeded in selecting and organizing precisely the ingredients required for her special concept of tragedy ... the weaver is her first full study of alienation ..." (p. 74).

is less personal; or rather, the author's own impulses and concerns are so perfectly accommodated to the narrative medium that no uneasiness or cleavage of the kind that mars the earlier novel can be found here. She has worked out and understood her feelings for the environment of her youth and, having rationalized and distilled her attachment to regional life, is now ready to move beyond it. After *Romola*, which proved to be a false start, she expands the scope of her regionalism and comes to concentrate on its general, universal potentialities.

George Eliot's new sense of ease and freedom in manipulating her materials is most clearly apparent in the directness and concentration with which she handles the time-span of *Silas Marner* (thirty years — longer than in any of her other books) and in the fluency with which she intertwines the novel's two plots — her first real attempt of this kind. As in *The Mill on the Floss*, she puts an intensified stress on subjective experience, but the links she makes between the tangible and intangible, between the material aspects of life and the moral, psychological, supernatural (or religious) ones, now have consistency and assurance.[2] In *The Mill on the Floss*, as I have argued, the balance is upset. Accompanying and perhaps resulting from the richness of psychological description and vivid particularization, is a conspicuous lack of specificity in the depiction of setting and occupation. The opening vista of the mill, with the town and the sea-going ships in the distance, is indistinct and hazy; the account of St. Ogg's itself is general. We never see precisely, intimately, as we do in *Adam Bede*, how the characters make their living — perhaps because in most cases work does not have the same profound importance for them. The details of the lawsuit that ruins the Tullivers are really irrelevant and therefore remain unexplained. Tom's venture with Bob Jakin into the export of "Laceham goods" to the Continent is also passed over rather quickly, though not as quickly as are his other "trading adventures." His rise in business is summarily treated throughout. The little we know of its high-

---

[2] See also Thomson on the "neat balance of realism and quasi-supernaturalism" (p. 72) in *Silas Marner*. Similarly, in "Structure and Quality in *Silas Marner*," *Studies in English Literature,1500–1900*, VI (1966), 720, Ian Milner writes: "In the tension between the 'legendary' and the 'realistic' components, considered in their joint relation to the structure of values unfolded in the tale, lies [the book's] full meaning and appeal."

lights comes mainly from generalized accounts or indirect allusions like Stephen's "They think of doing something for young Tulliver: he saved them from a considerable loss by riding home in some marvelous way . . ." Similar vagueness appears in trifling matters; for example, the wares that Maggie sells at the charity bazaar are with Jamesian fastidiousness referred to as "certain large plain articles."

Such a lack of particularity was almost unthinkable in *Adam Bede*; and *Silas Marner*, with its specific impressions of places and activity, its selective but concrete visualization, recalls the manner of the early novel. But the resemblance between the two books should not be overemphasized, for Raveloe is a different sort of village from Hayslope, and it is presented to us through a very different set of eyes. In *Silas Marner* the coordination of naturalistic and symbolic details is much more insistent and elaborate than in *Adam Bede*, and the exposition and background are strictly functional. The narrator, who does not intrude so blatantly into the story, is not as fond of the locale or the way of life as in the earlier novel. Thus the selection of details is not only much more rigorous but is directed by another, more impersonal and objective purpose: to create an atmosphere of material slackness, moral crudity, and spiritual torpor in the midst of a lavish landscape and a stable, hierarchical community — but a community that is closely knit without being benign or edifying.

The detachment and generalizing perspective that the narrator consistently maintains are well suited to the story of alienation and readjustment. They reinforce the distance between Silas and the village society and make clear their mutual ignorance and fear; they also show up the flaws of each by juxtaposing the intense withdrawal and yearning of the lapsed Dissenter to the rich but uninspired rusticity of Raveloe. Much of the time Silas is seen through the suspicions of the people in the village, but since they are themselves described from the outside, as it were, we are not asked to share, or even to trust, their point of view. Indeed the direct disclosure of the weaver's true background and character at the beginning of the story effectively undercuts their superstitious conjectures. From the very outset the narrator and the reader are elevated above the action and characters, and Raveloe as well as Silas are introduced

only after a brief survey in Chapter I of bygone days, peasant ignorance and parochialism, and the exotic air attached at that time
to itinerant weavers. General as this account is, it is also extremely
pointed and concise in its foreshadowing of the events of the narrative: Silas's appearance, loss of faith, and his situation in the village are all anticipated in the apparently neutral mention of "certain
pallid undersized men, who, by the side of the brawny countryfolk,
looked like remnants of a disinherited race." Thus, too, his alienness
and his reputation for sorcery are indirectly suggested as well as
the themes of communal closeness and family roots ("how was a
man to be explained unless you at least knew somebody who knew
his father and mother?") that will be so important in the rest of
the story.

The first description of Raveloe, which immediately follows that
survey and the account of Silas, is also filled with pregnant hints.
Initially it evokes simply a rural setting, fertile, pleasant, comfortable:

> And Raveloe was a village where many of the old echoes
> lingered, undrowned by new voices. Not that it was one of those
> barren parishes lying on the outskirts of civilisation — inhabited
> by meagre sheep and thinly-scattered shepherds: on the con-
> trary, it lay in the rich central plain of what we are pleased to
> call Merry England, and held farms which, speaking from a
> spiritual point of view, paid highly desirable tithes. But it was
> nestled in a snug well-wooded hollow, quite an hour's journey
> on horseback from any turnpike, where it was never reached
> by the vibrations of the coach-horn, or of public opinion.

Gradually, however, the irony of the tone, lightly scornful and patronizing, insinuates into the account a suggestion of undirected
lives, sloth, and prodigality:

> It was an important-looking village, with a fine old church and
> large churchyard in the heart of it, and two or three large brick-
> and-stone homesteads, with well-walled orchards and orna-
> mental weathercocks, standing close upon the road, and lifting
> more imposing fronts than the rectory, which peeped from
> among the trees on the other side of the churchyard: — a vil-
> lage which showed at once the summits of its social life, and
> told the practised eye that there was no great park and manor-
> house in the vicinity, but that there were several chiefs in

Raveloe who could farm badly quite at their ease, drawing enough money from their bad farming, in those war times, to live in a rollicking fashion, and keep a jolly Christmas, Whitsun, and Easter tide. (Chapter I)

The distraught and bewildered weaver is an obviously strange figure amid rural surroundings, but the earthiness of Raveloe, relaxed, self-indulgent, opposed in almost every particular to the only life he has ever known — the dark, earnest fervor of working-class Dissent — intensifies the incongruity. As the narrative unfolds and we learn of his tragedy of injustice, religious disillusionment, and exile, the impression of the village as a coarse and thoroughly dull place gathers strength. Prosperous and congenial as it is, Raveloe is incapable of awakening Silas out of his apathy or casting light on his confusion:

> And what could be more unlike that Lantern Yard world than the world in Raveloe? — orchards looking lazy with neglected plenty; the large church in the wide churchyard, which men gazed at lounging in their own doors in service-time; the purple-faced farmers jogging along the lanes or turning in at the Rainbow; homesteads, where men supped heavily and slept in the light of the evening hearth, and where women seemed to be laying up a stock of linen for the life to come. There were no lips in Raveloe from which a word could fall that would stir Silas Marner's benumbed faith to a sense of pain. (Chapter II)

The large view gradually gives way to particular description, but the account of the house and manner of life of the leading family in the village supports with revealing details the atmosphere of slovenliness and intemperance evoked at the outset. With ironic condescension, George Eliot places Squire Cass in a broad historical and social context:

> It was still that glorious war-time which was felt to be a peculiar favour of Providence towards the landed interest, and the fall of prices had not yet come to carry the race of small squires and yeomen down that road to ruin for which extravagant habits and bad husbandry were plentifully anointing their wheels . . . Raveloe lay low among the bushy trees and the rutted lanes, aloof from the currents of industrial energy and Puritan earnestness: the rich ate and drank freely, accepting gout and apoplexy as things that ran mysteriously in re-

spectable families, and the poor thought that the rich were entirely in the right of it to lead a jolly life . . . (Chapter III)

Although the shabby, dispirited interior of the Squire's home and his improvident economy are casually attributed to his widowed state, they reflect appropriately and with intensified force the laxness prevailing in the village. The Red House is the center of social activity in Raveloe,[3] just as the Hall Farm is in Hayslope. To grasp the difference between the two places, between the two kinds of rural life, and, in part, between *Silas Marner* and *Adam Bede*, we need only compare the descriptions of the two establishments. The first real look we get at the Cass household, with its stress on disorder and brutish inertia, contrasts depressingly with our memory of the neat, bright, cheerful, and active life of the Poysers (the contrast with the genteel elegance of Donnithorne Chase is even greater):[4] "The fading grey light fell dimly on the walls decorated with guns, whips, and foxes' brushes, on coats and hats flung on the chairs, on tankards sending forth a scent of flat ale, and on a half-choked fire, with pipes propped up in the chimney-corners: signs of a domestic life destitute of any hallowing charm . . ." (Chapter III).

Squire Cass's inconsistent and imprudent management of affairs, irascible relations with his sons, and parochial conceit round out the impression of domestic waste and squalor, and the whole atmosphere is illustrated in the events, conversations and gatherings (such as the conclave at the Rainbow and the New Year's dance) that follow the introductory expositions. Godfrey's one interview with his father, for example, is full of vivid details that enrich our sense of the life in Raveloe. The pervasive disorganization, waste-

---

[3] But cf. Thomson: "The real social center of Raveloe is . . . not Red House but the Rainbow . . ." (p. 83). In the sense that no crowds of villagers troop daily through the Squire's home, this is, of course, true, but it is still the Squire who in his behavior and establishment sets the social pattern in the village. Also, as the largest landowner and wealthiest citizen, he represents the local economic power as well as the social elite. Thus, in spite of its "rundown and gloomy" state (Thomson, p. 83), the Red House must still be considered central in the social life of Raveloe.

[4] The class difference that might invalidate my comparison of the Poyser and Cass households actually operates in its favor: not only is the gap between the two much smaller than between the Poysers and the Donnithornes, but the Poysers, in spite of their yeoman and tenant status, manage much more impressively than the Casses, who aspire to the rank of squires.

fulness, and bad temper seem to be concentrated in the Squire's character and appearance as well as his home:

> Every one breakfasted at a different hour in the Red House, and the Squire was always the latest, giving a long chance to a rather feeble morning appetite before he tried it. The table had been spread with substantial eatables nearly two hours before he presented himself — a tall, stout man of sixty, with a face in which the knit brow and rather hard glance seemed contradicted by the slack and feeble mouth. His person showed marks of habitual neglect, his dress was slovenly; and yet there was something in the presence of the old Squire distinguishable from that of the ordinary farmers in the parish, who were perhaps every whit as refined as he, but, having slouched their way through life with a consciousness of being in the vicinity of their "betters," wanted that self-possession and authoritativeness of voice and carriage which belonged to a man who thought of superiors as remote existences with whom he had personally little more to do than with America or the stars. The Squire had been used to parish homage all his life, used to the presupposition that his family, his tankards, and everything that was his, were the oldest and best; and as he never associated with any gentry higher than himself, his opinion was not disturbed by comparison. (Chapter IX)

As father and son face each other, their uneasy relationship and the coarse, undisciplined, ungenerous lavishness of their domestic habits are indicated with unobtrusive distinctness. The author's ear for living speech, her shrewd psychological insight and instinct for the significant physical detail are conspicuous in even a brief quotation:

> "Ah! well," said the Squire, throwing himself indifferently into his chair, and speaking in a ponderous coughing fashion, which was felt in Raveloe to be a sort of privilege of his rank, while he cut a piece of beef, and held it up before the deerhound that had come in with him. "Ring the bell for my ale, will you? You youngsters' business is your own pleasure, mostly. There's no hurry about it for anybody but yourselves."
> The Squire's life was quite as idle as his sons', but it was a fiction kept up by himself and his contemporaries in Raveloe that youth was exclusively the period of folly, and that their aged wisdom was constantly in a state of endurance mitigated by sarcasm. Godfrey waited, before he spoke again, until the ale had been brought and the door closed — an interval during

which Fleet, the deer-hound, had consumed enough bits of beef to make a poor man's holiday dinner. (Chapter IX)

ii

Squire Cass, whose appearance and that of his parlor so well embody the nature of Raveloe, whose temperament and conduct reflect the essential spirit of the place, is thus presented as a distinctively local type. The representative significance of his character is supported by the completeness with which his life, position, and self-estimation are rooted within the sheltered confines of the district; and it is decisively confirmed by the repeated contrast of his establishment with that of the Lammeters. The interesting thing about this opposition is not so much the frequency with which it occurs as the way in which it is made: in each case the exemplary ways of the Lammeters that redeem Raveloe from total slovenliness are seen as a remarkable exception. It is the Squire who sets the dominant tone, and the entire village (although it shares the general faults of the Casses) hopes for a match between Godfrey Cass and Nancy Lammeter as a sort of salvation of its first family. The common feeling is that "if she could come to be mistress at the Red House, there would be a fine change, for the Lammeters had been brought up in that way, that they never suffered a pinch of salt to be wasted, and yet everybody in their household had of the best, according to his place. Such a daughter-in-law would be a saving to the old Squire . . ." (Chapter III). That the saving is to be not merely material is suggested by the diction and imagery of Godfrey's thoughts about Nancy. As he yearns for her wholesomeness and redemptive influence, the mortification of his secret marriage (at the time, an apparently inextricable trap) and the disheveled gloom of his own home cause "the neatness, purity, and liberal orderliness of the Lammeter household, sunned by the smile of Nancy, to seem like those fresh bright hours of the morning when temptations go to sleep and leave the ear open to the voice of the good angel, inviting to industry, sobriety, and peace" (Chapter III).

As if to illustrate the rare excellence of his management, Mr. Lammeter's physical appearance, as singular in Raveloe as Squire Cass's is representative, is distinguished from the regional type: "His spare but healthy person, and high-featured firm face, that looked as if it had never been flushed by excess, was in strong contrast, not only with the Squire's, but with the appearance of the Raveloe farmers generally . . ." (Chapter XI). The regularity and enlightened discipline of the Lammeters do indeed transform the Red House after Nancy finally marries Godfrey. When we see it again in Part Two, fifteen years have passed since we caught our first glimpse of it, and it now bears the signs of Nancy's regimen:

> A great change has come over the dark wainscoted parlour since we saw it in Godfrey's bachelor days, and under the wife-less reign of the old Squire. Now all is polish, on which no yesterday's dust is ever allowed to rest, from the yard's width of oaken boards round the carpet, to the old Squire's gun and whips and walking-sticks, ranged on the stag's antlers above the mantelpiece. All other signs of sporting and outdoor oc-cupation Nancy has removed to another room; but she has brought into the Red House the habit of filial reverence, and preserves sacredly in a place of honour these relics of her hus-band's departed father. The tankards are on the side-table still, but the bossed silver is undimmed by handling, and there are no dregs to send forth unpleasant suggestions: the only prevailing scent is of the lavender and rose-leaves that fill the vases of Derbyshire spar. All is purity and order in this once dreary room, for, fifteen years ago, it was entered by a new presiding spirit. (Chapter XVII)

The change is real and for the best, yet if we compare this account with that of the Hall Farm interior in *Adam Bede*, we are at once struck by the reticence and sparseness with which George Eliot now describes a pleasant rural dwelling. Her economy and functional dispatch are dictated here not merely by the pall of disappointed childlessness that slightly dims Nancy and Godfrey's contentment, but also by the distance that she has moved since she waxed lyrical over the Poyser household and delighted in the largely happy life of Loamshire.

The chastened outlook and psychological emphasis, which are already prominent in *The Mill on the Floss* and which George Eliot later develops to dominance in *Felix Holt, Middlemarch,* and *Daniel Deronda,* can thus be seen behind the new attention with which she observes country life; they explain, at least in part, the stress in *Silas Marner* on the negligence and coarseness that mar the abundance and cohesiveness of rural society. The acerbic wit and aggressive feminism of Priscilla Lammeter, for example, jar unpleasantly, especially when we remember how amiable these qualities seemed in Mrs. Poyser. The fact that Priscilla is a spinster, while it need not have any precise sinister significance, does contribute, together with Nancy's childlessness, to the emotional bleakness of this world when contrasted with the world of *Adam Bede*. And it is difficult to ignore the difference between Mrs. Poyser's dairy, which is described in loving detail, and Nancy's dairy, which we never actually see. In *Adam Bede*, the dairy's cleanliness and beauty are hymned, and it is prized for itself as well as for its profit; in *Silas Marner*, Priscilla, with characteristic decision and energy, recommends it to Nancy for its therapeutic value:

> "There's nothing like a dairy if folks want a bit o' worrit to make the days pass. For as for rubbing furniture, when you can once see your face in a table there's nothing else to look for; but there's always something fresh with the dairy; for even in the depths o' winter there's some pleasure in conquering the butter, and making it come whether or no. My dear," added Priscilla, pressing her sister's hand affectionately as they walked side by side, "you'll never be low when you've got a dairy." (Chapter XVII)

The limited power of the Lammeters' bright competence and moral direction, which is indicated by their singularity in the village and by the underlying thread of melancholy that persists in the Red House, is confirmed by the fact that Raveloe's way of life has not been noticeably elevated by the reformation of the Cass household. The draining of the Stone-pit, which, together with Godfrey's other agricultural improvements, might perhaps have signified a resurgence of purposeful energy on a wide scale, is really no more than a device to disclose at last the identity and fate of the thief who fifteen years earlier had taken Silas Marner's gold. There is no sign that similar activity is going on elsewhere in the district, or that the dominant tone of local affairs and social intercourse has been in any way disciplined or purified.[5] Eppie's innocence and grace are attributed to the

---

[5] But cf. Thomson, who writes that as Godfrey Cass "restores the farm to stable prosperity the whole village recovers order and bloom" (p. 83). I think that Thomson mistakes the mood of much of the story's second part for the sub-

tender and peculiar love with which Silas had reared her in almost inseparable companionship with himself, aided by the seclusion of their dwelling, [which] had preserved her from the lowering influences of the village talk and habits, and had kept her mind in that freshness which is sometimes falsely supposed to be an invariable attribute of rusticity. (Chapter XVI)

In *Adam Bede*, the reminder of rustic crudeness, made in such a detached and humorless way, would have been practically unthinkable. It is almost an open acknowledgment of the difference between two two books, and underlines the dubiousness of regarding *Silas Marner* as merely a charming rustic idyll, a recreation of "the world of childhood and youth." [6]

Raveloe, then, remains unreformed, and if Nancy Lammeter, through her influence on Godfrey, fails to effect any general refinement, it is because her spiritual and material regularity, which sets the standard of excellence in the region, is not irradiated by any transfiguring impulse. Her principles are firm and righteous, and she applies them in a clear-headed way, but as the voice of provincial conscience at its best, she lacks the profound assurance and spontaneity of Mrs. Poyser or the imaginative thrust and enlightened impatience of Maggie Tulliver. Nancy, like Maggie, has an ethic of her own, one which her own moral instincts and the inadequacy of her culture have impelled her to stitch together. Her "religious theory," however, "pieced together out of narrow social traditions, fragments of church doctrine imperfectly understood, and girlish reasonings on her small experience," is not romantically inspired or strikingly heroic like Maggie's but resembles (at least in her resistance to the idea of adoption) "that of many devout people whose beliefs are held in the shape of a system quite remote from her knowledge" (Chapter XVII). She is sensitive, if not remarkably so (we recall her slight failure of sympathy with Silas in Chapter XIX), benign, upright, and genuinely conscientious, as her scrupulous, remniscent

---

stance. No real changes take place in the life of the village as a whole. The sense of coarseness, laxity, irascibility, and pettiness is still there at the end of the book, but it is overshadowed by the subdued happiness that Silas is allowed to enjoy. For a more enthusiastic view of the quality of life in Raveloe, see the fine essay by Q. D. Leavis (which I came upon too late to make use of its insights here) introducing the Penguin edition (1967) of the novel.

[6] Leavis, *The Great Tradition*, p. 46.

self-questioning in Chapter XVII shows. But the spiritual barrenness of her society and the haphazard and motley nature of her ethical beliefs restrict the efficacy of her virtues and obscure their impressiveness. The authority of the rural tradition, as she represents it, thus seems rather insecure, a little petty in its orderliness and decidedly short-sighted in its rigidity:

> It was as necessary to her mind to have an opinion on all topics, not exclusively masculine, that had come under her notice, as for her to have a precisely marked place for every article of her personal property: and her opinions were always principles to be unwaveringly acted on. They were firm, not because of their basis, but because she held them with a tenacity inseparable from her mental action. On all the duties and proprieties of life, from filial behaviour to the arrangements of the evening toilet, pretty Nancy Lammeter, by the time she was three-and-twenty, had her unalterable little code, and had formed every one of her habits in strict accordance with that code. (Chapter XVII)

The kindly condescending tone of this passage (evident particularly in the deflating Popean equation "from filial behaviour to the arrangement of the evening toilet" and in the diminutives applied to Nancy) reveals the distance between the author and character and emphasizes the want of sublimity and moral distinction in Nancy's world. Her meticulous, rigid, but not unfeeling integrity seems to be the best that provincial life can produce in the way of standards.

iii

Yet in spite of the atmosphere of pervasive mediocrity, George Eliot clearly is not hostile to Raveloe, nor does she intend that we should despise the weak, petty, and quarrelsome rustics that people the book. Once again, only this time with much more justification, she is striving to demonstrate the human importance, poignancy, and drama of the commonplace. "These fellow-mortals, every one, must be accepted as they are," she wrote in *Adam Bede*, "you can neither straighten their noses, nor brighten their wit, nor rectify their dispositions . . . It is so needful we should remember their existence, else we may happen to leave them quite out of our religion and philosophy, and frame lofty theories which only fit a world of extremes." In *Silas Marner*, the author's and the reader's tolerance for crooked noses, dull wits, and cantankerous dispositions is stretched further than in any of her other novels, and in the end, through a highlighting of the latent and redeeming human instincts for fellowship, love, and purposefulness, the tolerance is turned to sympathy. This movement begins with Silas Marner's intrusion into the village and our consciousness of the positive aspects of the contrast between Lantern Yard and Raveloe; it gathers force in Silas's attachment to Eppie, and rises to a sacramental climax in the wedding at the end, which celebrates the long-delayed integration of the alien weaver into the community as well as the marriage of the foundling who is the instrument of that integration.

But the second plot of the novel also exemplifies a qualified redemption of ordinary and fallible humanity; it, too, is related, perhaps even more directly than the first, to the flaws in the environment. For Silas, ignorant and confused as he is, moves, even in his passion for gold, on a more intense and heroic emotional plane than the villagers; but Godfrey Cass, the protagonist of the subplot, embodies in himself the very failings of the community as well as its potential virtues. Strong, healthy, energetic, and good-hearted, he is also undisciplined and indecisive, directed by impulse rather than informed purposefulness and self-control. "His easy disposition" is a natural foil to Silas's narrow and passionate dedication (whether to the faith that he loses, the gold that is stolen from him, or the child that stumbles into his cottage and responds to his love). Where Silas is miserly and abstemious, Godfrey is wasteful and self-indulgent, where Silas is a recluse, Godfrey, though not a complete rake, is gregarious and dissolute. Yet both begin as social outcasts: the weaver because of his strangeness and the young Squire, in his own mind at least, because of his degrading marriage. Their lives are strangely intertwined, and the prodigality and sin of the one are made not only to recoil against him but also to reward the suffering, the emotional craving and spiritual need, of the other. Godfrey's unacknowledged child becomes Silas Marner's link with society and the means of his salvation; eventually she reconciles both men, in their distinct ways, to the significance of their past lives.[7]

[7] The connection between Silas and Godfrey has also been noticed by Robert B. Heilman, in "Return to Raveloe: Thirty-Five Years After," *English Journal*, XLIV (1957), 1–10, and Jerome Thale, in his Introduction to *Silas Marner* (Rinehart Editions, 1962), pp. xv-xvi, xix-xxi. I cannot help feeling that Ian

With his good intentions and wavering will, Godfrey Cass is an appropriately fallible figure; his flaws are common human imperfections, and it is on his behalf that George Eliot makes her characteristic plea for understanding and compassion and insists on the moral drama played out in the most obscure lives:

> The subtle and varied pains springing from the higher sensibility that accompanies higher culture, are perhaps less pitiable than that dreary absence of impersonal enjoyment and consolation which leaves ruder minds to the perpetual urgent companionship of their own griefs and discontents. The lives of those rural forefathers, whom we are apt to think very prosaic figures — men whose only work was to ride round their land, getting heavier and heavier in their saddles, and who passed the rest of their days in the half-listless gratification of senses dulled by monotony — had a certain pathos in them nevertheless. (Chapter III)

She elaborates this insight, evoking a genuine sympathy for "these flushed and dull-eyed men," whose only hope of visionary excitement, of access to "purity, order, and calm," is precariously dependent on a woman's elevating affection. Before he marries Nancy — when indeed he has no real hope of marrying her — Godfrey wastes his life in what George Eliot now regards as the prevailing routine of country squires, the monotonous alternation between anger and dissipation. His own better instincts, however, preserve him from utter degradation; as she says, he is one of those "whom — thanks to their native human-kindness — even riot could never drive into brutality" (Chapter III). Thus it is the pathos of his position that she stresses when she describes the psychological corruption to which Godfrey, with all his admirable qualities, has made himself

---

Milner, in the generally perceptive essay already cited, allows his ideological preconceptions to distort the nature of the link between Silas and Godfrey. Believing their relationship to manifest George Eliot's interest in class conflict in the contrast between "folk" and "bourgeois" values, he takes a harsher view of the young squire than the author herself. His language, moreover, seems to me extreme: "Godfrey and Silas are fatal opposites brought into a fatal conjunction. The thematic development of Marner's loss and recovery of his humanity is counterpointed with the stages of Cass's moral deception and defeat" (p. 725). The best treatment of the relationship between Silas and Godfrey is to be found in David R. Carroll's "*Silas Marner*: Reversing the Oracles of Religion," *Literary Monographs*, ed. Eric Rothstein and Thomas K. Dunseath (Madison, Milwaukee, and London, 1967), I, 165–200 — an excellent essay which I read too late to apply to the present work.

susceptible. Her pity and understanding act to soften not his delinquency but our attitude to him, so that we become concerned about his predicament even though it seems squalid:

> The yoke a man creates for himself by wrong-doing will breed hate in the kindliest nature; and the good-humoured, affectionate-hearted Godfrey Cass was fast becoming a bitter man, visited by cruel wishes, that seemed to enter, and depart, and enter again, like demons who had found in him a ready-garnished home. (Chapter III)

There are no comparable explicit apologies for the low moral tone of Raveloe, but here also, in spite of the village's glaring imperfections, George Eliot guides the reader's feelings away from disdain and toward sympathy — though never toward the enchanted affection and admiration with which she depicts Hayslope. It is near the end of Part One, with Mrs. Winthrop's first visit to Silas's cottage (Chapter X) and, much more decisively, with the condensed account of the weaver's joyous tribulations with the growing Eppie and his awakening responsiveness to his surroundings, that our feelings about the community begin to alter. The community itself, however, is not different at this stage from what it had been earlier. In Chapter X, for example, when Dolly Winthrop comes to comfort Silas (who, desolate after the loss of his gold, is no longer feared by his neighbors but pitied "as a 'poor mushed creatur' "), the villagers are still described as relaxed in their churchgoing, gluttonous in their celebrations, and petty in their relations with one another. After the requisite Christmas Day service, "the red faces [make] their way through the black biting frost to their own homes, feeling themselves free for the rest of the day to eat, drink, and be merry, and using that Christian freedom without diffidence." And Squire Cass's New Year's Eve dance brings together "all the society of Raveloe and Tarley, whether old acquaintances separated by misunderstandings concerning run-away calves, or acquaintances founded on intermittent condescension."

But at the same time that she continues to mock the loose habits and trivial minds of the villagers, George Eliot also begins to show them in a more flattering light. The crucial indication of the change is the "kindlier feeling" with which his neighbors come to regard the disconsolate weaver. Mr. Macey, crusty, complacent, and self-centered, is one spokesman of the general sentiments after Silas's loss; Mrs. Winthrop is another. Her solicitude, "simple theology," and quaint good sense show that the village mentality is capable of transcending its ordinary level. She is actually called a "good wholesome woman" and she personifies, in her quickness of feeling and readiness to help, the ties of fellowship and communal warmth that the monotony, abrasiveness, and slackness of daily intercouse tend to obscure or wear away:

> . . . she was in all respects a woman of scrupulous conscience, so eager for duties that life seemed to offer them too scantily unless she rose at half-past four . . . Yet she had not the vixenish temper which is sometimes supposed to be a necessary condition of such habits: she was a very mild, patient woman, whose nature it was to seek out all the sadder and more serious elements of life, and pasture her mind upon them. (Chapter X)

Although there is something almost compulsive about Mrs. Winthrop's restless good nature — her benevolence seems to wear the protective coloring of eccentricity, a little in the manner of Dickensian "do-gooders" like Mr. Jarndyce — she does help to save Raveloe from complete disgrace in the eyes of the author and reader. If Godfrey Cass has redeeming qualities, so has the village as a whole, and Dolly Winthrop embodies them.

But the emphasis on the congenial aspects of rural life that becomes apparent as the villagers respond to Silas's isolation does not cancel out the earlier ironic presentation of its dreary side. The community remains essentially the same, but the author now provides it with an opportunity to demonstrate its humanity, good will, and potential for genuine sociability, which serve to soften, if not erase, our awareness of its crudeness. The movement to elicit the reader's sympathy for the village becomes conspicuous in Chapter X, gains impetus in Chapter XIV (the penultimate chapter in Part One), and reaches its height in Part Two, where Silas Marner's assimilation is amply demonstrated and connected with his past. It is clear that George Eliot, in spite of her ironic presentation of the flaws of Raveloe, approves of Silas's progressive affiliation with its life. She shows systematically how his participation in social intercourse humanizes him; at the same time, quite naturally and without contradicting her previous characterizations, she brings to light the warmth and friendliness of the residents of the village. As

Silas appears in church for the first time and shares "in the observances held sacred by his neighbours," as Eppie creates "fresh and
fresh links between his life and the lives from which he had hitherto
shrunk," we become aware, together with him, of "the ties and chari-
ties that bound together the families of his neighbours" (Chapter
XIV).

The interest that the villagers take in Eppie and, through her,
in Silas makes them appear much more amicable than they did
earlier. And their aroused benevolence, corresponding to Silas's revived attentiveness to his environment, imbues the copious, untidy
land with the radiance of human affection:

> Hitherto he had been treated very much as if he had been a use-
> ful gnome or brownie — a queer and unaccountable creature,
> who must necessarily be looked at with wondering curiosity and
> repulsion . . . But now Silas met with open smiling faces and
> cheerful questioning, as a person whose satisfactions and diffi-
> culties could be understood. Everywhere he must sit a little and
> talk about the child, and words of interest were always ready
> for him: "Ah, Master Marner, you'll be lucky if she takes the
> measles soon and easy!" . . . Elderly masters and mistresses,
> seated observantly in large kitchen arm-chairs, shook their
> heads over the difficulties attendant on rearing children, felt
> Eppie's round arms and legs, and pronounced them remarkably
> firm, and told Silas that, if she turned out well (which, however,
> there was no telling), it would be a fine thing for him to have
> a steady lass to do for him when he got helpless . . . No child
> was afraid of approaching Silas when Eppie was near him:
> there was no repulsion around him now, either for young or
> old; for the little child had come to link him once more with the
> whole world. There was love between him and the child that
> blent them into one, and there was love between the child and
> the world — from men and women with parental looks and
> tones, to the red lady-birds and the round pebbles.[8] (Chapter
> XIV)

It is significant that after this point in the narrative the two
social occasions that occur in Part Two stand in striking contrast to
the conversation at the Rainbow and the dance at the Red House:
both take place around the church, and though the second presently
shifts to the Rainbow, the occasion, Eppie's wedding-feast, is still

---

[8] The passage (especially in its climax and conclusion) resonantly echoes and
confirms the epigraph of the book from Wordsworth's "Michael": ". . . a child,
more than all other gifts/That earth can offer to declining man,/Brings hope
with it, and forward-looking thoughts . . ."

a sacrosanct one. The difference between the group scenes in Part One and Part Two does not signify a change or refinement in the rustic temper, but rather sustains a mood appropriate to the affirmation of social ties and coherence. At the very end there is indeed an apparent acknowledgement of the familiar strain of grossness and pugnacity that persists but is for the moment absorbed by the genial spirit of Silas's triumph:

> In the open yard before the Rainbow the party of guests were already assembled, though it was still nearly an hour before the appointed feast-time. But by this means they could not only enjoy the slow advent of their pleasures; they had also ample leisure to talk of Silas Marner's strange history, and arrive by due degrees at the conclusion that he had brought a blessing on himself by acting like a father to a lone motherless child. Even the farrier did not negative this sentiment: on the contrary, he took it up as peculiarly his own, and invited any hardy person present to contradict him. But he met with no contradiction; and all differences among the company were merged in a general agreement with Mr. Snell's sentiment, that when a man had deserved his good luck, it was the part of his neighbours to wish him joy. (Conclusion)

The inconspicuous way in which George Eliot here succeeds — through the guests' reminiscences about Silas's history, their open declaration of the story's moral, and their veiled benediction — in reinforcing the sense of a completed narrative does not dim the echo of the first Rainbow scene and its argumentative nature. The rural character responds to conviviality and ceremony, but its gnarled bluntness is incorrigible.[9]

iv

So far I have been chiefly concerned with the realistic aspects of *Silas Marner*, with the more or less naturalistic presentation of rural society. I have suggested that the view of regional life that we get

[9] In his Introduction to the Rinehart Edition, Thale writes that "the portrait of Raveloe life is relatively free of pastoral glamorization. The famous Rainbow scene may suggest community, but it also suggests dullness and bad temper. Silas may gain happiness by his reintegration, but the community which he becomes part of is neither ideal nor idealized" (p. xiii). Milner emphasizes mainly "the warmth and vitality of the Raveloe popular community," its "pulsing communal life" (p. 720).

here is strangely caustic, particularly when set against the predominantly favorable tone of George Eliot's earlier novels. At the same time, however, we have seen that there is no real antagonism in her picture of Raveloe. The movement of the novel is in part directed to bring out the capacity of a most mediocre and complacent community to respond to the personal distress, to satisfy the emotional needs and spiritual craving of an alien, exceptionally intense nature. But with all the damaging disclosures about the real character of rusticity, its latent depth and possible contentment cannot be made significant and credible by conventionally direct and concrete narrative methods alone. Moreover, while George Eliot wishes to show the rural coarseness transcended, it is important to her purpose, I believe, that we never forget it altogether. For she is now primarily interested not in singing the praises of pastoral life but in dramatizing the universal aspects of the human condition that have always stirred her imagination. In *Silas Marner*, as to some extent in *The Mill on the Floss*, the themes of loneliness and fellowship, fallibility and forgiveness, the inescapable working of moral cause and effect, and above all, the need of guiding principles, the difficulty of faith, and the redemptive power of selfless love begin to dominate her work explicitly, irresistibly.[10] Amid such concerns, the particular failings of country life are made to appear essentially irrelevant and superficial. Thus, while the realistic portrait of Raveloe emphasizes narrowness, ignorance, crudity, even gluttonous dissipation, the dominant moral and psychological perspective reduces the importance of those vices. The portrait is based on an extraordinarily successful amalgam of realistic and symbolic techniques in order to show the impossibility of escaping the consequences of one's deeds, the interconnectedness of individual destinies, and the human need of sociality. The theme of the book is that "life is with people," regardless of how obscure and trivial they may be.

The fairy-tale quality of *Silas Marner*, which derives from the co-ordination of naturalism with a vaguely religious supernaturalism,

---

[10] Thale contrasts the deceptive simplicity and charm of the novel with the ambitiousness of its central concern: "an elaborate examination of human happiness" (p. ix). Although the contrast is a real one, Thale, simply by his way of putting it, exaggerates the importance in the novel of the "inquiry into the conditions of happiness" (p. xi). If there is such an inquiry, it arises almost incidentally out of the narrative.

has often been noticed. George Eliot indirectly acknowledged its supernatural element when she wrote to John Blackwood:

> I have felt all through as if the story would have lent itself best to metrical rather than prose fiction, especially in all that relates to the psychology of Silas; except that, under that treatment, there could not be an equal play of humour. It came to me first of all, quite suddenly, as a sort of legendary tale, suggested by my recollection of having once, in early childhood, seen a linen-weaver with a bag on his back; but, as my mind dwelt on the subject, I became inclined to a more realistic treatment. (*Letters*, III, 382)

But since the sense of supernatural contrivance remains conspicuous in the narrative, the "realistic treatment" of which George Eliot speaks in her letter never achieves decisive dominance. In part it is the condensed simplicity of the story's structure and its rich symbolic symmetry that indicate the control of Providence over human fate. The sheltered isolation of Raveloe separates it almost completely from the wider current of national life (of which we hear less in *Silas Marner* than in any of George Eliot's other fiction). The temporal setting ("In the days when spinning wheels hummed busily in the farmhouses," "In the early years of this century"), while not entirely vague, is also less precise than is usual in her work; and the few historical allusions that occur are extremly general in nature. The impression of indefiniteness thus created combines with the concentrated attention devoted to the twofold story to invest the recounted events with a heightened reality.

The main action is set with some precision between late November, when Dunsey Cass disappears with Silas's gold, and New Year's Eve, when Eppie crawls into Silas's cottage. After fifteen years in the parish, Silas's new life begins, appropriately, with the coming of a new year, and it is celebrated fifteen years later still, with Eppie's wedding, which takes place "when the great lilacs and laburnums in the old-fashioned gardens showed their golden and purple wealth above the lichen-tinted walls, and when there were calves still young enough to want bucketfuls of fragrant milk" (Conclusion). The spring wedding at the end is thus effectively set against the rain and darkness of the opening's raw autumn, when Silas loses his gold. The formal division of the books supports the juxtaposition, for Part One deals with the disappearance of the gold and the appearance of Eppie, while Part Two, fifteen years later, accounts for both. The disclosures are, of course, unimportant to the reader, who has been kept informed about almost everything from the outset. In this story, the author deliberately neglects all opportunities for conventional suspense and mystery. Dwelling no more than is necessary on the linking means, she chooses to stress instead cause and effect, the relentless working out of moral implications.

But there are more insistent indications of supernatural design than the somewhat stylized arrangement of the book. Dunsey's rash confidence in his good luck, for example, has a hubristic ring and recoils ironically against him. "I'm always lucky in my weather," he boasts to Godfrey. "You never hold trumps, you know — I always do. You've got the beauty, you see, and I've got the luck . . ." (Chapter III). As events show, of course, it is Godfrey who has the great and undeserved good luck, although he too cannot escape the consequence of his actions. Although his first wife's death and Silas's devotion to Eppie save him from disgrace and enable him to marry Nancy, he comes to regard his childlessness as a punishment for his "vicious folly" and disingenuousness: "Everything comes to light . . . sooner or later. When God Almighty wills it, our secrets are found out" (Chapter XVIII). After he reveals himself to Eppie and she refuses to leave Silas for him, Godfrey himself notes the justice of his situation: "I wanted to pass for childless once, Nancy — I shall pass for childless now against my wish" (Chapter XX).

But however qualified and incomplete his "good fortune" is, Godfrey is rewarded for his better nature and for the sensitivity, limited and irresolute though it is, with which he confronts his own character. His brother, a crude and dull egoist, is utterly without capacity for insight and introspection. When he stakes Godfrey's horse, Dunsey thinks himself fortunate in the absence of witnesses to his mishap, and regards the darkness and mist, which will presently cause him to slip to his death, as part of his good luck. As he begins to ransack Silas's cottage for the money that he guesses to be hidden there, he wonders quite mindlessly whether "the weaver had perhaps gone outside his cottage to fetch in the fuel . . . and had slipped into the Stone-pit." It never occurs to him that under the circumstances this may easily be his own fate, and he steals away still relishing his luck: "The rain and darkness had got thicker, and he was glad of it; though it was awkward walking with both hands filled, so that it was as much as he could do to grasp his whip along with one of the bags. But when he had gone a yard or two, he might take his time. So he stepped forward into the darkness" (Chapter IV). When Dunstan's skeleton is discovered fifteen years later, wedged between two stones in the pit, together with the bags of money and the whip (which he had taken from Godfrey), we recognize the ironic implications and resonance of that passage.

The signs of supernatural design, however, are most prominent in the story of Silas. Disillusioned in his faith and exiled from the Dissenting community in Lantern Yard because God did not intervene to vindicate him before his accusers, Silas lives for fifteen years as an alien in Raveloe, shunned for his strangeness and feared for his reputed ghostly powers. His passionate spirituality, even when in revulsion from religion it attaches itself to his gold, as well as his cataleptic trances, endow him with an extraordinary aura. And the author insistently strengthens this impression. When Silas comes to the Rainbow in search of help to find his gold, the company has been excitedly arguing about the existence of ghosts, and his appearance seems for a moment to settle the question. With his "strange unearthly eyes," he looks not like "Silas Marner in the flesh, but an apparition," and the landlord addresses him as if he were "adjuring the ghost" (Chapter VII). When Silas, with Eppie in his arms, comes to the Squire's house during the dance, he is again described as a ghost, "an apparition from the dead." And to Godfrey, who sees him first, "It *was* an apparition from that hidden life which lies, like a dark by-street, behind the goodly ornamented façade that meets the sunlight and the gaze of respectable admirers. It was his own child carried in Silas Marner's arms" (Chapter XIII).

The omens of supernatural ordinance and direction are most strikingly suggested in connection with Eppie's appearance in Silas's cottage and, to a lesser extent, the reaction to the theft that precedes it. We are made to feel in the account of the coincidences governing both events that nothing that happens is accidental, that everything is preordained by some supervisory agency and according to fixed moral laws. When Silas leaves his home unattended, he does not reckon with the possibility of such intervention: "What thief would find his way to the Stone-pits on such a night as this? and why should he come on this particular night, when he had never come through all the fifteen years before?" (Chapter V). Why, indeed, if not in fulfillment of some divine plan? That this is the case actually occurs to the disconsolate weaver when he returns to find his gold gone, but he is afraid of the suggestion and rejects it. The reticence with which his response is described is equivocal and almost supports the supernatural interpretation: "*Was* it a thief who had taken the bags? or was it a cruel power that no hands could reach, which had delighted in making him a second time desolate? He shrank from this vaguer dread, and fixed his mind with struggling effort on the robber with hands, who could be reached by hands" (Chapter V). Mr. Macey, however, and his adherents in the village arrive at the supernatural explanation independently and assert it with great vigor (Chapters VII, VIII, and X). And although the author mocks the simple-minded assurance of both sides in the running debate about the robbery, it is clear that the rational "advocates of the tinder-box-and-peddler view" are much further from the truth than "the adherents of the inexplicable." Even the rector, Mr. Crackenthorp, is not far wrong when he admonishes "Silas that his money had probably been taken from him because he thought too much of it" (Chapter X).

When Eppie finally toddles through Silas's open door, the insistent connection between her arrival and the loss of the gold makes it impossible to avoid the feeling that strings are being pulled here. If they are no more than aesthetic strings, they nevertheless suggest a larger, more comprehensive control: the author seems actually to urge on us the view that the concatenation of events is the work of an omniscient power. The nature of this power, however, she never tries to describe but leaves enigmatic, thus intensifying the sense of the transcendent mysteriousness of the world. It may be a coincidence that Eppie's mother dies near Silas's home, the door of which just happens to be open, or that Silas has one of his trances just as Eppie, attracted by the light from his fire, stumbles inside the cottage, but we are discouraged by the whole tenor of the book from regarding these circumstances as merely fortuitous. The author describes the incident as if there was something fateful and predetermined about it:

But where was Silas Marner while this strange visitor had come to his hearth? He was in the cottage, but he did not see the child. During the last few weeks, since he had lost his money, he had contracted the habit of opening his door and looking out from time to time, as if he thought that his money might be somehow coming back to him . . . Since the on-coming of twilight he had opened his door again and again, though only to shut it immediately at seeing all distance veiled by the falling snow. But the last time he opened it the snow had ceased, and the clouds were parting here and there. He stood and listened, and gazed for a long while — there was really something on the road coming towards him then, but he caught no sign of it . . . He went in again, and put his right hand on the latch of the door to close it — but he did not close it: he was arrested, as he had been already since his loss, by the invisible wand of catalepsy, and stood like a graven image, with wide but sightless eyes, holding open his door, powerless to resist either the good or evil that might enter there. (Chapter XII)

When he comes to himself, Silas at first mistakes the luster of Eppie's hair for his gold. After he recognizes the sleeping child, he believes that it has been sent in the place of the gold, and with that belief his dormant religious instincts begin to revive: "he had a dreamy feeling that this child was somehow a message come to him from that far-off life: it stirred fibres that had never been moved in Raveloe — old quiverings of tenderness — old impressions of awe at the presentiment of some Power presiding over his life . . ." (Chapter XII). More and more firmly associating the little girl with his gold (as the author also comes to do), Silas refuses to give her up: "My money's gone, I don't know where — and this is come from I don't know where. I know nothing — I'm partly mazed" (Chapter XIII). As he repeatedly expresses the thought, it almost acquires the force of an invocation.[11]

[11] Thale (pp. xv-xvii, xix-xxi) and Thomson (pp. 83–84) both dismiss too easily the sense of supernatural ordinance at work in the novel. Thale sees *Silas Marner* as a moral fable based on secular theology; Thomson finds that George Eliot, "instead of referring to some cosmic or metaphorical source for the sense of mysterious power . . . implants it in the organism of society itself." But it is not society that leads Eppie to Silas's cottage or arranges for Silas to fall into a trance at just the right moment. Neither critic, in denying the importance of the supernatural element, discusses that crucial episode or the author's way of presenting it. Thale also simplifies when he says "whereas the Silas story is like a fairy tale, the Godfrey story is basically realistic" (p. xix). Both stories, it seems to me, contain realistic details as well as suggestions of transcendent design: it is Silas's greater intensity and spiritual impulse that make his story

v

The supernatural element in *Silas Marner* does not exist for its own sake; its assertion of a transcendental order enforcing moral laws is too equivocal for that. The closest the book comes to a directly religious affirmation is in Dolly Winthrop's "exposition of her simple Raveloe theology" and Silas Marner's eventual acceptance of it:

> ". . . you're i' the right, Mrs. Winthrop — you're i' the right. There's good i' this world — I've a feeling o' that now; and it makes a man feel as there's a good more nor he can see, i' spite o' the trouble and the wickedness. That drawing o' the lots is dark; but the child was sent to me: there's dealings with us — there's dealings." (Chapter XVI)

As an interpretation of George Eliot's religious convictions, which are not orthodox, assured, explicit, or simple, this is obviously an inadequate account, but it is not basically misleading. It is commonly recognized that her work provides illuminating studies in the difficulties of Victorian religious belief: generally, her protagonists are caught between their need of faith and the inadequacies of conventional religion. They try, as she herself and so many of her contemporaries tried, to fulfill their spiritual drive through emotional and intellectual channels, through a painfully worked out and conscientiously pursued moral vision and high-minded social dedication; usually their ambitious commitments are subdued in encounters with actual experience. Silas Marner is not one of these heroic figures, thwarted by their own flaws and the tragic mediocrity of their time, but his experience is related to theirs and reflects George Eliot's exploration of the individual condition in a social context. The apparently supernatural design of his integration into the community of Raveloe is not significant in its own right as much as in its compelling corroboration of his psychological and moral growth. Just as the

---

appear the more supernatural of the two. Milner, though he does not discuss it in any significant detail, recognizes that "the 'legendary' element . . . enters deeply into the structure of *Silas Marner*" and, as he says, "is most evident in the narration of Silas' finding of the child on his cottage hearth" (pp. 721–722). He is right, I think, when he notes later in the essay that "the drama of Marner's re-humanization is expressed in a more realistic vein that contrasts significantly with the legendary and numinous atmosphere of his earlier alienation" (pp. 723–724). At that point, "the religion of humanity" has been affirmed with sufficient force and drama, so that it can be presented without loss of authority (perhaps even with a gain) in its psychological and social operation.

attainment of social harmony and congeniality seems to imply a higher spiritual fulfillment, so the sense of divine direction lends persuasion and authority to the human events. And for Silas Marner (as in a way for Maggie Tulliver), regeneration comes through a resurgent memory and a revived sense of continuity with his life of long ago. The precise forms through which social connections are established and enjoyed are unimportant in this process of reawakening. Only the continued maintenance of sociality matters.

Even Silas's Dissenting faith expresses itself through his attachment to familiar observances, surroundings, and friends more than through an otherworldly vision. When he first comes to Raveloe, it is the habitual expressions and ties of Lantern Yard that he misses.

> The whitewashed walls; the little pews where well-known figures entered with a subdued rustling, and where first one well-known voice and then another, pitched in a peculiar key of petition, uttered phrases at once occult and familiar, like the amulet worn on the heart; the pulpit where the minister delivered unquestioned doctrine, and swayed to and fro, and handled the book in a long-accustomed manner; the very pauses between the couplets of the hymn, as it was given out, and the recurrent swell of voices in song: these things had been the channel of divine influences to Marner — they were the fostering home of his religious emotions — they were Christianity and God's kingdom upon earth. (Chapter II)

When he is deprived of these associations in his exile, his memory and imagination as well as his "faith in the invisible" are starved: the "past becomes dreamy because its symbols have all vanished, and the present too is dreamy because it is linked with no memories" (Chapter II). The author even compares his state of mind to "the feeling of primitive men," who "believed that each territory was inhabited and ruled by its own divinities, so that a man could cross the bordering heights and be out of the reach of his native gods, whose presence was confined to the streams and the groves and the hills among which he had lived from his birth" (Chapter II).

The religious distillation of regional attachments that this comparison expresses is implicitly amplified by the design of the narrative. It is not that George Eliot now regards local roots as unimportant — they are obviously still crucial — but she does show that they can be transplanted and that exile and alienation can, indeed must, be overcome. Even during the stupor of fifteen years, as he drags out a lonely existence, Silas dimly, instinctively casts about for an emotional center, and attaches his devotion to the most likely inanimate things: "his brown earthenware pot," his work, and his gold. Through these objects his "sap of affection" still runs fitfully: when the pot breaks after twelve years, he carries the pieces "home with grief in his heart," sticks them together, and props "the ruin in its old place for a memorial" (Chapter II). And, of course, when his gold is stolen, he is profoundly heartsick; significantly, he hardly thinks of it as money or wealth but as a focus for his emotions. In vain does Dolly Winthrop try to console him:

> Her simple view of life and its comforts, by which she had tried to cheer him, was only like a report of unknown objects, which his imagination could not fashion. The fountains of human love and of faith in a divine love had not yet been unlocked, and his soul was still the shrunken rivulet, with only this difference, that its little groove of sand was blocked up, and it wandered confusedly against dark obstruction. (Chapter X)

It is only after he takes Eppie into his house that Silas begins to revive and in a sense becomes "the dead man come to life again" that he is reputed to be. The wondering possessiveness and jealous affection with which he first regards her stir his memories of long-forgotten feelings and attachments, so that as the child draws his love to itself, it also directs it inward, to his past, and outward, to his neighbors:

> The gold had kept his thoughts in an ever-repeated circle, leading to nothing beyond itself; but Eppie was an object compacted of changes and hopes that forced his thoughts onward . . . The gold had asked that he should sit weaving longer and longer, deafened and blinded more and more to all things except the monotony of his loom and the repetition of his web; but Eppie called him away from his weaving, and made him think all its pauses a holiday, reawakening his senses with her fresh life . . . and warming him into joy because *she* had joy . . . As the child's mind was growing into knowledge, his mind was growing into memory: as her life unfolded, his soul, long stupefied in a cold narrow prison, was unfolding too, and trembling gradually into full consciousness. (Chapter XIV)

Almost consciously now Silas takes to the process of assimilation and transplantation, trying to absorb, for Eppie's sake, the nature of Raveloe life:

> ... he listened docilely, that he might come to understand better what this life was, from which, for fifteen years, he had stood aloof as from a strange thing, wherewith he could have no communion: as some man who has a precious plant to which he would give a nurturing home in a new soil, thinks of the rain, and the sunshine, and all influences, in relation to his nursling, and asks industriously for all knowledge that will help him to satisfy the wants of the searching roots, or to guard leaf and bud from invading harm. (Chapter XIV)

Part One ends with the impulse toward readjustment already in full force; when Part Two opens, Silas, exhibiting all the signs of additional years, also shows evidence of his integration and fulfillment. In the charming social scene in which the congregation leaves the church after the Sunday service, "it is impossible to mistake Silas Marner. His large brown eyes seem to have gathered a longer vision ... and they have a less vague, a more answering gaze ..." (Chapter XVI). The transformation of his cottage, with its cheerful animal life and new furniture, is as striking as the changes in the Red House, to which it corresponds. But the transplantation is seen as successful and entire because he has managed to cultivate in his new life the all-important sense of continuity with the old:

> By seeking what was needful for Eppie, by sharing the effect that everything produced on her, he had himself come to appropriate the forms of custom and belief which were the mould of Raveloe life; and as, with reawakening sensibilities, memory also reawakened, he had begun to ponder over the elements of his old faith, and blend them with his new impressions, till he recovered a consciousness of unity between his past and present. (Chapter XVI)

The completeness of Silas Marner's transplantation is signified in the journey which he makes with Eppie back to the manufacturing town in which he was born. Not only has Lantern Yard vanished, swept before the advance of the Industrial Revolution — there is a large factory in its place; the date must be in the early 1830s — but the town as a whole is grim and noisy, a depressing contrast with Raveloe. Even if he desired it, there is no returning to the old life;

but having already come to terms with the past, he is able to maintain his ties to it and preserve unimpaired his restored emotional wholeness. Thus, only minimally disturbed at the disappointing outcome of his trip, he goes back to the community in which he had once been an alien: " 'The old place is all swep'away,' Silas said to Dolly Winthrop on the night of his return — 'the little graveyard and everything. The old home's gone; I've no home but this now' " (Chapter XXI).

Silas Marner is George Eliot's first treatment of alienation, immigration, and resettlement; its regionalism is genuine but slanted in a new way, a way that ultimately leads beyond it and discounts its importance. After the laborious and painfully uncongenial task of writing *Romola*, George Eliot returned to the depiction of English life, and, until *Daniel Deronda*, particularly English provincial life. But it was a return with a difference, for it marked an advancement of vision, an extension of scope and form. The question of local roots counts for much less in the late novels than in the early ones: what is important there is individual fulfillment through social dedication and involvement. Felix Holt, Dorothea Brooke, Daniel Deronda, all have in their distinct ways essentially the same sense of mission, which springs originally from a somewhat theoretical idealism, but is tested, chastened, and refined in the furnace of actual experience. From the suffering of personal relations and the complex interconnections of social intercourse, from the painful reappraisals that derive from these, George Eliot's most moving and successful characters (not in every case the nominal protagonists) gain a new strength and a new self-knowledge. The problems they face are more intricate than those of their predecessors in the early novels; they are decisively more articulate and sophisticated, and their societies are recognizably modern — larger, appreciably urban, considerably cosmopolitan, hypersensitive to historical trends, more impersonal and less satisfying.

But though the sense of coherent communal life is not strong here, though the closely knit rural society is implicitly recognized as old-fashioned and anachronistic, it is not difficult to see how George Eliot's interest in regional life is transferred and adapted to her late work. It appears there in the high value she places on personal connection and social responsibility, in her nostalgic admiration, often quite clear, for the cohesiveness, strength, and fellowship of a bygone day, and in her protagonists' individualistic, frequently isolated and frustrated efforts to snatch these lost virtues and plant them amid modern surroundings. It is, after all, in *Daniel Deronda*, her last great work, a novel dealing with the fragmented, materialistic, and corrupt aspects of the society of her own day, that she wrote:

> A human life, I think, should be well rooted in some spot of a native land, where it may get the love of tender kinship for the face of earth, for the labours men go forth to, for the sounds and accents that haunt it, for whatever will give that early home a familiar unmistakable difference amidst the future widening of knowledge: a spot where the definiteness of early memories may be inwrought with affection, and kindly acquaintance with all neighbours, even to the dogs and donkeys, may spread not by sentimental effort and reflection, but as a sweet habit of the blood. (Chapter III)

Bibliography

In this selected list of works discussed, cited, and consulted, I have not included the standard reference guides and surveys of writings that seemed to me decidedly irrelevant or unhelpful. In listing paperbacks I give the name of the series instead of the place of publication.

I. Primary Works

Cross, John W. *George Eliot's Life as Related in Her Letters and Journals.* 3 volumes. Edinburgh and London, 1885.

Eliot, George. *Essays of George Eliot*, ed. Thomas Pinney. London: Routledge and Kegan Paul, 1963.

———— *The George Eliot Letters*, ed. Gordon S. Haight. 7 volumes. New Haven and London: Yale University Press, 1954–55.

———— *The Standard Edition of the Works of George Eliot.* 21 volumes. Edinburgh and London [1897].

II. Secondary Works: Books, Essays, Articles and Reviews Concerned with George Eliot

Acton, John Emerich Edward Dalberg, First Baron. "George Eliot," *Nineteenth Century*, XVII (1885), 464–485.

Allen, Walter. *George Eliot.* New York: Macmillan, 1964.

Allott, Miriam. "George Eliot in the 1860's," *Victorian Studies*, V (1961–62), 93–108.

Annan, Noel. "Books in General," *New Statesman and Nation*, XXV–XXVI n.s. (1943), 355.

Arthos, John. "George Eliot: 'The Art of Vision'," *Rivista di Letterature Moderne et Comparate*, III n.s. (1952), 260–270.

Axon, William Edward Armitage. "George Eliot's Use of Dialect," *Stray Chapters in Literature, Folklore, and Archeology.* Manchester, 1888.

Bald, Marjory A. "George Eliot," *Women Writers of the Nineteenth Century.* Cambridge: Cambridge University Press, 1923.

Barry, James D. "The Literary Reputation of George Eliot's Fiction," *Bulletin of Bibliography*, XXII, no. 8 (January–April 1959), pp. 176–182.

Bassett, John J. "The Purpose in George Eliot's Art," *Anglia*, LIV (1930), 338–350.

Bennett, Joan, *George Eliot: Her Mind and Art.* Cambridge: Cambridge University Press, 1948.

Berle, Lina W. *George Eliot and Thomas Hardy: A Contrast.* New York: M. Kennerley, 1917.

Bethell, S. L. "The Novels of George Eliot," *Criterion*, XVIII (1938–39), 39–57.

Bissell, Claude T. "Social Analysis in the Novels of George Eliot," *ELH* XVIII (1951), 221–239.

Bibliography

Bisson, L. A. "Proust, Bergson, and George Eliot," *Modern Language Review*, XL (1945), 104–114.

Blind, Mathilde. *George Eliot*, with an introduction and bibliography by Frank Waldo and G. A. Turkington. Boston: Little, Brown, 1904.

Bourl'honne, P. *George Eliot: Éssai de biograpie intellectuelle et morale, 1819–1854.* Paris: H. Champion, 1933.

Brownell, W. C. "George Eliot," *Victorian Prose Masters*. New York: C. Scribner's Sons, 1901.

Browning, Oscar. *Life of George Eliot*, with a checklist of early literature about George Eliot by J. P. Anderson. London, 1890.

Buchanan, Robert. "A Talk with George Eliot" and "George Eliot's Life," *A Look Around Literature*. London, 1887.

Bullett, Gerald. *George Eliot: Her Life and Books*. New Haven: Yale University Press, 1948.

Carroll, D. R. "An Image of Disenchantment in the Novels of George Eliot," *Review of English Studies*, XI n.s. (1960), 29–41.

Casson, Allan Perham. "The Early Novels of George Eliot," Unpublished Ph.D. dissertation. Harvard University, 1960.

Cockshut, A. O. J. "George Eliot: The Search for Justice," *The Unbelievers: English Agnostic Thought, 1840–1890*. London: Collins, 1964.

Cooke, George Willis. *George Eliot: A Critical Study of Her Life, Writings, and Philosophy*. Boston and New York, 1883.

Cox, C. B. "George Eliot: The Conservative-Reformer," *The Free Spirit: A Study of Liberal Humanism in the Novels of George Eliot, Henry James, E. M. Forster, Virginia Woolf, Angus Wilson*. London and New York: Oxford University Press, 1963.

Cross, Wilbur L. "George Eliot in Retrospect," *Yale Review*, IX n.s. (1920), 256–270.

Daiches, David. "The Return of George Eliot," *The Nation*, CXCIV (1962), 518–519.

Dangerfield, George. "A Great Victorian Intelligence," *The Nation*, CLXXIX (1954), 333–335.

Deakin, Mary H. *The Early Life of George Eliot*. Manchester: Manchester University Press, 1913.

Dodds, Dorothy. *The George Eliot Country*, ed. F. J. Cross. Nuneaton: The George Eliot Fellowship, 1952.

Dowden, Edward. "George Eliot"; "'Middlemarch' and 'Daniel Deronda'," *Studies in Literature, 1789–1877*. London: Kegan Paul, Trench, Trübner, 1906.

"The Eliot Novels," Anon., *Christian Examiner*, LXX (1861), 227–251.

Evans, B. Ifor. "George Eliot," *Contemporary Review*, CLXXII (1947), 153–156.

Feltes, N. N. "George Eliot and the Unified Sensibility," *PMLA*, LXXIX (1964), 130–136.

Foard, James T. "Features of Fact and Fancy in the Works of George Eliot," *Manchester Quarterly*, IX (1890), 28–54.

Fremantle, Anne. *George Eliot.* London: Duckworth, 1933.

Gardner, Charles. "George Eliot's 'Quarries,'" *Atlantic Monthly,* CXXXVI (1925), 659–665.

Gary, Franklin. "In Search of George Eliot: An Approach through Marcel Proust," *Symposium,* IV (1933), 182–206.

"George Eliot." Anon., *Blackwood's Edinburgh Magazine,* CXXIX (1881), 255–268.

"George Eliot." Anon., *British Quarterly Review,* LXXXI (1885), 316–333.

"George Eliot." Anon., *London Quarterly Review,* LVII (1881), 154–176.

"George Eliot." Anon., *London Quarterly Review,* LXIV (1885), 197–222.

"George Eliot." Anon., *The Nation* (London), XXVI (1919), 70–74.

"George Eliot." Anon., *Saturday Review,* LI (1881), 12–13.

"George Eliot." Anon., *The Times* (London), 24 December 1880, pp. 7, 9.

"George Eliot." Anon., *Westminster Review,* LXVIII n.s. (1885), 161–208.

"George Eliot as a Novelist." Anon., *Westminster Review,* LIV n.s. (1878), 105–135.

"George Eliot's Novels." Anon., *Quarterly Review,* CVIII (1860), 469–499.

Gosse, Edmund. "George Eliot," *The London Mercury,* I (1918–19), 34–43.

H., C. H. "A Hundred Years of George Eliot," *The Living Age,* CCCII (1919), 595–598.

Haight, Gordon S., ed. *A Century of George Eliot Criticism.* Boston: Houghton Mifflin, 1965.

———— *George Eliot: A Biography.* New York and Oxford: Oxford University Press, 1968.

———— *George Eliot and John Chapman.* New Haven: Yale University Press, 1940.

———— "George Eliot: The Moralist as Artist," *Victorian Newsletter,* no. 16 (Fall 1959), pp. 25–27.

———— " 'George Eliot' Reviewed," *The Trollopian,* III (1948), 127–131.

———— "George Eliot's Originals," *From Jane Austen to Joseph Conrad,* ed. Robert C. Rathburn and Martin Steinmann. Minneapolis: Minnesota University Press, 1958.

———— "George Eliot's Theory of Fiction," *Victorian Newsletter,* no. 10 (Fall 1956), pp. 1–2.

———— "The George Eliot and the George Henry Lewes Collections," *Yale University Library Gazette,* XXXV (1961), 170–171.

———— "Main MS Locations of George Eliot Material," *Victorian Newsletter,* no. 13 (Spring 1958), p. 23.

———— "The Tinker Collection of George Eliot Manuscripts," *Yale University Library Gazette,* XXIX (1955), 148–150.

Haldane, Elizabeth S. *George Eliot and Her Times: A Victorian Study.* London: Hodder and Stoughton, 1927.

Hampshire, Stuart. "The Horses on the Common," *New Statesman,* LXVI (1963), 783.

Hanson, Lawrence, and Elisabeth Hanson. *Marian Evans and George Eliot.* London: Oxford University Press, 1952.

Hardwick, Elizabeth. "George Eliot's Husband," *Partisan Review*, XII (1955), 260–264.
Hardy, Barbara. *The Novels of George Eliot.* London: University of London, Athlone Press, 1959.
Harper, Charles G. "The George Eliot Country," *The Living Age*, CCCIII (1919), 416–419.
Harrison, Frederic. "George Eliot's Place in Literature," *The Forum*, XX (1895), 66–78.
———— "The Life of George Eliot," *Fortnightly Review*, XXXVII n.s. (1885), 309–322.
Harvey, W. J. *The Art of George Eliot.* London: Chatto and Windus, 1961.
———— "George Eliot," *Victorian Fiction: A Guide to Research*, ed. Lionel Stevenson. Cambridge, Mass.: Harvard University Press, 1964.
———— "Ideas in George Eliot," *Modern Language Quarterly*, XXVII (1966), 86–92.
Henley, William Ernest. "George Eliot," *Views and Reviews.* New York, 1890.
Holloway, John. "George Eliot," *The Victorian Sage.* London: Macmillan, 1953.
Holmstrom, John, and Laurence Lerner, ed. *George Eliot and Her Readers: A Selection of Contemporary Reviews.* London: Bodley Head, 1966.
Hough, Graham. "Novelist-Philosopher: George Eliot," *Horizon*, XVII (1948), 50–62.
House, Humphry. "Qualities of George Eliot's Unbelief," *All in Due Time.* London: Hart Davis, 1955.
Howe, Irving. "A Great Writer's Evolution," *New Republic*, CXXXI (1954), 18–20.
Howells, William Dean. "George Eliot's Maggie Tulliver and Hetty Sorrel"; "George Eliot's Rosamond Vincy and Dorothea Brooke"; "George Eliot's Gwendolen Harleth and Janet Dempster," *Heroines of Fiction.* Vol. II. New York and London: Harper and Brothers, 1901.
Hutton, Richard Holt. "George Eliot," *Contemporary Review*, XLVII (1885), 372–391.
———— "The Novels of George Eliot," *National Review*, XI (1860), 191–219.
———— "George Eliot as Author"; "George Eliot's Life and Letters," *Essays on Some of the Modern Guides of English Thought.* London, 1887.
Hyde, William J. "George Eliot and the Climate of Realism," *PMLA*, LXXII (1957), 147–164.
James, Henry. "George Eliot's Life," *Atlantic Monthly*, LV (1885), 668–678.
———— "The Novels of George Eliot," *Atlantic Monthly*, XVIII (1866), 479–492.
Kaminsky, Alice R. "George Eliot, George Henry Lewes, and the Novel," *PMLA*, LXX (1955), 997–1013.
Katona, Anna. "Problems of Adjustment in George Eliot's Early Novels," *Acta Litteraria Academiae Scientiarum Hungaricae*, VI (1963), 149–162.

Kebbel, T. E. "Miss Austen and George Eliot," *National Review*, II (1883), 259–273.

———— "Village Life According to George Eliot," *Fraser's Magazine*, XXIII n.s. (1881), 263–276.

Kingsley, Rose G. "George Eliot's Country," *Century Magazine*, XXX (1885), 339–352.

Kitchel, Anna T. *George Lewes and George Eliot: A Review of Records.* New York: John Day, 1933.

Knoepflmacher, U. C. *George Eliot's Early Novels: The Limits of Realism.* Berkeley and Los Angeles: University of California Press, 1968.

———— *Religious Humanism and the Victorian Novel: George Eliot, Walter Pater, and Samuel Butler.* Princeton: Princeton University Press, 1965.

Lancaster, Henry H. "George Eliot's Novels," *North British Review*, XLV (1866), 197–228.

Leavis, F. R. *The Great Tradition.* London: Chatto and Windus, 1948.

Lemke, Frederick D. "George Eliot and Her Predecessors in Village Literature." Unpublished Ph.D. dissertation. University of Illinois, 1933.

Lerner, Laurence. "The Cool Gaze and the Warm Heart," *The Listener*, LXIV (1960), 518–522.

———— *The Truthtellers: Jane Austen, George Eliot, D. H. Lawrence.* London: Chatto and Windus, 1967.

Levine, George. "Determinism and Responsibility in the Works of George Eliot," *PMLA*, LXXVII (1962), 268–279.

"The Life and Letters of George Eliot." Anon., *Blackwood's Edinburgh Magazine*, CXXXVII (1885), 155–176.

"The Life and Letters of George Eliot." Anon., *Edinburgh Review*, CLXI (1885), 514–553.

McKenzie, K. A. *Edith Simcox and George Eliot*, with an introduction by Gordon S. Haight. London: Oxford University Press, 1961.

Mansell, Darrel, Jr. "George Eliot's Conception of 'Form'," *Studies in English Literature, 1500–1900*, V (1965), 651–662.

———— "George Eliot's Conception of Tragedy," *Nineteenth-Century Fiction*, XXII (1967), 155–172.

———— "A Note on Hegel and George Eliot," *Victorian Newsletter*, no. 27 (Spring 1965), pp. 12–15.

———— "Ruskin and George Eliot's Realism," *Criticism*, VII (Summer 1965), 203–216.

Masters, Donald C. "George Eliot and the Evangelicals," *Dalhousie Review*, XLI (1962), 505–512.

Merton, Stephen. "George Eliot and William Hale White," *Victorian Newsletter*, no. 25 (1964), pp. 13–15.

Minchin, H. C. "George Eliot: Some Observations," *Fortnightly Review*, CXII (1919), 896–903.

Montégut, Emile. "George Eliot: L'âme et le talent"; "Les Oeuvres et la doctrine morale," *Revue des deux mondes*, LVI (1883), 77–96 and 305–346.

Morley, John. "George Eliot's Novels," *Macmillan's Magazine*, XIV (1866), 272–279.

———— "The Life of George Eliot," *Macmillan's Magazine*, LI (1885), 241–256.

Mudge, Isadore Gilbert, and M. E. Sears. *A George Eliot Dictionary*. London: G. Routledge and Sons, 1924.

Myers, Frederic William Henry. "George Eliot," *Essays, Modern*. London, 1883.

Naumann, Walter. "The Architecture of George Eliot's Novels," *Modern Language Quarterly*, IX (1948), 37–50.

"The Novels of George Eliot." Anon., *British Quarterly Review*, XLV (1867), 141–178.

Olcott, Charles S. *George Eliot: Scenes and People in Her Novels*. New York: Crowell, 1910.

Paris, Bernard J. *Experiments in Life: George Eliot's Quest for Values*. Detroit: Wayne State University Press, 1965.

———— "George Eliot and the Higher Criticism," *Anglia*, LXXIV (1966), 59–73.

———— "George Eliot's Unpublished Poetry," *Studies in Philology*, LVI (1959), 539–558.

Parkinson, S. *Scenes from the "George Eliot" Country*. Leeds, 1888.

Parlett, Mathilde. "George Eliot and Humanism," *Studies in Philology*, XXVII (1930), 25–46.

———— "The Influence of Contemporary Criticism on George Eliot," *Studies in Philology*, XXX (1933), 103–132.

Parry, Edward A. "The Humour of George Eliot," *Fortnightly Review*, CXII (1919), 881–895.

Paul, C. Kegan. "The Rustic of George Eliot and Thomas Hardy," *Merry England*, I (1883), 40–51.

Pinney, Thomas. "The Authority of the Past in George Eliot's Novels," *Nineteenth-Century Fiction*, XXI (1966), 131–147.

———— "George Eliot's Reading of Wordsworth: The Record," *Victorian Newsletter*, no. 24 (Fall 1963), pp. 20–22.

———— "More Leaves from George Eliot's Notebook," *Huntington Library Quarterly*, XXIX (1966), 353–376.

Pond, E. J. *Les Idées morales et religieuses de George Eliot*. Paris: Les presses universitaires de France, 1927.

Pritchett, V. S. "George Eliot," *The Living Novel*. London: Chatto and Windus, 1946.

Purdy, Richard Little. "Journal and Letters of George Eliot," *Yale University Library Gazette*, VII (1932), 1–4.

Renwick, Ralph, Jr. "The Intellectual Background of George Eliot's Early Writings." Unpublished Ph.D. dissertation. Harvard University, 1950.

Royce, Josiah. "George Eliot as a Religious Teacher," *Fugitive Essays*. Cambridge, Mass.: Harvard University Press, 1920.

Rubinstein, Elliot L. "A Forgotten Tale by George Eliot," *Nineteenth-Century Fiction*, XVII (1962–63), 175–183.

Russell, George W. E. "George Eliot Revisited," *Contemporary Review*, LXIX (1896), 357–373.

Rust, James D. "The Art of Fiction in George Eliot's Reviews," *Review of English Studies*, VII n.s. (1956), 164–172.

Sackville-West, Edward. "Books in General," *New Statesman and Nation*, XX (1940), 518.

Sackville-West, Vita. "George Eliot," *The Great Victorians*, ed. H. J. Massingham and Hugh Massingham. London: Ivor Nicholson and Watson, 1932.

Sambrook, A. J. "The Natural Historian of Our Social Classes," *English*, XIV (1962–63), 130–134.

Scherer, Edmond, "George Eliot," *Études sur la littérature contemporaine*. Paris, 1886.

Seccombe, Thomas. "George Eliot," *Encyclopaedia Britannica*, 11th ed. (New York, 1910), IX, 274–277.

Sharp, William. "The Country of George Eliot," *Literary Geography*. London: Pall Mall Publications, 1904.

Sibbald, William A. "George Eliot's Place in Literature," *Westminster Review*, CLXIII (1905), 330–338 and 431–448.

Simon, Irène. "Innocence in the Novels of George Eliot," *English Studies Today, Second Series*, ed. G. A. Bonnard. Bern: Francke Verlag, 1959.

Speaight, Robert. *George Eliot*. London: Barker, 1954.

Stang, Richard, ed. *Discussions of George Eliot*. Boston: Heath, 1960.

———— "The Literary Criticism of George Eliot," *PMLA*, LXXII (1957), 952–961.

Stephen, Leslie. *George Eliot*. New York and London: Macmillan, 1902.

Stone, Wilfred H. "Hale White and George Eliot," *University of Toronto Quarterly*, XXV (1955–56), 437–451.

Stump, Reva. *Movement and Vision in George Eliot's Novels*. Seattle: Washington University Press, 1959.

Svaglic, M. J. "Religion in the Novels of George Eliot," *Journal of English and Germanic Philology*, LIII (1954), 145–159.

Thale, Jerome. *The Novels of George Eliot*. New York: Columbia University Press, 1959.

Thomson, Patricia. "The Three Georges," *Nineteenth-Century Fiction*, XVIII (1963–64), 137–150.

Tupper, Frederick. "George Eliot: 1819–1919," *The Nation*, CIX (1919), 683–685.

Wheatley, James Holbrook. "George Eliot and the Art of Thought: Studies in the Early Novels." Unpublished Ph.D. dissertation. Harvard University, 1960.

White, William Hale. "George Eliot as I Knew Her," *Last Pages from a Journal*. London: Oxford University Press, 1915.

Whiting, Lilian. "The Centenary of George Eliot," *The Bookman* (New York), L (1919), 315–322.

Wilkinson, W. C. "George Eliot's Novels," *Scribner's Monthly*, VIII (1894), 685–703.

Willey, Basil. "George Eliot," *Nineteenth Century Studies: Coleridge to Matthew Arnold*. London: Chatto and Windus, 1949.

Willey, Frederick William. "George Eliot and the Conventions of the Novel: Studies of a Writer in the Traditions of Fiction." Unpublished Ph.D. dissertation. Harvard University, 1962.

Williams, Blanche Colton. *George Eliot*. New York: Macmillan, 1936.

———— "George Eliot: Social Pressure on the Individual," *Sewanee Review*, XLVI (1938), 235–241.

Woolf, Virginia. "George Eliot," *The Common Reader* [*First Series*]. London: Hogarth Press, 1925.

Worth, George J. "The Intruder Motif in George Eliot's Fiction," *Six Studies in Nineteenth-Century Literature and Thought*, ed. Harold J. Orel and George J. Worth. Lawrence, Kansas: University of Kansas Press, 1962.

Wright, Walter Francis. "George Eliot as Industrial Reformer," *PMLA*, LVI (1941), 1107–15.

Wyatt, Edith Franklin. "George Eliot, 1819–1919," *North American Review*, CCX (1919), 837–848.

III. Secondary Works: Studies of Individual Novels

Scenes of Clerical Life (1858)

Reviews: *Edinburgh Review*, CX (1859), 223–246; *Saturday Review*, V (1858), 685–703; *The Times* (London), 2 January 1858 [by Samuel Lucas].

Deneau, Daniel P. "A Note on George Eliot's 'Amos Barton' — Reticence and Chronology," *Notes and Queries*, VI n.s. (1959), 450–451.

———— "Imagery in the *Scenes of Clerical Life*," *Victorian Newsletter*, no. 28 (Fall 1965), pp. 18–22.

Knoepflmacher, U. C. "George Eliot's Anti-Romantic Romance: 'Mr. Gilfil's Love-Story,'" *Victorian Newsletter*, no. 31 (Spring 1967), pp. 15–19.

Laski, Marghanita. "Some Words from George Eliot's 'Scenes of Clerical Life,'" *Notes and Queries*, IX n.s. (1962), 304–305.

Newdigate-Newdegate [Anne Emily Garnier], Lady. *The Cheverels of Cheverel Manor*. London, 1898.

Noble, Thomas A. *George Eliot's "Scenes of Clerical Life."* New Haven: Yale University Press, 1965.

Tomlinson, May. "The Beginning of George Eliot's Art: A Study of *Scenes of Clerical Life*," *Sewanee Review*, XXVII (1919), 320–329.

Adam Bede (1859)

Reviews: *Blackwood's Edinburgh Magazine*, LXXXV (1859), 490–504; *Dublin Review*, XLVII (1859), 33–42; *Edinburgh Review*, CX (1859),

Bibliography

223–246; *Harper's New Monthly Magazine*, XVIII (1859), 691; *Revue des deux mondes*, XXI (1859), 867–897 [by Émile Montégut]; *Spectator*, XXXI (1859), 194; *The Times* (London), 12 April 1859, p. 5; *Westminster Review*, XV n.s. (1859), 486–512.

Adam, I. W. "Restoration through Feeling in George Eliot's Fiction: A New Look at Hetty Sorrel," *Victorian Newsletter*, no. 22 (Fall 1962), pp. 9–12.

Buchen, Irving A. "Arthur Donnithorne and *Zeluco*: Characterization via Literary Allusion in *Adam Bede*," *Victorian Newsletter*, no. 22 (Fall 1962), pp. 18–19.

Burton, Thomas G. "Hetty Sorrel, the Forlorn Maiden," *Victorian Newsletter*, no. 30 (Fall 1966), pp. 24–26.

Casson, Allan Perham. " 'Thee' and 'You' in *Adam Bede*," *Notes and Queries*, VI n.s. (1959), 451.

Colby, Robert A. "Miss Evans, Miss Mulock, and Hetty Sorrel," *English Language Notes*, III (March 1965), 206–211.

Creeger, George R. "An Interpretation of *Adam Bede*," *ELH*, XXIII (1956), 218–236.

Deneau, Daniel P. "Inconsistencies and Inaccuracies in *Adam Bede*," *Nineteenth-Century Fiction*, XIV (1959–60), 71–75.

Diekhoff, J. S. "The Happy Ending of *Adam Bede*," *ELH*, III (1936), 221–227.

Foakes, R. A. "Adam Bede Reconsidered," *English*, XII (1958–59), 173–176.

Fyfe, A. J. "The Interpretation of *Adam Bede*," *Nineteenth-Century Fiction*, IX (1954–55), 134–139.

Gregor, Ian. "The Two Worlds of *Adam Bede*," *The Moral and the Story*, with Brian Nichols. London: Faber and Faber, 1962.

Hussey, Maurice. "Structure and Imagery in *Adam Bede*," *Nineteenth-Century Fiction*, X (1955–56), 115–129.

Jones, W. Garet. "George Eliot's *Adam Bede* and Tolstoy's *Anna Karenina*," *Modern Language Review*, LXI (1966), 473–481.

Jones, William M. "From Abstract to Concrete in *Adam Bede*," *College English*, XVII (1955–56), 88–89.

Knoepflmacher, U. C. "George Eliot, Feuerbach, and the Question of Criticism," *Victorian Studies*, VII (1963–64), 306–309.

Leavis, F. R. Foreword to *Adam Bede*. Signet Classics, 1961.

Milner, Ian. "The Structure of Values in *Adam Bede*," *Philologica Pragensia*, IX (1966), 281–291.

Mottram, William. *The True Story of George Eliot in Relation to "Adam Bede," Giving the Real Life History of the More Prominent Characters.* London: T. Fisher Unwin, 1905.

Ryals, Claude de L. "The Thorn Imagery in the Novels of George Eliot," *Victorian Newsletter*, no. 22 (Fall 1962), pp. 12–13.

Thale, Jerome. "*Adam Bede*: Arthur Donnithorne and *Zeluco*," *Modern Language Notes*, LXX (1955), 263–265.

Van Ghent, Dorothy. "On *Adam Bede*," *The English Novel: Form and Function*. New York: Rinehart, 1953.

The Mill on the Floss (1860)

Reviews: *Athenaeum*, 7 April 1860, pp. 467–468; *Atlantic Monthly*, V (1860), 756–757; *Blackwood's Edinburgh Magazine*, LXXXVII (1860), 611–623; *Dublin University Magazine*, LVII (1861), 192–200; *Harper's New Monthly Magazine*, XXI (1860), 117; *Macmillan's Magazine*, III (1861), 441–448; *Saturday Review*, IX (1860), 470–471; *Spectator*, XXXII (1860), 330–331; *The Times* (London), 19 May 1860, p. 10; *Westminster Review*, XVIII n.s. (1860), 24–33.

Bellringer, A. W. "Education in *The Mill on the Floss*," *Review of English Literature*, VII (1966), 52–61.

Bolton, F. "Le Manuscrit du *Mill on the Floss*," *Études Anglaises*, XVIII (1965), 53–58.

Brown, Keith. "The Ending of *The Mill on the Floss*," *Notes and Queries*, XI (1964), 226.

Drew, Elizabeth. "*The Mill on the Floss*," *The Novel: A Modern Guide to Fifteen Masterpieces*. New York: Dell Laurel Classics, 1963.

Haight, Gordon S. Introduction to *The Mill on the Floss*. Boston: Houghton Mifflin, 1961.

Levine, George. "Intelligence as Deception: *The Mill on the Floss*," *PMLA*, LXXX (September 1965), 402–409.

Rubin, Larry, "River Imagery as a Means of Foreshadowing in *The Mill on the Floss*," *Modern Language Notes*, LXXI (1956), 18–22.

Smith, David. "Incest Patterns in Two Victorian Novels," *Literature and Psychology*, XV (1965), 135–162.

Steinhoff, William R. "Intention and Fulfillment in the Ending of *The Mill on the Floss*," *The Image of the Work: Essays in Criticism* by B. H. Lehman et al. Berkeley and Los Angeles: University of California Press, 1955.

Tomlinson, May. "Dodsons and Tullivers," *Sewanee Review*, XXVI (1918), 319–327.

Welsh, Alexander. "George Eliot and the Romance," *Nineteenth-Century Fiction*, XIV (1959-60), 241–254.

Silas Marner: The Weaver of Raveloe (1861)

Reviews: *Athenaeum*, 6 April 1861, pp. 464–468; *Revue des deux mondes*, XXXV (1861), 188–210 [by Cucheval-Clarigny]; *Saturday Review*, XI (1861), 369–370; *The Times* (London), 29 April 1861, p. 12; *Westminster Review*, LXXVI (1861), 280.

Carroll, D. R. "*Silas Marner*: Reversing the Oracles of Religion," *Literary Monographs*, ed. Eric Rothstein and Thomas K. Dunseath, I, 165–200. Madison, Milwaukee, and London: University of Wisconsin Press, 1967.

Fairley, Edwin. "The Art of George Eliot in 'Silas Marner,'" *English Journal,* II (1913), 221–230.

Heilman, Robert B. "Return to Raveloe: Thirty-Five Years After," *English Journal,* XLVI (1957), 1–10.

Leavis, Q. D. Introduction to *Silas Marner: The Weaver of Raveloe.* Penguin Books, 1967.

Milner, Ian. "Structure and Quality in *Silas Marner,*" *Studies in English Literature, 1500–1900,* VI (1966) 717–729.

Parsons, Coleman O. "Background Material Illustrative of *Silas Marner,*" *Notes and Queries,* CXCI (1946), 266–270.

Thale, Jerome. Introduction to *Silas Marner: The Weaver of Raveloe.* Rinehart Editions, 1962.

Thomson, Fred C. "The Theme of Alienation in *Silas Marner,*" *Nineteenth-Century Fiction,* XX (June 1965), 69–84.

Romola (1863)

Reviews: *Athenaeum,* 11 June 1863, p. 46; *Revue des deux mondes,* XLVIII (1863), 939–967 [by E. D. Forgues]; *Saturday Review,* XVI (1863), 124–125; *Westminster Review,* XXIV n.s. (1863), 344–351.

De Laura, David J. "*Romola* and the Origin of the Paterian View of Life," *Nineteenth-Century Fiction,* XXI (1961), 225–233.

Poston, Lawrence, III. "Setting and Theme in *Romola,*" *Nineteenth-Century Fiction,* XX (1966), 355–366.

Robinson, Carole. "*Romola*: A Reading of the Novel," *Victorian Studies,* VI (1962–63), 29–42.

Felix Holt, The Radical (1866)

Reviews: *Athenaeum,* 23 June 1866, p. 828; *Blackwood's Edinburgh Magazine,* C (1866), 94–109; *Contemporary Review,* III (1866), 51–70; *Edinburgh Review,* CXXIV (1866), 435–449; *London Quarterly Review* XXVII (1866), 100–124; *The Nation,* III (1866), 127–128 [by Henry James]; *North American Review,* CIII (1866), 557–563 [by G. Sedgwick]; *Saturday Review,* XXI (1866), 722–724; *Spectator,* XXXIX (1866), 692–693; *The Times* (London), 26 June 1866, p. 6; *Westminster Review,* XXX n.s. (1866), 200–207.

Carroll, D. R. "*Felix Holt*: Society as Protagonist," *Nineteenth-Century Fiction,* XVII (1962–63), 237–252.

Myers, W. F. T. "Politics and Personality in *Felix Holt,*" *Renaissance and Modern Studies* (University of Nottingham), X (1966), 5–33.

Thomson, Fred C. "The Genesis of *Felix Holt,*" *PMLA,* LXXIV (1959), 4–5 and 576–584.

———— "*Felix Holt* as Classic Tragedy," *Nineteenth-Century Fiction,* XVI (1961–62), 47–58.

Middlemarch (1871–72)

Reviews: *Academy*, IV (1873), 1–4 by H. Lawrenny [i.e., Edith Simcox]; *Athenaeum*, 2 December 1871, pp. 713–14; 3 February 1872, pp. 137–138; 30 March 1872, p. 393; 1 June 1872, p. 681; 27 July 1872, p. 112; 7 December 1872, pp. 725–726; *Blackwood's Edinburgh Magazine*, CXII (1872), 727–745; *British Quarterly Review*, LVII (1873), 407–429; *Contemporary Review*, XIX (1877), 348–369; *Canadian Monthly*, III (1873), 549–552; *Catholic World*, XVII (1873), 775–792 [by Justin McCarthy]; *Edinburgh Review*, CXXXVII (1873), 246–263; *Fortnightly Review*, XIII n.s. (1873), 143–148 [by Sidney Colvin]; *Galaxy*, XV (1873), 424–428 [by Henry James, reprinted in *Nineteenth-Century Fiction*, VIII (1953), 161–170]; *Harper's New Monthly Magazine*, XLVI (1873), 775; *The Nation*, XVI (1873), 60–62, 76–77 [by A. V. Dicey]; *North American Review*, CXVI (1873), 432–440 [by T. S. Perry]; *Quarterly Review*, CXXXIV (1873), 336–369; *Revue des deux mondes*, CIII (1873), 667–690 [by Thomas Bentzon]; *Saturday Review*, XXXIV (1872), 733–734, 794–796; *Spectator*, XLIV (1871), 1528–29; XLV (1872), 147–148, 404–406, 1554–56; *The Times* (London), 7 March 1873, pp. 3–4; *Westminster Review*, XCII (1872), 276–277; XCIX (1873), 325.

Anderson, Quentin. "George Eliot in *Middlemarch*," *From Dickens to Hardy*, ed. Boris Ford. Vol. VI of *The Pelican History of English Literature*. Penguin Books, 1958.

de Banke, Cecily. "A Week-end with *Middlemarch*," *Queen's Quarterly*, LII (1945–46), 346–351.

Beaty, Jerome. "The Forgotten Past of Will Ladislaw," *Nineteenth-Century Fiction*, XIII (1958–59), 159–163.

———— "History by Indirection: The Era of Reform in *Middlemarch*," *Victorian Studies*, I (1957–58), 173–179.

———— "*Middlemarch*" *from Noebook to Novel*. Urbana, Illinois: University of Illinois Press, 1960.

Briggs, Asa. "*Middlemarch* and the Doctors," *Cambridge Journal*, I (1947–48), 749–762.

Carroll, D. R. "Unity through Analogy: An Interpretation of *Middlemarch*," *Victorian Studies*, II (1958–59), 305–316.

Daiches, David. *George Eliot: Middlemarch*. London: Arnold, 1963.

Feltes, N. N. "George Eliot and the Unified Sensibility," *PMLA*, LXXIX (1964), 130–136.

Ferguson, Suzanne C. "Mme. Laure and Operative Irony in *Middlemarch*: A Structural Analogy," *Studies in English Literature, 1500–1900*, III (1963), 509–516.

Fernando, Lloyd. "George Eliot, Feminism, and Dorothea Brooke," *Review of English Literature*, IV (1963), 76–90.

Ferris, Sumner J. "*Middlemarch*: George Eliot's Masterpiece," *From Jane Austen to Joseph Conrad*, ed. Robert C. Rathburn and Martin Steinmann. Minneapolis: University of Minnesota Press, 1958.

Goldfarb, Russell. "Caleb Garth of *Middlemarch*," *Victorian Newsletter*, no. 26 (Fall 1964), pp. 14–19.

Greenberg, Robert A. "The Heritage of Will Ladislaw," *Nineteenth-Century Fiction*, XV (1960–61), 355–358.

Hagan, J. "*Middlemarch*: Narrative Unity in the Story of Dorothea Brooke," *Nineteenth-Century Fiction*, XVI (1961–62), 17–32.

Haight, Gordon S. Introduction to *Middlemarch*. Boston: Houghton Mifflin, 1956.

Hardy, Barbara, ed. *Approaches to "Middlemarch."* London: University of London, Athlone Press, 1967.

Harvey, W. J. Introduction to *Middlemarch*. Penguin Books, 1965.

Hornback, Bert G. "The Organization of *Middlemarch*," *Papers on Language and Literature*, II (1966), 169–175.

Isaacs, Neil. "*Middlemarch*: Crescendo of Obligatory Drama," *Nineteenth-Century Fiction*, XVIII (1963–64), 21–34.

Jerman, B. R. "On the Discovery of Two New *Middlemarch* Notebooks in the Folger Library," *Victorian Newsletter*, no. 22 (Fall 1962), p. 23.

Kitchel, Anna T., ed. "Quarry for *Middlemarch*," Supplement, *Nineteenth-Century Fiction*, IV (1949–50).

Leavis, Q. D. "A Note on Literary Indebtedness: Dickens, George Eliot, Henry James," *Hudson Review*, VIII (1955), 423–428.

Levine, George. "Isabel, Gwendolen, and Dorothea," *ELH*, XXX (1963), 244–257.

Lyons, Richard S. "The Method of *Middlemarch*," *Nineteenth-Century Fiction*, XXI (1966), 35–47.

Luecke, Sister Jane Marie. "Ladislaw and the *Middlemarch* Vision," *Nineteenth-Century Fiction*, XIX (1964–65), 55–64.

Monod, Sylvère. "George Eliot et les personages de *Middlemarch*," *Études Anglaises*, XII (1959), 306–314.

O'Clair, Robert Matheson. "A Critical Study of George Eliot's *Middlemarch*." Unpublished Ph.D. dissertation. Harvard University, 1956.

Pinney, Thomas. "Another Note on the Forgotten Past of Will Ladislaw," *Nineteenth-Century Fiction*, XVII (1962–63), 69–73.

Pritchett, V. S. "The Pains of Others," *New Statesman*, LXX (12 November 1965), 737–738.

Reiner, A. P. "Ariadne and Cleopatra: The Treatment of Dorothea in *Middlemarch*," *Southern Review* (University of Adelaide), II (1966), 50–58.

Robbins, Larry M. "Mill and Middlemarch: The Progress of Public Opinion," *Victorian Newsletter*, no. 31 (Spring 1967), pp. 37–39.

Schorer, Mark. "Fiction and the 'Matrix of Analogy,'" *Kenyon Review*, XI (1949), 540–560.

Stallknecht, Newton P. "Resolution and Independence: A Reading of *Middlemarch*," *Twelve Original Essays on Great English Novels*, ed. C. Shapiro. Detroit: Wayne State University Press, 1960.

Steiner, F. George. "A Preface to *Middlemarch*," *Nineteenth-Century Fiction*, IX (1954–55), 262–279.

Daniel Deronda (1876)

Reviews: *Athenaeum*, 29 January 1876, p. 160; 4 March 1876, p. 327; 1 April 1876, pp. 461–462; 29 April 1876, pp. 593–594; 3 June 1876, p. 762; 1 July 1876, pp. 14–15; 29 July 1876, p. 143; 2 September 1876, p. 303; *British Quarterly Review*, LXIV (1876), 472–492; *Edinburgh Review*, CXLIV (1876), 442–470; *Fortnightly Review*, XX n.s. (1876), 601–616 [by Sidney Colvin]; *Gentleman's Magazine*, XVII n.s. (1876), 411–427 [by R. E. Francillon]; *North American Review*, CXXIV (1877), 31–52 [by E. P. Whipple]; *Saturday Review*, XL (1876), 12–13; *The Times* (London) 31 January 1876, p. 6, and 5 June 1876, p. 5; *Westminster Review*, CV (1876), 579, and CVI (1876), 280, 575.

Adam, I. W. "Character and Destiny in George Eliot's Fiction," *Nineteenth-Century Fiction*, XX (1965), 127–143.

Beaty, Jerome. "*Daniel Deronda* and the Question of Unity in Fiction," *Victorian Newsletter*, no. 15 (Spring 1959), pp. 17–19.

Beebe, M. " 'Visions are Creators': The Unity of *Daniel Deronda*," *Boston University Studies in English* (1955).

Beeton, D. R. "George Eliot's Greatest and Poorest Novel: An Appraisal of *Daniel Deronda*," *English Studies in Africa*, IX (1966), 8–27.

Carroll, D. R. "*Mansfield Park*, *Daniel Deronda*, and Ordination," *Modern Philology*, LXII (1965), 217–226.

———— "The Unity of *Daniel Deronda*," *Essays in Criticism*, IX (1959), 369–380.

Cirillo, Albert R. "Salvation in *Daniel Deronda*: The Fortunate Overthrow of Gwendolen Harleth," *Literary Monographs*, ed. Eric Rothstein and Thomas K. Dunseath, I, 201–244. Madison, Milwaukee, and London: University of Wisconsin Press, 1967.

Fisch, Harold. "*Daniel Deronda* or *Gwendolen Harleth*," *Nineteenth-Century Fiction*, XIX (March 1965), 345–346.

Hardy, Barbara. Introduction to *Daniel Deronda*. Penguin Books, 1966.

Hester, Erwin. "George Eliot's Use of Historical Events in *Daniel Deronda*," *English Language Notes*, IV (1966), 115–118.

James, Henry. "*Daniel Deronda*: A Conversation," *Atlantic Monthly*, XXVIII (1876), 684–694.

Lainoff, Seymour. "James and Eliot: The Two Gwendolens." *Victorian Newsletter*, no. 21 (Spring 1962), pp. 23–24.

Leavis, F. R. Introduction to *Daniel Deronda*. Harper Torchbooks, 1960.

Lerner, Laurence. "The Education of Gwendolen Harleth," *Critical Quarterly*, XII (1965), 355–364.

Peterson, Virgil A. "Forgotten Bastards: A Note on *Daniel Deronda*," *Victorian Newsletter*, no. 15 (Spring 1959), p. 29.

Pryer, Robert. "Beyond the Liberal Imagination: Vision and Unreality in *Daniel Deronda*," *Victorian Studies*, IV (1960–61), 33–54.

Robinson, Carole. "The Severe Angel: A Study of *Daniel Deronda*," *ELH*, XXXI (1964), 278–300.

IV. Secondary Works: Background Material

Allott, Miriam, ed. *Novelists on the Novel*. New York: Columbia University Press, 1959.

Altick, Richard D. *The English Common Reader: A Social History of the Mass Reading Public, 1800–1900*. Chicago: Chicago University Press, 1957.

Appleman, Philip, William A. Madden, and Michael Wolff, ed. *1859: Entering an Age of Crisis*. Bloomington, Indiana: University of Indiana Press, 1959.

Auerbach, Erich. *Mimesis: The Representation of Reality in Western Literature*, trans. Willard Trask. Princeton: Princeton University Press, 1953.

Becker, George J. "Realism: an Essay in Definition," *Modern Language Quarterly*, X (1949), 184–197.

Beer, Gillian. "Charles Kingsley and the Literary Image of the Countryside," *Victorian Studies*, VIII (March 1965), 243–254.

Bentley, Phyllis Eleanor. *The English Regional Novel*. London: George Allen and Unwin, 1941.

────── "The Significance of Haworth," *The Trollopian*, II (1947), 127–136.

Bernard, Harry. *Le Roman régionaliste aux États-Unis, 1913–1940*. Montréal: Fides, 1949.

Bethell, S. L. *Essays on Literary Criticism and the English Tradition*. London: Dobson, 1948.

Booth, Wayne C. *The Rhetoric of Fiction*. Chicago: Chicago University Press, 1961.

Bourne, George [George Sturt]. *Change in the Village*. London: Duckworth, 1912.

────── *The Wheelwright's Shop*. Cambridge: Cambridge University Press, 1923.

Bowron, Bernard R., Jr. "Realism in America," *Comparative Literature*, III (1951), 268–285.

Briggs, Asa. *The Age of Improvement*. London: Longmans, 1959.

Brown, Douglas. *Thomas Hardy*. London: Longmans, 1954.

Brown, E. K. *Rhythm in the Novel*. Toronto: Toronto University Press, 1950.

Brunetière, Ferdinand. *Le Roman naturaliste*. 7th ed. Paris: C. Lévy, 1896.

Buckley, Jerome Hamilton. *The Victorian Temper: A Study in Literary Culture*. Cambridge, Mass.: Harvard University Press, 1951.

Carter, Everett. "The Meaning of, and in, Realism," *Antioch Review*, XII (1952), 78–94.

Cazamian, Louis. *L'Évolution psychologique et la litterature en Angleterre, 1660–1914*. Paris: F. Alcan, 1920.

———— *Le Roman social en Angleterre, 1830–1850.* Paris: Société Nouvelle de Librairie et d'Édition, 1903.

Cazamian, Madeleine L. *Le Roman et les idées en Angleterre, 1860–1914.* Strasbourg: Istra, 1923.

Cecil, Lord David. *Early Victorian Novelists.* New York: Bobbs-Merrill, 1935.

———— *The Fine Art of Reading and Other Literary Studies.* Indianapolis: Bobbs-Merrill, 1957.

Chase, Richard. *The American Novel and Its Tradition.* Garden City, New York: Doubleday, 1957.

Cobbett, William. *Rural Rides; Together with Tours in Scotland and Letters from Ireland,* ed. G. D. H. and Margaret Cole, 3 vols. London: P. Davies, 1930.

Creighton, Mandell. "The Northumbrian Border," *Reviews and Addresses.* London, 1884.

Cross, Wilbur L. *The Development of the English Novel.* New York: Macmillan, 1899.

Cruse, Amy. *The Victorians and Their Reading.* Boston: Houghton Mifflin, 1962.

Davis, Robert Gorham. "The Sense of the Real in English Fiction," *Comparative Literature,* III (1951), 200–217.

Ellmann, Richard, and Charles Feidelson, eds. *The Modern Tradition: Backgrounds of Modern Literature.* New York: Oxford University Press, 1965.

Elton, Oliver. *Survey of English Literature, 1780–1880.* 4 vols. New York: Macmillan, 1920.

"English Realism and Romance." Anon., *Quarterly Review,* CLXXIII (1891), 468–494.

Flanagan, Thomas. *The Irish Novelists, 1800–1850.* New York: Columbia University Press, 1959.

Forster, E. M. *Aspects of the Novel.* London: Arnold, 1928.

Freeman, John. *Literature and Locality.* London: Cassell, 1963.

Friedman, Norman. "Criticism and the Novel," *Antioch Review,* XVIII (Fall 1959), 343–370.

———— "Point of View in Fiction: the Development of a Critical Concept," *PMLA,* LXX (1955), 1160–84.

Frierson, William C. *The English Novel in Transition, 1885–1940.* Norman, Oklahoma: University of Oklahoma Press, 1942.

Frye, Northrop. *Anatomy of Criticism.* Princeton: Princeton University Press, 1957.

Gissing, George. *Letters of George Gissing to Members of His Family,* ed. Algernon and Ellen Gissing. London: Constable, 1927.

Greenhut, Morris. "George Henry Lewes as a Critic of the Novel," *Studies in Philology,* XLV (1948), 491–511.

Hannigan, D. F. "Prospective Transformations of the Novel," *Westminster Review,* CXL (1893), 257–260.

Hardy, Barbara. *The Appropriate Form: An Essay on the Novel*. London: University of London, Athlone Press, 1964.
Hardy, John Edward. *Man in the Modern Novel*. Seattle: University of Washington Press, 1964.
Hardy, Thomas John. "Regional Romance," *Books on the Shelf*. London: P. Allan, 1934.
Hatfield, Henry. "Realism in the German Novel," *Comparative Literature*, III (1951), 234–252.
Henkin, Leo J. *Darwinism in the English Novel, 1860–1910*. New York: Corporate Press, 1940.
Hoskins, William George. *Midland England*. London: B. T. Batsford, 1949.
Houghton, Walter E. *The Victorian Frame of Mind, 1830–1870*. New Haven: Yale University Press, 1957.
Hudson, William Henry. *Hampshire Days*. London: J. M. Dent, 1923.
Hyde, William J. "Hardy's View of Realism: A Key to the Rustic Characters," *Victorian Studies*, II (1958–59), 45–59.
James, Henry. *The Art of the Novel: Critical Prefaces*. New York: C. Scribner's Sons, 1934.
James, Louis. *Fiction for the Working Man, 1830–1850*. London: Oxford University Press, 1963.
Kettle, Arnold. *An Introduction to the English Novel*. 2 vols. London: Hutchinson's University Library, 1951–1953.
Lawrence, D. H. *Phoenix: The Posthumous Papers of D. H. Lawrence*, ed. Edward D. McDonald. London: Heinemann, 1936.
Leavis, F. R. and Denys Thompson. *Culture and Environment: the Training of Critical Awareness*. London: Chatto and Windus, 1933.
Leavis, Q. D. *Fiction and the Reading Public*. London: Chatto and Windus, 1932.
———— "Regional Novels," *Scrutiny*, IV (1935–36), 440–470.
Leclaire, Lucien. *A General Analytical Bibliography of the Regional Novelists of the British Isles*. Paris: Les Belles Lettres, 1954.
————*Le Roman régionaliste dans les Îles Britanniques*. Paris: Les Belles Lettres, 1954.
Levin, Harry. *The Gates of Horn*. New York: Oxford University Press, 1963.
———— "What is Realism?" *Comparative Literature*, III (1951), 193–198.
Lewes, George Henry. "The Lady Novelists," *Westminster Review*, LVIII (1852), 129–141.
———— "Realism in Art: Recent German Fiction," *Westminster Review*, LXX (1858), 488–518.
Liddell, Robert. *A Treatise on the Novel*. London: Jonathan Cape, 1947.
———— *Some Principles of Fiction*. London: Jonathan Cape, 1953.
Lubbock, Percy. *The Craft of Fiction*. London: Jonathan Cape, 1921.
Lukács, Georg. *The Historical Novel*, trans. Hannah and Stanley Mitchell. London: Merlin Press, 1962.
———— *Studies in European Realism*, translated by Edith Bone, with a foreword by Roy Pascal. London: Hillway, 1950.

McCarthy, Mary. "The Fact in Fiction," *On the Contrary*. New York: Farrar, Strauss and Cudahy, 1961.

McCormick, John Owen. *Catastrophe and Imagination*. London: Longmans, 1957.

McKillop, Alan Dugald. *The Early Masters of English Fiction*. Lawrence, Kansas: Kansas University Press, 1956.

Martin, Ernest William Lunn. *Where London Ends: English Provincial Life after 1750*. London: Phoenix House, 1958.

Masson, David. *British Novelists and Their Styles*. Cambridge, 1859.

Meadowcroft, Charles William, Jr. *The Place of Eden Phillpotts in English Peasant Drama*. Ph.D. dissertation. University of Pennsylvania, 1924.

Mizener, Arthur. *The Sense of Life in the Modern Novel*. Boston: Houghton Mifflin, 1964.

Morgan, F. W. "Three Aspects of Regional Consciousness," *Sociological Review*, XXI (1939), 68–88.

Muir, Edwin. *The Structure of the Novel*. London: Hogarth Press, 1928.

O'Connor, William Van, ed. *Forms of Modern Fiction: Essays Collected in Honor of Joseph Warren Beach*. Minneapolis: University of Minnesota Press, 1948.

O'Faolain, Sean. *The Vanishing Hero: Studies in Novelists of the Twenties*. London: Eyre and Spottiswoode, 1956.

Pizer, Donald. "Late Nineteenth-Century American Realism: An Essay in Definition," *Nineteenth-Century Fiction*, XVI (1961–62), 263–269.

Praz, Mario. *The Hero in Eclipse in Victorian Fiction*, translated by Angus Davidson. London: Oxford University Press, 1956.

Prest, John M. *The Industrial Revolution in Coventry*. London: Oxford University Press, 1960.

"The Progress of Fiction as an Art." Anon., *Westminster Review*, LX (1853), 342–374.

Rahv, Philip. "Fiction and the Criticism of Fiction," *Kenyon Review*, XVIII (1956), 276–299.

Raleigh, John Henry. "What Scott Meant to the Victorians," *Victorian Studies*, VII (1963–64), 7–34.

Raleigh, Sir Walter. *The English Novel*. New York, 1894.

Saintsbury, George. *Corrected Impressions: Essays on Victorian Writers*. London, 1895.

——— *The English Novel*. London: J. M. Dent and Sons, 1913.

Schorer, Mark. "Foreword: Self and Society," *Society and Self in the Novel: English Institute Essays, 1955*, ed. Mark Schorer. New York: Columbia University Press, 1956.

Sherman, George W. "Thomas Hardy and the Agricultural Laborer," *Nineteenth-Century Fiction*, VII (1952–53), 111–118.

Simon, Irène. *Formes du roman anglais de Dickens à Joyce*. Liège: Faculté de philosophie et lettres, 1949.

Simpson, Claude M., ed. *The Local Colorists: American Short Stories, 1857–1900*. New York: Harper, 1960.

Somervell, D. C. *English Thought in the Nineteenth Century.* London: Methuen and Company, 1929.

Speare, Morris Edmund. *The Political Novel: Its Development in England and in America.* New York: Oxford University Press, 1924.

Stang, Richard. *The Theory of the Novel in England, 1850–1870.* New York: Columbia University Press, 1959.

Swinburne, Algernon C. *A Note on Charlotte Brontë.* London, 1877.

Tillotson, Kathleen. *Novels of the Eighteen-Forties.* Oxford: Oxford University Press, 1954.

Trilling, Lionel. *The Liberal Imagination: Essays on Literature and Society.* New York: Viking Press, 1950.

Wain, John. "Oysters and a Novelist's Art," *New Republic,* CLI (1964), 23–24.

Watt, Ian. *The Rise of the Novel: Studies in Defoe, Richardson, and Fielding.* London: Chatto and Windus, 1957.

Willey, Basil. *More Nineteenth Century Studies: A Group of Honest Doubters.* London: Chatto and Windus, 1956.

———— " 'Nature' in Wordsworth," *The Eighteenth Century Background: Studies in the Idea of Nature in the Thought of the Period.* London: Chatto and Windus, 1940.

———— "Postscript: On Wordsworth and the Locke Tradition," *The Seventeenth Century Background: Studies in the Thought of the Age in Relation to Poetry and Religion.* London: Chatto and Windus, 1934.

Williams, Raymond. *Culture and Society, 1780–1950.* London: Chatto and Windus, 1958.

———— *The Long Revolution.* London: Chatto and Windus, 1961.

———— "Thomas Hardy," *Critical Quarterly,* VI (1964), 341–351.

Index

Index